Through the Prism
of Slavery

WORLD SOCIAL CHANGE
Series Editor: Mark Selden

Through the Prism of Slavery

Labor, Capital, and World Economy

Dale W. Tomich

ROWMAN & LITTLEFIELD PUBLISHERS, INC.
Lanham • Boulder • New York • Toronto • Oxford

ROWMAN & LITTLEFIELD PUBLISHERS, INC.

Published in the United States of America
by Rowman & Littlefield Publishers, Inc.
A wholly owned subsidiary of The Rowman & Littlefield Publishing Group, Inc.
4501 Forbes Boulevard, Suite 200, Lanham, MD 20706
www.rowmanlittlefield.com

P.O. Box 317, Oxford OX2 9RU, UK

British Library Cataloguing in Publication Information Available

Library of Congress Cataloging-in-Publication Data

Tomich, Dale W., 1946–
   Through the prism of slavery : labor, capital, and world economy /
Dale W. Tomich.
      p.   cm. — (World social change)
   Includes bibliographical references and index.
   ISBN   978-0-7425-2939-7
alk. paper)
      1. Slave labor—Caribbean Area—History—19th century.   2.
Slavery—Caribbean Area—History—19th century.   3. Sugarcane
industry—Caribbean Area—History.   4. Slave labor—History—19th
century.   I. Title.   II. Series.
   HD4865 .C27 T66   2004
   331.11'734'0972909034—dc21   2003013079

Printed in the United States of America

♾ ™ The paper used in this publication meets the minimum requirements of American
National Standard for Information Sciences—Permanence of Paper for Printed Library
Materials, ANSI/NISO Z39.48-1992.

For Phil, Steve, Jim,
and in memory of Terry

Contents

Acknowledgments

I have enjoyed a great deal of support from many people during the period in which the ideas expressed in these essays evolved. First, I must thank Mark Selden who first suggested that I gather them into a book and patiently kept after me until the project became a reality. I would also like to acknowledge my gratitude to a community of support that includes Bob Antonio, Carlos Antonio Aguirre Rojas, Giovanni Arrighi, César Ayala, Ronald Aminzade, Farshad Araghi, David Bartine, Ira Berlin, Steve Bunker, Charles Burroughs, Manuel Cerdà, Jane Collins, Cathérine Coquery-Vidrovitch, Michaeline Crichlow, Anna Davin, Edgar DeDecca, Karen Dhanda, Shelly Feldman, Maria Sylvia de Carvalho Franco, Carolyn Fick, Robert Forster, Mark Frezzo, Harriet Friedmann, Antoní Furio, Juan Giusti, Barry Gaspar, Janet Gouldner, John R. Hall, John Higginson, Darlene Clarke Hine, Terry Hopkins, Carl Johnson, Vasant Kaiwar, Tony Kaye, Augustín Lao, Julie Lirus-Galap, José Mota Lopes, Fouad Makki, Rafael de Bivar Marquese, Sucheta Mazumdar, Phil McMichael, Russell Menard, Sidney Mintz, Philip Morgan, Jim O'Connor, Erick Pérez, Marta Petrusewicz, Aníbal Quijano, João Reis, Ravi Sundaram, Francisco O. Ramirez, Roberto Romano, Kelvin Santiago, Francisco Scarano, Joan Scott, Rebecca Scott, Chris Schmidt Nowara, Bob Slenes, David Smith, Nicoletta Stame, Richard Tardanico, Pedro Ruiz Torres, Italo Tronca, Rolph Trouillot, Mary Turner, Immanuel Wallerstein, John Walton, Richard Yidana, and my colleagues and students at Binghamton University. Finally, my greatest debt is to Laura and Luiza.

Introduction

This volume brings together chapters that were written as part of an effort to comprehend the role of New World slavery in the making of the capitalist world economy. My purpose in writing them has been to understand how the histories of particular slave formations in the Americas have been shaped by the ways in which they were integrated into the world market, the division of labor, and the interstate system, and, conversely, to rethink from the perspective of New World slavery the historical development of modern capitalism as a world economy.

Slavery is one of a multiplicity of forms of economic exploitation and social domination that are central to the historical development of capital and the formation of the modern world economy (Quijano 2000). The establishment of slave production in the Americas beginning in the sixteenth century was a formative moment of the world division of labor and world market. The productive activity of African slaves in the Americas created a new organization and hierarchy of labor, trade, and power and put Europe at the center of an unprecedented world economy. The slave regimes of the Americas were made and remade as part of the historical expansion and recomposition of the social relations of capital on a global scale. Which states founded individual zones of slave production and where and when they were established were products of world economic developments. At the same time, these factors had much to do with determining the particular character of each zone. My concern is with understanding not only the ongoing unevenness, asymmetry, and tension between highly specific *local* slave societies and the *global* processes that produce them but also the ways in which such asymmetries and tensions contribute to the historically formed complexity and heterogeneity of the capitalist world economy as a whole.

The immediate objective of these chapters is the interpretation of slavery as part of the historical formation of the capitalist world economy. In addressing this problem, however, they also raise methodological and conceptual issues whose resolutions have acquired a new urgency, in order not only to understand the past but also to comprehend the present. The profound social and economic transformations of the past thirty years have reintegrated all forms of class exploitation and coerced labor within new configurations of world market and states. The processes of globalization have provoked a variety of responses. One, of course, has been to simply abandon a historical perspective and to focus on the universal triumph of "the market" (itself conceived narrowly), which in its most extreme interpretation is identified with "the end of history" (Fukuyama 1992). In contrast, others have cautioned against overgeneralization about globalization and have emphasized historical shifts of regimes of accumulation as well as the importance of both geographical specificity and local difference (Arrighi 1996; McMichael 2000; Hoogvelt 1997; Stiglitz 2002; Dicken 1998). Through critical engagement with methodological and conceptual problems raised by slave labor (and, by extension, unwaged labor more generally), the chapters presented here contribute to a theoretical understanding of the historical development of the capitalist world economy as a whole. They not only call attention to the diversity and specificity of forms of labor that constitute the world economy, but by viewing capitalist development from the perspective of slave labor, the chapters also reveal spatial and temporal complexity and the production of local differences by world-scale processes.

The first chapter develops the theoretical perspective employed throughout the book. It takes as its point of departure three influential approaches to the political economy of slavery: new economic history, Marxism, and world-systems theory. Through a critical appraisal of the work of Robert Fogel and Stanley Engerman, Eugene Genovese, and Immanuel Wallerstein, it argues that none of these perspectives is able to incorporate into a unified analytical framework the complex historical combinations of specific forms of wage *and* non-wage production together with the world market. Rather, each of these approaches takes abstract and partial categories for complex sociohistorical wholes and confuses analytical priority with historical causality. Their common failure to recognize the necessarily constructed nature of their analyses prevents them from going beyond their own abstractions. Paradoxically, these approaches share theoretical assumptions and methodological conditions that preclude adequately comprehending of the specific character of diverse production relations and the particularity of individual local histories within a unified theoretical-historical account of capitalist development as a world-historical process. The accumulation of empirical evidence from diverse cases will not, and cannot, by itself resolve the issues and controversies that emerge from these competing perspectives. Rather, it is necessary to confront the conceptual frameworks themselves and to pose once again the problem of the relation of theory to history.

The first chapter seeks to *critically think through* the methodological and theoretical premises of these perspectives in order to formulate a new approach to the question of slavery and capitalism and, through it, to the historical development of the modern world economy as a whole. At issue is the need to move beyond the abstract conceptions of capitalism that are presented in these approaches in order to establish the historical terrain of (world) capitalist development. It is insufficient, however, to simply add slavery to an already given and completed concept of capital. Rather, the first chapter proposes to rethink the totality of relations of capital in a way that is inclusive of slavery and diverse non-waged relations. This entails reconceptualizing the ways that the slave formations of the New World are constituted by the capitalist world economy and are themselves productive of capital even while they retain their particular characteristics.

The remaining chapters in the first section of the book, and, indeed, the book as a whole, pursue this approach through the historical reconstruction of slavery as it relates to the capitalist world economy. They call attention to the spatial and temporal constitution of new zones of slave production as part of the material expansion of the nineteenth-century world economy. By emphasizing making, remaking, and unmaking slave relations over historical time and in geographical space, they draw attention to the heterogeneity and complexity of world economic relations and processes. They establish the distinction between those slave regimes that precede, and are partly responsible for, the emergence of industrial capital and wage labor as dominant poles of the world economy and those slave regimes that were created as part of the processes restructuring the nineteenth-century world economy. From this perspective, they reinterpret the crisis of slavery in the Americas not as the result of the unilinear expansion of industrial capitalist modernity, but as a result of the expansion and differentiation of slave regimes during the nineteenth century.

The chapters in the second part build upon these insights. They examine particular zones of slave production as local sites of global transformation. Through comparison of old and new slave zones, they emphasize the importance of the historical constitution of specific geographies of production in differentiating slave zones from one another and in shaping the temporalities of the world economy. Central to their concerns is how the expansion of world sugar production and geographical relocation of sugar making recast slave labor and transformed particular natural environments. This confluence of global and local conditions produced particular configurations of land, slave labor, and technologies of production and transport that were articulated differently in the world division of labor. Each such configuration was subject to new and varied possibilities and constraints for both sugar production and slave labor. The local response to world market pressures was itself a mechanism of differentiation. This focus on the spatiotemporal differentiation of zones of slave production calls attention to the active role of colonial elites and laboring productions and the changing relations among slave regimes and altering the world division of labor and shaping the crisis of slavery in the Caribbean region.

The final section looks at the consequences of global expansion in an old sugar region, the French West Indian colony of Martinique. The chapters presented here demonstrate not only the ways in which world economic changes created the conditions for local agency but also the ways in which the contingent outcomes of local struggles contributed to the transformation of global structures. They focus on slavery as a specific form of production in the capitalist world economy and analyze the ways that the combination of the world market, the material processes of sugar production, and the social relations of slavery shaped the organization of labor-time on Martinican sugar estates. They seek to go beyond notions of "protopeasantry" to examine the specific combination of estate agriculture, provision ground cultivation, and small-scale marketing that characterized slave relations in Martinique. In particular, they are concerned with local response to pressures to increase productivity resulting from the impact of industrialization and market integration on the world economy. Under these pressures, planters attempted to increase productivity through the reorganization of production and the modification of labor discipline. These efforts were at once causes of and responses to slave initiatives to both delimit the working day and appropriate the time and space of the plantation for provision ground cultivation and independent petty marketing activities. Day-to-day slave struggles over the working day and subsistence cultivation in Martinique altered the relation between master and slave, created crises of both slavery and sugar cultivation, and created the local conditions for the transition to a postslavery economy and society. With emancipation, the former slaves did not abandon estate agriculture. Instead, they attempted to make it subordinate to their economy of small-scale production and petty marketing. The problem of postemancipation Martinique was that of containing the initiatives of the freed population. Failure to do so imposed new and perhaps fatal conditions on the recovery of the sugar industry in the island.

By interpreting slavery as an integral part of the capitalist world economy, the chapters in this book do not simply emphasize the persistence of slavery and other forms of unwaged labor. Rather, they demonstrate the fundamental historical interconnection and interdependence of the diverse relations and processes whose interaction forms and reforms the world economic whole. The approach presented here allows us to apprehend this development through the ongoing interplay of material processes and social relations, production and exchange, and structure and agency across diverse spatial and temporal scales. It thereby allows us to reconstruct the interaction of varied yet interrelated forms of relations, social and material needs, capacities, constraints, and possibilities that shaped the course of historical development of both individual slave formations and the world economy as a whole. In this way, it reveals the constant asymmetry, unevenness, and tension between particular local histories and the diverse but unified temporal rhythms and spatial extensions of world economic processes.

Part One

Slavery in the World Economy

Chapter One

Capitalism, Slavery, and World Economy

Historical Theory and Theoretical History

Slavery in the Americas was the historical product of the expansion of the European world economy. It entailed systematic production for the market by means of a non-waged form of labor. Thus, it is neither a "traditional" social relation nor a formally capitalist relation of production. Rather, it represents a generalized form of commodity production effected through specific relations of domination. Consequently, the attempt to theoretically comprehend the social-historical character of modern slavery puts in sharp relief the problem of conceptualizing the relation between market and production within the historical trajectory of the capitalist world economy.

This chapter examines the theoretical categories through which the world market and social relations of slavery are represented in neo-classical, Marxist, and world-system theories and discusses the implications of each conceptual framework for the theoretical reconstruction of historical processes. It thereby seeks both to highlight the implicit and explicit assumptions about production and exchange relations within each paradigm and to assess the methodological strategies and theoretical implications of each for the analysis of a particular historical phenomenon. It argues that none of these approaches is capable of adequately comprehending the specific character of diverse production relations and the particularity of individual local histories as part of unified historical processes of capitalist development on a world scale. The way that these perspectives formulate the problem offers little possibility of going beyond the repeated opposition of the specificity of the capital—wage labor relation to the market and division of labor. In each approach, abstract and partial categories orchestrate historical narratives in ways that eliminate

3

from consideration complex and contingent causal relations. Their limits are
to be found not in the adequacy or appropriateness of the theoretical category
that is privileged by the proponents of each approach and the evident interpretive differences between them. Rather, their limits reside in their commonly held assumptions about the nature of theoretical categories and their
role in the reconstruction of historical processes of capitalist development.

The purpose of focusing the discussion on slave relations is not only to
address particular problems involved in their analysis but also to use slavery
to shed light on more general conceptual problems entailed in studying market and production relations as part of the historical development of the capitalist world economy. Through a critical appraisal of these approaches, this
chapter proposes a strategy to go beyond simple dichotomies such as production for the market vs. wage labor and capitalist vs. precapitalist, which have
characterized much historical analysis and interpretation from all three perspectives. It suggests a method for conceptualizing market and production
relations as constructs, at once theoretical and historical, that are capable of
comprehending the specificity and complexity of local histories within processes of world economy.

SLAVERY AND THE
"NEW ECONOMIC HISTORY"

The "New Economic History" or, as it is more boldly known, "Cliometric
History" has had a great impact on writing on slavery from the pioneering
work of John H. Conrad and John R. Meyer (1964) to the more recent works
of Robert W. Fogel and Stanley L. Engerman (1974). The originality of this
approach is in the application of sophisticated econometric models and statistical methods of social science to the study of historical problems. In the view
of its practitioners, the use of these value-neutral analytical techniques allows
ideological bias to be separated from the scientific analysis of facts. Much of
the debate over this approach has centered on the adequacy and interpretation
of data as well as the conclusions derived from it. (Most critiques have
emphasized the nature of the data, the character of the models and their application, and the adequacy for interpretation of substantive problems. See, for
example, David et al. [1976] and Gutman [1975]. A methodological critique
is undertaken by Greenberg [1977]). Here, however, I wish to focus more
explicitly on the method of New Economic History and on the use of neo-
classical theory for historical interpretation and analysis.

Neo-classical economic theory presents itself as a purely technical instrument for determining the optimal allocation of scarce resources independent of any particular social or historical context. Taking price formation as its central object and point of departure, modern capital theory abstracts from social relations and constructs categories of economic analysis that are presumed to have universal validity. Within the neo-classical model, social relations, and more particularly social relations of production, are excluded from consideration. Production itself is only treated from a purely technical point of view. Economic science is concerned only with the technical determination of the proportions in which factors of production are employed in order to produce goods and otherwise regards production as beyond its scope. Hence, slavery presents no special analytical problems. In the words of Conrad and Mayer: "From the standpoint of the entrepreneur making an investment in slaves, the basic problems in determining profitability are analytically the same as those met in determining the returns from any other kind of capital investment"(Conrad and Meyer 1964, 47).

From the perspective of economic theory, slaves are treated simply as "capital." They are regarded as a "production function" that is to be understood in terms of inputs of slaves and the materials required to maintain the slaves to staple crop production and to the production of slave labor. In accordance with these premises, slavery itself is conceived simply as a juridical relation of property. It is treated as a category that is related to the categories of economic analysis only in a contingent and external manner. The origins of slavery are non-economic—"the outcome of force and compulsion practiced by one group against others and not the outcome of a set of voluntarily exchanged property rights"—while slave relations are economically important only insofar as they affect "the allocation and distribution of economic resources," and therefore the "level and pattern of output in the economy, as well as the distribution of income and utility"(Conrad and Meyer 1964, 45; Engerman 1973, 43–45).

Thus, in neo-classical theory, categories of economic analysis are not regarded as specific historical categories nor are they constituted as substantive political-social relations. Rather, they are treated as technically determined universals. By the same token, those categories that refer to social, political, cultural, or ideological relations are conceived as external and contingent to "the economy" and are of interest only insofar as they affect production functions. As a result, neo-classical theory separates the slaves as factors of production from the institution of slavery and assigns a different theoretical status to each; it thus separates the products from the processes—material and social—of their production, and the producers from the social relations—to one another and to nature—through which they act. The economy and production are thereby abstracted from history and social relations and viewed in isolation as technical processes. By means of this logical oper-ation, history and social relations, rather than being formative of economic processes, are transformed into "contexts" whose relation to the universally valid economic categories is conjunctural. The specificity of production rela-tions is thereby eliminated.

In accordance with the premises of this model, the analysis and interpreta-tion of slavery focus not on the historical conditions of the reproduction of the social relations of slavery, but rather on the technical evaluation of the "profitability" and "efficiency" of the slave "economy." It is presumed that continued profitability and efficiency are sufficient to maintain the viability of slavery as an economic institution. Significantly, the major studies based on this approach have emphasized the positive performance of slavery according to these criteria and have attributed slave emancipation to the suc-cess of contingent "extra-economic factors," most notably politics and ideol-ogy, in undercutting the economic system (Conrad and Meyer 1964, 45, 47, 83–84; Drescher 1977; Fogel and Engerman 1974; Fogel 1989).

Nonetheless, by reducing economy and production to technical processes, neo-classical theory disregards the social character of slave production and the specific social conditions of profitability and efficiency under a regime of slave labor. Within the framework of neo-classical theory, profitability and efficiency are themselves understood as technical terms. The calculation of profitability is based upon the comparison of the price of factor inputs to the price of output. It depends upon staple prices and the price sensitivity of the rational entrepreneur in efficiently allocating production factors. On the other hand, efficiency is measured by either output per worker (labor productivity) or by output per average unit of all inputs—here, land, labor, and capital (total factor productivity). Thus, these two categories are conceptually independent of one another. Profitability measures the cost of producing things without regard to their physical production, while efficiency measures the physical production of things without regard to their cost. Production costs and output are thus treated as exogenous variables; the relation between them is only established by the market price of the product. This comparison with market price permits the rational calculation of the optimal allocation of production factors.

In accordance with these theoretical premises, in calculating the profitabil-ity of slavery and the exploitation of the slave, the cost of the slave and the cost of slave maintenance are treated as the cost of labor, which is compared to the earnings from the sale of the product. The social relations of slavery enter into this equation only insofar as they affect the allocation and distribu-tion of production factors. Thus, in this view, the rationale of a slave regime and the particular source of its profitability rests, first, on the compulsion of labor into a branch of industry and a work regime that would not have been voluntarily accepted and, second, on the ability of the slave owner to hold down the return to labor and to appropriate "the excess of the value of the output produced by the slave labor force above the value of the consumption allowed." Consistent with this formulation, the exploitation of the slave is calculated as the difference between the real return to the slave (maintenance costs) and the optimal or average return to labor under conditions of free exchange. According to these criteria, econometric historians have demonstrated both the profitability of slavery and the efficiency of slave owners in allocating their resources among alternative investments in order to exploit opportunities for profit (Stanley Engerman, for example, attempts to measure slave exploitation on the basis of slave price. He takes current slave price as the expression of the relation between discounted future earnings and discounted future costs [Engerman 1976, 258–275; Engerman 1973, 43–47; Fogel 1989, 73]).

However, force and compulsion are not simply contingent extra-economic factors. Rather, they are constitutive of slave production. Through the property relation, the slaveholder asserts dominion over the slave's person, the labor process, and the whole product of labor. At the same time, the appropriation of the person of the slave and the production of goods by means of slave labor are two independent moments of the process of social production. While the person of the laborer takes the form of commodity, the activity of labor (in Marx's terms "labor-power") does not. Thus, the property relation and the labor process presuppose one another as given, external conditions. There is no economic relation of exchange mediating between the two. While ownership of the slave is the condition for production, it does not by itself secure the expenditure of the slave's labor. Rather, the process of production is organized through the direct domination of the slaveholder. Work is an activity imposed upon slaves and carried out independently of their subsistence.

Because the capacity to labor does not take the form of commodity under slavery, the category labor-power cannot appear as a social relation independent of the person of the laborer. Instead, the value of labor is subsumed under the value of the slave, and all the slave's labor appears as surplus (unpaid) labor (Marx 1976, I, 680). Consequently, within the slave relation, the activity of laboring has no cost, while the price of the slave is independent of the process of production. The former is not a commodity and has no exchange value. The latter is an investment in the means of production. It is a deduction from the capital available for production, and the personal domination of the slave owner, whether through force and compulsion or through paternalistic strategies, is necessary to set the slave's labor in motion.

Similarly, while the slave owner has to bear the costs of reproducing the laborer, what is reproduced is the person of the slave, which remains separate from the activity of labor. Even that portion of labor, which reproduces the slave's physical existence—whether directly or indirectly—does not correspond to the reproduction of labor-power as in the case of wage labor, rather it renews the stock of constant capital. It is, therefore, equivalent to the cost of maintenance, fuel, or parts for machines. The cost of slave maintenance does not appear directly as the price of labor-power, but rather takes the form of a series of investments in constant capital (housing, food, clothing, purchase of new slaves, etc.). These costs must be paid whether the slave works or not, or else the investment in his person will be lost.

Consequently, slave price is independent of the creation of new value by the slave, and, therefore, of the exploitation of the slave. On the other side of the coin, the costs of slave maintenance—although they may be manipulated through a system of rewards and punishments in order to manage labor more effectively—are not received in exchange for laboring and do not represent slave income or a return to labor any more than the feed for a horse is a wage. Thus, while the social relations of slavery do permit measurement of the expenses and revenues of the budgetary unit, the cost of labor remains incalculable (see Tomich 1990, esp. 129–138; also Hall 1961).

Under slavery, the appropriation of the labor force as slaves shapes the organization of the labor process and constrains its development. The specific relations of production mediate the conditions of profitability and of efficiency. Any increase in the output of labor distributes the labor expended over a greater number of commodities, but such a change has no necessary relation to the value of the slave or the value of the product. (Indeed, depending on market structure, increased output per unit of labor may have the negative effect of lowering the price of staple commodities without reducing costs.) Despite increased product per worker, labor is not expelled from the production process. The size and composition of the resident slave population and the cost of slave maintenance remain unchanged. The master retains possession of the laborers and is compelled to provide for the physical renewal of the slave population. He remains surrounded by superfluous laborers whose labor is always at his disposition at no extra cost. The very presence of this excess labor limits the further rationalization of production. Thus, profitability and efficiency cannot be regarded simply as independent technical categories. Rather, they move within parameters defined by slave relations of production and are dependent upon the social conditions under which these relations are reproduced.

By presuming the universal validity of economic categories, neo-classical theory constructs and maintains a persistent dualism between economic analysis and historical process. Economic categories are treated as being independent of history, while all social, political, cultural, or ideological phenomena are regarded as contingent and are judged against universal categories of economic rationality. Consequently, changing data about the past are passed through a static analytical scheme. The social relations of slavery are reduced to purely technical considerations or are all treated one-sidedly in terms of "not yet complete" market relations, while the historical moment is at best seen as a deviation from the pure market situation. Conversely, politics and ideology are abstractly juxtaposed against a technically conceived economy rather than mediated through social relations. Such an ahistorical approach obscures relations of power and domination that constitute economic activity behind the facade of pure exchange and the rational actor. The problem of the specific historical origins of economic relations disappears from view. Instead, history itself is conceived as the progressive loosening of constraints on factor realities: the continual development of the division of labor in response to changes in price and productivity. The market and market rationality become at once the beginning and end point of historical change as well as the prime force behind it. Through a linear process of rationalization, time and space are progressively subordinated to the universal criteria of the market. Thus, despite the accomplishments of this approach, it leaves unanswered deeper questions of historical interpretation and the formation of social relations.

A MARXIST VIEW OF SLAVERY

While the neo-classical approach presumes the universality of exchange relations, Marxism insists upon the historical specificity of social relations of production. Yet despite this expressed opposition, much Marxist writing mirrors the methodological and theoretical presuppositions of the neo-classical approach. (Writing on this subject has been voluminous and contentious, and there is much serious disagreement among Marxists. I shall not attempt to rehearse the variety of approaches here, but merely illustrate the type of difficulties that commonly appear as a result of either particular theoretical formulations or the way the concepts are handled in practice.) A Marxist interpretation that appears as in many ways diametrically opposed to the abstract and technical approach to the slave economy of neo-classical theory illustrates both the pervasiveness of viewing theoretical categories as though they refer to discrete empirical entities and the difficulties resulting from this procedure. Eugene D. Genovese's influential *The Political Economy of Slavery* (1967), produces an account of slavery in which the backward, "irrational" characteristics of "precapitalist" social relations inhibit the development of productive forces within the U.S. South and impede the appearance of capitalism in the region. In this interpretation, slavery is not treated as formative of categories of production and exchange, but remains a "socio-political structure" altering the operation of universally valid "economic" laws from the "outside." "Capitalism" and "slavery" are transformed into abstract, static, ahistorical categories. The conceptual autonomy of each remains intact, and the "slave economy" is judged against universal standards of efficiency and profitability. Despite substantive differences in interpretation and evaluation, there is an unexpected convergence between Genovese and the neo-classical approach.

Genovese's interpretation of slavery rests upon the assumed conceptual independence of capitalism and slavery on the one hand and the fragmentation of production and exchange relations on the other. Operating within a conception of a hierarchy of analytical levels, Genovese argues for the importance of social relations in determining the character of the slave South. He writes:

> Slavery provided the basis for a special Southern economic and social life, special problems and tensions, and special laws of development. . . . The fact of slave ownership is central to our problem. This seemingly formal question of whether the owners of the means of production command labor or purchase the labor power of free workers contains in itself the content of Southern life. The essential features of Southern particularity, as well as of Southern backwardness, can be traced to the relationship of master to slave. (Genovese 1967, 16, 23)

In contrast to the neo-classical approach, Genovese emphasizes the decisive importance of superstructural elements in shaping social relations of slavery and the character of Southern life. He stresses that the "slaveholders' domination made possible by their command of labor" created "a powerful, largely autonomous civilization, with aristocratic pretensions and possibilities." (Here relations are subtly transposed into the ascribed attributes of masters—their ideology, culture, and psychology. "The hegemony of the slaveholders, presupposing the social and economic preponderance of the great slave plantations, determined the character of the South. . . . [T]hey imparted to Southern life a special social, economic, political, ideological, and psychological content" [Genovese 1967, 13].) Thus, the slave economy is defined by the master-slave relation, and capitalism is identified exclusively with wage labor. Each of these two relations is conceived as the "content" of a distinctive socio-economic system. "Slavery" and "capitalism" are thereby made to stand in isolation from one another and from the historical whole and are contrasted to one another in terms of what are conceived as their particular internal attributes (Genovese 1967, 13, 15–16, 23).

Genovese's analysis of the precapitalist character of the South and Southern backwardness is an artifact of this theoretical separation of capitalism and slavery—and results in the disjunction of production and exchange. Genovese conceives of production relations (broadly understood to include superstructural elements) and exchange relations as discrete and exclusive categories and assigns each to a different theoretical level. According to Genovese: "Many precapitalist economic systems have had well-developed commercial relations, but if every commercial society is to be considered capitalist, the word loses all meaning. In general, commercial classes have supported the existing system of production" (Genovese 1967, 15–16). Thus, even though Genovese recognizes that the Southern slave economy "developed within, and was in a sense exploited by the capitalist world market," the market is relegated to a secondary position outside the sphere of production, and analytical priority is assigned to production relations. As a result, the master-slave relation takes precedence over exchange relations in explaining the character of the slave economy, and the conceptual boundaries of slavery are viewed as coincident with the boundaries of the South as a geographical region. The constitution of slave relations is attributed to processes within this region. In turn, these relations define a separate "system" that is explicable by particular "internal laws." Slavery is regarded as a feature of "Southern society," and slave relations give "Southern reality" its distinguishing content. In this way, the slave South is constructed as a thing apart, an isolated local enclave cut off from world market and capital. Its particularity as a backward, premodern, and precapitalist region is emphasized (Genovese 1967, 19).

Having separated slavery from capitalism, the latter becomes the measure of the backwardness of the former. In this comparison, Marxian historical analysis takes a decidedly Weberian bent. The categories of the capitalist economy are judged to possess a universally valid rationality while the slave economy is characterized by "irrational tendencies that inhibit economic development and endanger social stability." In this interpretation, the peculiarity of slavery and the nature of Southern "backwardness" is defined through the opposition of the master-slave relation to what are taken to be the "normal" features of capitalism—presumably those of the Anglo-North American metropolitan centers.

If for a moment we accept the designation of the planters as capitalists and the slave system as a form of capitalism, we are then confronted by a capitalist society that impeded the development of every normal feature of capitalism. The planters were

not mere capitalists; they were precapitalist, quasi-aristocratic landowners who had
to adjust their economy and ways of thinking to a capitalist world market. Their
society in its spirit and fundamental direction, represented the antithesis of capitalism, however many compromises it had to make. (Genovese 1967, 15–18)

The relation of the slave South to the market is here construed as one of compromise with and adjustment to an external force. The planters remain
"quasi-aristocrats" who must nonetheless "adjust their economy and ways of
thinking" and "compromise" with the capitalist world market. Thus, even
though the slave South "remained tied to the capitalist world by bonds of
commodity production," its internal, superstructural features assume greater
analytical importance. The "special laws" of slave development turn upon
the "irrationality" of slavery, that is, the ways in which the "precapitalist"
planter culture and ideology impede the operation of "economic rationality"
within the South. The peculiarity of slavery is to be understood through its
deviation from the presumed "normal" course of capitalist development and
the laws of the market. Southern backwardness is seen as a result of the failure to modernize and industrialize in ways characteristic of "capitalist development." Here material production becomes external and contingent to social
relations.

The external relation of analytical categories to one another in Genovese's
approach thus creates a hierarchy of levels—material production and social
relations, economic structure and political-juridical superstructure. This
scheme is then generalized as a permanent feature of all social formations.
The social-historical difference between societies has to do with the content
of these categories, while the categories themselves remain conceptually
independent of one another and assume the fixed characteristics of "things."
They are viewed in isolation from one another and from the historical whole
and treated as though they refer to discrete empirical entities. Characteristically, production relations and productive forces are taken to refer narrowly
to the immediate process of material production and are used to produce distinctions between base and superstructure and what is "internal" and what is
"external" to the unit of analysis. Thus, for example, capitalism is identified
with the prevalence of wage labor in the immediate process of production.
The particular historical "laws" derived from production relations are
regarded as internal and primary, while the "market" or the broader "economic system" is treated as external and secondary.

All too often, theoretical boundaries are conflated with geographical
boundaries and analytical categories are treated as though they are direct attributes of a particular national or regional society. Consequently, the relatedness

of slavery and the transformation of the world economy is de-emphasized. Instead, slavery and capitalism are regarded as two distinct and conceptually and practically autonomous categories. These two terms are conjoined to construct the complexity and heterogeneity of the historical processes under consideration. However, there is no historical synthesis. Instead, their simple coexistence defines the spatial and temporal boundaries of nineteenth-century Southern history. Within this duality, the slave relation is treated as if it were a local phenomenon that is situated in the South and is impinged upon from the outside by a capitalist world market. In turn, the world market is construed as spatially "somewhere else." The market is therefore treated as if it were independent of the relations of production that form one of its essential poles. In this way, conceptually linked and mutually interdependent social processes such as production and exchange are theoretically or geographically or both bounded in such a way that their unity and interdependence are fragmented. Historical processes whose explanation and alteration is the very point of theory are thereby eliminated from consideration.

A hierarchy of causality is created within which change is conceived narrowly and one-sidedly. The "application" of theory becomes an operation of classification. Particular phenomena are placed in the appropriate boxes, while the relation between boxes is already established, not through historical inquiry, but through inference from theoretical knowledge (Cohen 1978, 95). Theory becomes a surrogate for historical analysis and interpretation. It aims at the derivation of "historical laws" (usually understood abstractly as causal principles emanating from particular production relations). These "laws" impose themselves on empirical material and choreograph a historical narrative as "facts" are selected and arranged to illustrate the predetermined outcome.

SLAVERY AND THE MODERN WORLD-SYSTEM

Immanuel Wallerstein's conception of the modern world-system offers an alternative formulation of the relation of slave production and world market. Wallerstein regards the capitalist world economy as an empirically specific historical structure. In his view, this system has been defined from its origins in the sixteenth century onward by a single division of labor between core, semiperipheral, and peripheral zones. Each zone is characterized by distinct modes of labor control, including, respectively: wage labor and self-employment; tenancy and sharecropping; and coerced cash crop production and slavery. These various modes of labor control, each concentrated in a particular zone, are integrated through the world market. Wallerstein contends that within this framework production is overwhelmingly for exchange, and "value is created greater than the socially necessary amount needed to reproduce the labor that created the product, there is surplus value, whatever the nature of the social relation at the work place" (Wallerstein 1979, 276).

In Wallerstein's view, this system is historically unique in that its structure promotes the constant accumulation of capital and permits the maximization of surplus production over time and space:

> Capitalism is the only mode of production in which the maximization of surplus creation is rewarded per se. In every historical system, there has been some production for use and some production for exchange, but only in capitalism are all producers rewarded primarily in terms of the exchange value they produce and penalized to the extent they neglect it. The "rewards" and "penalties" are mediated through a structure called a "market." . . . Not only is surplus maximized for its own sake, but those who use the surplus to accumulate more capital to produce still more surplus are further rewarded. (Wallerstein 1979, 285)

This approach thus emphasizes the diversity of modes of labor within a unified global structure. The capitalist character of production is neither identified with an abstract universal nor confined to relations of waged labor. Rather, the structure of the modern world-system embraces a multiplicity of forms of labor control whose common thread is participation in the production and appropriation of surplus value through the world market.

For Wallerstein, the key methodological issue is the unit of analysis: The relations of production that define the system are the relations of production of the whole system (Wallerstein 1974, I, 127). From this point of view, Wallerstein reinterprets the arguments of Fogel and Engerman and of Genovese regarding the character and role of modern American slavery:

> The slave owners were then indeed capitalists, as Fogel and Engerman argue, not however, because all rational men are, but because they were operating in a capitalist world economy. And a slave owner who did not allow market considerations to loom large in his firm's operation would sooner or later go bankrupt and be replaced by one who did. That southern planters developed a different ideology from that of New England mill owners (and were they as different as Genovese implies?) is simply the reflection of differing interests within a single capitalist world-system. That they tried to use the state (whether within the Union or by creating the Confederacy) to defend their interests, that is the name of the game. (Wallerstein 1979, 218–219)

Consequently, in this perspective, Southern slavery is not only compatible with but is necessarily a part of modern capitalism. Thus, Wallerstein contends that "the forms Genovese is describing are not transitional or remnants or pockets of resistance but the heart and essence of capitalism as a mode of production" (Wallerstein 1979, 218).

This conceptual framework calls attention at once to the unity, complexity, and long-term structural continuity of the historical processes forming capitalist modernity. However, it does so by abstracting from fundamental differences in form between the various social relations of production and by reducing all economic phenomena to a common content, the production of surplus value. Thus, Wallerstein argues:

> If we have defined the bourgeoisie as those who receive surplus value they do not themselves create and use some of it to accumulate capital, it follows that the proletariat are those who yield part of the value they have created to others. In this sense there exists in the capitalist mode of production only capitalists and proletarians. The polarity is structural. (Wallerstein 1979, 288–289)

In this formulation, the concept "surplus value" loses all qualitative distinctions and simply describes a homogeneous quantitative relation. (I have discussed the importance of forms of social relations and surplus value as a qualitatively specific social form in greater detail in Tomich 1980, esp. 540–545.) It thereby becomes the lowest common denominator through which the diverse relations of production encompassed within the capitalist world economy are equated with one another. Thus, capitalist and wage worker, landlord and tenant, master and slave, among others, are subsumed under the bipolar division between bourgeoisie and proletariat. In each instance, qualitative distinctions between relations of production and exchange are dissolved into variations in the proportion of economic and extra-economic factors and the distribution of resources to be mobilized. Differences in kind are subtly transformed into differences in degree as the emphasis falls upon the essential production of surplus value, and all producers within the "historical structure" of this capitalist world economy are seen as attempting to maximize the surplus value at their disposal.

On the other side of the coin, to the degree that differences between distinct forms of labor organization are recognized within the terms of the theory, they are treated as particular instances of the given general conditions of the system. Wage labor, tenancy, coerced cash cropping, and other forms of social labor are thus regarded as attributes of core, semiperiphery, and periphery. (For example, Wallerstein writes: "Thus coerced or semicoerced semiwage labor is, and has been from the beginning of capitalism as a world-system, a phenomenon of peripheral areas of the capitalist world-economy, while contractual labor is concentrated largely (but not exclusively) in core areas" [1979, 219].) Through this procedure, Wallerstein assimilates historically specific social relations into fixed general categories that define the structure of the modern world-system. He thereby transforms the diversity among production relations into a priori properties of general theoretical categories. The structural requirements (e.g., core, semiperiphery, periphery) must of necessity be present in order to constitute the system: The problem of which particular individual or collective actors—entrepreneurs, classes, states, etc.—fill which box is regarded as simply conjunctural.

Consequently, slavery appears here simply as one among several forms of coerced labor that characterize peripheral arenas of the world economy. Within this framework, the more general term, coerced cash crop production, is given analytical priority over the particularities of slavery as a defining feature of the periphery. While this general category serves to differentiate slavery from types of labor prevailing in other zones, it fails to distinguish among forms of coerced labor within the periphery. Thus, for example, slavery is treated as the equivalent of "serfdom," and the abolition of slavery connotes simply a change from one type of "coerced or semicoerced semi-wage labor" to another. From the point of view of world-systems theory, the historical significance of such a transformation is of less importance than the theoretically necessary persistence of the general category of coerced cash crop production.

In this theoretical schema, the relation between the general structural categories is functionally determined by the requirements of surplus extraction and maximization:

> Why different modes of organizing labor—slavery, "feudalism," wage labor, self-employment—at the same point in time within the world-economy? Because each mode of labor control is best suited for particular types of production. And why were these modes concentrated in different zones of the world-economy—slavery and "feudalism" in the periphery, wage labor and self-employment in the core, and as we shall see sharecropping in the semiperiphery? Because the modes of labor control greatly affect the political system (in particular the strength of the state apparatus) and the possibility for an indigenous bourgeoisie to thrive. The world-economy was based precisely on the assumption that there were in fact these three zones and that they did in fact have different modes of labor control. Were this not so, it would not have been possible to assure the kind of flow of the surplus which enabled the capitalist system to come into existence. (Wallerstein 1974, I, 87)

From this perspective, the modern world-system appears as an invariant and functionally defined structure in which the parts are subordinated to the system as a whole. The requirements of the "unequal exchange" of surplus value through the world market determine relations between core, semiperiphery, and periphery and create an overriding logic of endless capital accumulation for the system as a whole.

Thus, this conceptual framework constructs abstract fixed categories of production and exchange that disregard empirical variation and therefore operate independently of any specific historical content. The premises of the theory conjoin an abstract functionalist view of capitalism as a system with an equally abstract methodological individualism. The profit-maximizing individual rationality of neo-classical theory is reproduced here, not as a presumed universal, but as bounded by the "system." On the one hand, the theory's instrumental conception of surplus value fragments social relations into myriad disaggregated individuals, each acting in their self-interest. On the other hand, the activities of the various producers are integrated and regulated by the tripartite structure of the world market: The zero-sum relation between core, semiperiphery, and periphery unequally distributes "rewards" and "penalties" and functionally determines the possibilities and limits of capital accumulation (and therefore the particular context of individual action).

This formulation fails adequately to grasp the specific character of individual forms of social relations—the distinctive social and historical conditions under which labor is brought together with the instruments and material of labor to engage in social production within each form. Consequently, it is unable to comprehend either the differences between the various relations of production or the historically changing relations among them within the processes constituting world economy. The question of the social origins of society and history—how social relations are produced, how they produce, and how they are reproduced—is excluded from consideration. Instead, the theory presumes both the availability of appropriate social relations and an automatic, functional process of their adoption. The diversity of empirical relations merely illustrates an unchanging structure, while the conception of production and market relations remains static. Implicit in this approach is a dualistic conception of history. By treating particular forms as if they were simply conjunctural elements, Wallerstein proposes a "historical system" that has no history or whose historical development is predetermined by a static structure. He then counterposes this system to the virtually infinite empirical details of "real history."

MARX AND *CAPITAL:*
HISTORICAL THEORY

In their different ways, each of the approaches discussed here theoretically fragments the inner connection between slavery, the world market, and capitalist development. In so doing they obscure both the world economic origins of slavery and the slave origins of the world economy. In them, analytical categories are taken as given; they are seen as things in themselves and remain conceptually independent from one another and from the historical whole. While they may be judged by their contents and conditioned by their contexts, the categories themselves do not change. Thus, slavery can be only one thing with only one meaning. On the one hand, production for the market is privileged, and slavery is regarded as capitalist (and capitalism itself is construed broadly either as a universally valid concept or as the historically singular structure of the world market). On the other, the particularity of slave production relations is emphasized, and slavery is regarded as precapitalist or non-capitalist (while capitalism is identified narrowly with the waged form of labor). In each case, analytical abstraction is substituted for the variability and complexity of historical process rather than serving as a means for grasping and constituting it. Slavery is not seen in organic interdependence with and changing historical relation to other forms of social labor within a complex of interrelated processes of production and exchange. Instead, it is isolated from the ensemble of relations that comprise the world economy and is either subsumed under presumedly universal economic laws or conceptualized as a distinct socio-economic system with its own universal laws. Thus, the historical development of each individual form of social production and the relationships among forms are eliminated as subject matter. The world economy is treated either as merely the sum of its parts, any one of which can be removed and treated in isolation or as an autonomous whole that predominates over its parts.

The historical conditions of slave production require theoretical and methodological premises different from those discussed above. In order to reconstruct slavery within the interrelated and interdependent relations and processes forming the world economy as a whole, it is necessary to move beyond such partial and abstract conceptions of capitalism. Instead, we must rethink the totality of relations of capital in a way that is not simply inclusive of slavery and diverse non-waged relations but also is capable of comprehending their specific character. The limitations of the approaches discussed above bring us back to questions about the nature and role of theoretical categories and their relation to historical processes of capitalist development. The remainder of this chapter pursues these questions through an examination of the problem of Marx's method of abstraction in order to suggest an alternative conception of the role of political economic categories in reconstructing world historical processes of capitalist development. This discussion emphasizes the distinction between historical theory which is concerned with formulating theoretical categories that are appropriate for the comprehension of a historically distinct object of inquiry and theoretical history which is concerned with using such categories to reconstruct processes of historical development

Marx's *Capital* poses a specific relation between theory and history that allows us to break out of the false choices of production vs. market and precapitalist vs. capitalist, which have characterized these debates. The purpose of Marx's *critique* of political economy is to disclose the historically specific character of capital as social relation. His approach is determined by the character of his subject matter. He attempts to comprehend a reality that is already structured and therefore requires methodological procedures and theoretical categories that are appropriate to it (Schmidt 1983, 7–8; also Hopkins 1982b, esp. 152–158). Through a continual process of abstraction from a social-historical reality that possesses its own (inner) coherence and (self)-movement, he seeks to establish the historical conditions under which the categories of analysis are valid (Korsch 1963, 24–44; Schmidt 1983).

Marx's conceptualization of capital is, in Engels words, "ultimately a historical one, stripped of its historical form and disturbing accidents" (in Rosdolsky 1974, 65). The concepts of *Capital* form what Marx terms "rational abstractions" (Marx 1973, 85). The categories of wage labor and capital are not arbitrary logical models or ideal types in any conventional sense. Rather, they are construed as abstract reflections derived from developing historical relations. Capitalist social relations provide the ongoing historical premise of Marx's theory, and the categories of this theory obtain only under specified historical conditions. This conceptual approach provides what Engels describes as, "a corrected mirror image [of the historical process], but corrected according to principles which permit us to grasp the real historical processes so that every moment can be viewed *at the developmental point of its full maturity, at the moment of its classical perfection*" (Engels in Rosdolsky 1974, 65). These concepts are intended "to fix the common element" of relations of varying scope and duration. Thus, in conceptualizing "production," Marx argues: "Some determinations belong to all epochs, others only to a few. . . . [N]evertheless, just those things which determine their development, i.e., the elements which are not general and common, must be separated out from the determinations valid for production as such, so that in their unity . . . their essential difference is not forgotten" (Marx 1973, 85).

Thus, in Marx's conception, categories are at once historical and logical. Engels emphasizes that "only the historical gives determinate form to abstraction and predetermines its place and its role in [Marx's] theoretical system (Schmidt 1985, 35–36). Consistent with his method, Marx regards the emergence of industrial capital and, more importantly, the wage-earning proletariat, as the practical precondition for his methodological abstractions. The historical presence of the capital-wage labor relation on a scale sufficient to reproduce itself from its own processes allows him to develop his concept of capital. In his view, the capital–wage labor relation represents the full development of commodity production and "announces from the outset a new epoch in the process of social production" (Marx 1976, 274; Marx 1973, 277). Only when labor becomes wage labor does the "sale and purchase embrace not just excess produce, but its very substance, and the various conditions of production themselves appear as *commodities* which leave circulation and enter production only on the foundations for capitalist production" (Marx 1976, 950). Only when the working population sells its labor-power "can it be said that production has become the *production of commodities* through its entire length and breadth. Only then does all produce become commodity and the objective conditions of each and every sphere of production enter into it as commodities themselves. Only on the basis of capitalist commodity production [i.e., the capital–wage labor relation] does the commodity actually become the *universal elementary form of wealth*" (Marx 1976, 950–951).

Concomitant with the generalization of commodity production and the full development of the commodity form, the wage form develops the universal character of labor:

> As a rule, the most general abstractions arise only in the midst of the richest possible concrete development, where one thing appears as common to many, to all. Then it ceases to be thinkable in a particular form alone. On the other side, this abstraction of labor as such is not merely a mental product of the concrete totality of labors. Indifference towards specific labors corresponds to a form of society in which individuals can with ease transfer from one labor to another, and where the specific kind is a matter of chance for them, hence of indifference. Not only the category labor, but labor in reality has here become the means of creating wealth in general, and has ceased to be organically linked with particular individuals in any specific form. . . . Here, then, for the first time, the point of departure of modern economics, namely the abstraction of the category "labor," "labor as such," becomes true in practice. The simplest abstraction, then, which modern economics places at the head of its discussions, and which expresses an immeasurably ancient relation valid in all forms of society, nevertheless achieves practical truth as an abstraction only as a category of the most modern society. (Marx 1973, 104–105)

Marx's understanding of (abstract) labor as at once a specific attribute of the capital–wage labor relation and a universal category provides the conceptual underpinning of his critique of political economy. It allows him to apprehend capital as a particular *historical* form of social relation of production and labor as its content. By treating the capital–wage labor relation as the most fully developed form of social (commodity) production, he is able to theoretically reconstruct less developed forms of social relations of production (slavery, serfdom, etc.) where labor is concealed by particular forms of social domination and to conceptualize history as the changing relation between form and content, that is to say, the history of forms of social labor.

For Marx, the wage labor form gives capital its specific social-historical character and distinguishes it from other modes of social production: "What distinguishes the various economic formations of society—the distinction between for example a society based on slave-labor and a society based on wage-labor—is the form in which this surplus labor is in each case extorted from the immediate producer, the worker" (Marx 1976, 325; also 174n). This emphasis on the importance of the *form* of social relations is one of the defining elements of Marx's critique of political economy: "Political economy has indeed analyzed value and its magnitude, however incompletely, and has uncovered the content [labor] concealed within these forms. But it has never once asked why this content has assumed that particular form, that is to say, why labor is expressed in value, and why the measurement of labor by its duration is expressed in the magnitude of the value of the product" (Marx 1976, 173–174). This passage demonstrates how central the concept of form is to Marx's argument. By presenting capital as a distinct social form, Marx is able to conceptualize it as a social process undergoing continual transformation and development rather than as something eternal and natural, or, to quote his formulation as "a particular kind of social production of a historical and transitory nature" (Marx 1976, 174n).

The capital–wage labor relation, which is the focal point of the theoretical inquiry, provides the methodological ground for Marx's critical reconstruction both of capital as historical social relation and of antecedent forms of political economic relations. He regards the capital–wage labor form as "the most developed and the most complex historic organization of production" (Marx 1973, 105) and treats it as the "specific kind of production which dominates over all the rest, whose relations thus assign rank and influence the others, it is a general illumination which bathes all the other colors and modifies their particularity. It is a particular ether which determines the specific gravity of every being which has materialized within it" (Marx 1973, 106–107). As the most fully developed form of social labor, the capital–wage labor relation provides the privileged perspective from which Marx organizes the order and sequence of categories used to analyze both capital and antecedent forms of social labor. "It would . . . be unfeasible and wrong," he writes, "to let the economic categories follow one another in the same sequence as that in which they are historically decisive. Their sequence is determined rather, by their relation to one another in modern bourgeois society, which is precisely the opposite of that which seems to be their natural order or which corresponds to historical development" (Marx 1973, 107). Rather than comprehending history as an evolutionary sequence, Marx regards it as a critical reconstruction to be grasped from the vantage point of the most fully developed relations and the theoretical categories derived from them. As he states in a well-known passage, "Human anatomy contains a key to the anatomy of the ape."(Marx 1973, 105). Earlier formations are construed as less developed forms of the capital relation, and historical development is theoretically interpreted as the movement from simple to complex relations. History here is a theoretical construct; it is not given. Far from being predictive in any conventional sense, theory must be continually reinterpreted and reformulated in the light of the ongoing development of the capitalist form.

Although Marx conceives of the capital–wage labor relation as itself historical, the outcome of a long process of historical development, his purpose is not to provide a historical account of the capital relation. Rather, in *Capital*, he grants cognitive primacy to the logical relation among categories over the historical (Schmidt 1983, 33, 37). In the *Grundrisse*, he describes his methodological approach: "In order to develop the laws of bourgeois economy, therefore, it is not necessary to write the *real history of the relations of production*. But the correct observation and deduction of these laws, as having themselves become in history, always leads to primary equations—like the empirical numbers, e.g., in natural science—which points towards a past lying behind this system. These indications, together with a correct grasp of the present, then also offer the key to the understanding of the past—a work in its own right which, it is to be hoped, we shall be able to undertake as well" (Marx 1973, 460–461).

Thus, Marx focuses on the theoretical exposition of specifically capitalist social relations. By abstracting the formal characteristics of the capital–wage labor relation from the historical conditions of its existence, he establishes the concept of capital "*at the developmental point of its full maturity, at the moment of its classical perfection.*" This process of abstraction entails stripping the concept of its "historical form" and eliminating "contingencies and disturbing accidents" and emphasizing the necessary logical connection between categories. Throughout the text Marx indicates definite historical conditions and presuppositions for the development of the capital–wage labor relation but at the same time excludes them from the presentation, pursuing instead the logical development of the concept of capital. Thus, he regards material production, the human interchange with nature through labor, as the ongoing premise of capitalist production and indeed of all human production. Indeed, he boldly proposes: "Technology reveals the active relation of man to nature, the direct process of production of his life, and thereby it also lays bare the production of the social relations of his life, and of the mental conceptions that flow from those relations" (1976, 493n). Nonetheless, he provides no sustained and integral account of the particular use values, material processes of production, and technological organization that shaped the course of capitalist development. Instead, with the exception of examples intended to illustrate particular relationships, material processes only appear abstractly under the heading of "use-value" as Marx devotes his attention to the theoretical exposition of specifically capitalist forms of socially constructed objectivity (fetishism).

Similarly, the history of capitalist social relations remains external to the theoretical account. For example, in a well-known passage, Marx writes:

> While the cotton industry introduced child-slavery into England, in the United States it gave impulse for the transformation of the earlier, more or less patriarchal slavery into a system of commercial exploitation. *In fact, the veiled slavery of the wage-laborers in Europe needed the unqualified slavery of the New World as its pedestal.* (Marx 1976, 925; my emphasis)

This remark calls attention to a particular historical condition of the development of capital. Yet, there is no extended discussion of the historical role of slavery in the development of capitalism or of the interrelation of slavery and wage labor. Rather, Marx's concern is to delineate the theoretical structure of the capital relation. He therefore gives priority to the logical development of its form. Theoretically, capital requires a given mass of commodities in circulation and a given division of labor for its development, but it does not necessarily "require" slavery. Therefore, Marx treats slavery as an external contingency and excludes it from the logical exposition. Nonetheless, historically, slavery was a key means of expanding commodity production, creating a world market, and providing the substantive conditions for the development of the capital–wage labor form.

The architecture of *Capital* reveals its theoretical structure. Marx's presentation of his theory of capital begins with the commodity form, which is presented as its necessary *logical starting point*. In contrast, the *historical beginnings* of capital, its origins in non-capitalist relations, are relegated to the end of the text. Marx regards this "original accumulation" as necessarily a part of the concept of capital understood as a historically specific relation, but as not in any way a part of its ongoing processes and relations (see Korsch 1963; Marx 1973, 459–461). (Here we should also note that the section on the original accumulation of capital is itself a theoretically constructed sketch of the historical origins of capital, the separation of the direct producers from the means of production, and the concentration of the means in the hands of a class of capitalists but is by no means identical with the real history of the formation of capitalist social relations.)

The presentation of the logical structure of the capital relation (*darstel-*

lung) appears in *Capital* as what Roman Rosdolsky (1974, 65) calls a "dialectic of concepts." The organization of the text follows the dialectical
movement from simple to complex and from abstract to concrete. This exposition proceeds from its logically necessary starting point, the commodity as
the cell-form of capitalist relations, to the fully developed concept of capital.
In the succession of categories—Commodity–Value–Money–Capital—each
relation is regarded as the simpler and more elemental form of the category
that succeeds it. Each builds upon the preceding ones and goes beyond them.
At the same time, the prior categories only attain their full development on
the basis of the later ones (Rosdolsky 1977, 167–168). Taken together, these
categories form a complex and heterogeneous totality, "the concentration of
many determinations," that integrates diverse relations and processes into a
unified theoretical scheme and allows us to understand their interrelation.

The organizing pivot of this theoretical exposition is, of course, the capital–wage labor relation. For Marx, the concept of wage labor and the commodification of *labor power* represent the specific form of the capital relation.
Through the commodity form, he establishes the contradictory unity of capital and (wage) labor and discloses the inner structure of capital as social relation. All the elements of the production process—materials and instruments
of labor, the *activity* of labor, as well as the entire product of labor—take the
form of commodities and can be related to one another through their value.
The wage labor form thus establishes the inner coherence of the totality of
relations of capital; and it allows each of its elements to be related to one
another through their value. The formal attributes of this relation allow Marx
to formulate his key concepts—labor-power, abstract labor, socially necessary labor time, value—and to analyze the relations they represent. The specific form of capital–wage labor is necessary for the appearance of the
categories in the preceding as objective social relations: in turn, these relations develop the form.

As the conceptual hub of *Capital*, the wage relation unifies production and
exchange and brings into focus the movement of categories from simple to
complex and abstract to concrete. It thereby establishes a logical hierarchy of
political economic forms. Relations are construed either as external presuppositions of capital and wage labor or as the results of its processes. From
this perspective, the meaning of concepts is not static and their progression
is not linear. Later formulations of concepts assume greater complexity and
new meanings within a more fully developed whole, even as the earlier ones
remain necessary for the comprehension of the totality of relations. In the
logical succession of categories, the simpler categories may express either
"the dominant relation of a less developed whole" or "the subordinate relations of a more developed whole" (Marx 1973, 102). Through a movement

of "dialectical inversion," equivalent exchange is revealed as the form of appropriation and the character and significance of categories such as "commodity," "exchange," and "labor" are transformed when they are viewed as the products of capitalist production and expanded reproduction (Marx 1973, 458; Marx 1976, 729–730, 733–734, 949–954). In this conceptual framework, meaning is not intrinsic to concepts, but derives from their relation to other concepts forming the totality. The key to understanding Marx's concept of capital is not to be found in any definition given at a particular point in the presentation, nor is it in any single category viewed in isolation; it is given, rather, by the structure and movement of the whole.

Instead of treating the categories of political economy as if they were natural or universal, this methodological approach allows Marx to "establish the specific form in which it [capital] is posited at a *certain* point" (Marx 1973, 310). From this perspective, he delineates the relation of categories to one another and specifies the conditions under which they are valid. Marx reveals the internal structure of the capital relation by tracing its logically necessary development from abstract to concrete. In this way, he establishes the (contradictory) unity of diverse relations of production *and* exchange and gives coherence and content to the conceptual whole. This logical hierarchy of concepts allows him to distinguish simple from complex expressions of the same relation. He is thereby able to specify the capital relation and differentiate it from more elementary forms of commodity production and exchange.

By determining the necessary logical structure of categories Marx is able to theoretically comprehend the historical formation of capital as a specific relation. His analysis of the commodity form establishes commodity circulation, not production, as the starting point of capital. Thus, he argues that world trade and the world market of the sixteenth century form the historic presuppositions of the capital–wage labor relation, and from that point on, "the modern history of capital starts to unfold" (Marx 1973, 259–264, 450–458; Marx 1976, 247). Although Marx identifies the world market as the *historical* premise and condition of capital, he presents a *theoretical* account of the movement from the market to the capital–wage labor relation and the categories of capitalist production, not a historical one. The wage relation, that is the purchase and sale of labor-power, resolves what Marx posits as the contradiction in the general formula for capital: the need to reconcile the appropriation of surplus with the assumption of equivalent exchange. It thereby discloses the specifically capitalist form of social relations of production (Marx 1973, 268–269, 279–306). Nonetheless, the world market remains the ongoing theoretical and practical condition for the wage labor relation and capitalist production and the product of their action. Marx distinguishes between the world market as the condition for the emergence of wage labor and capital and the (reformation of the) world market as the outcome of capitalist production (Marx 1973, 259–264, 450–458; Marx 1976, 247). Although world market frames the entire theoretical exposition of capital, it is constantly changing in relation to other concepts that at once are shaped by it and shape it, above all, wage labor and capital. Consistent with the logic of Marx's method, the capital–wage labor relation itself is continually reinterpreted in the light of the ongoing transformations of the material processes and social organization of production (see especially Marx 1976, appendix, "Immediate Results of the Production Process").

This theoretical construction of capital as a complex and structured historical relation takes us well beyond the abstract and partial choices of production vs. market, which have informed the perspectives discussed above. The history of capitalist development appears neither as the linear unfolding of the inner-logic of the capital–wage relation nor as the product of an all-embracing world market that is both cause and result of all historical development (Merrington in Hilton 1976, 173–174). Rather, market and the wage labor form of production represent substantive social relations that are continuously made and remade in a spiral of development through their interaction with one another.

Thus, Marx's method posits a close and necessary relation between theory and history. On the one hand, his theoretical categories are valid only under specified historical conditions. On the other hand, the conceptual movement of *Capital* reproduces *in theory* the historical development of capital. However, according to its own methodological assumptions, the theoretical structure of *Capital* cannot be treated as if it were identical with the history of capitalist development. One cannot be reduced to the other. The general theory of capital, however interpreted, is distinct from the particular history of capitalist development. Although Marx regards England as the *locus classicus* of the "capitalist mode of production, and the relations of production and forms of intercourse that correspond to it" and uses it as "the main illustration of [his] theoretical developments," *Capital* in no way presents a history of capital in England (Marx 1976, 90). Nor does it provide theoretical support for an already given conception of capitalist world economy. The organizing principle of *Capital* is logical. History retains its independent movement.

A discussion of Marx's treatment of the working day serves to emphasize the constant and productive tension between history and theory in his work as well as his insistence on the limits of theory. In the chapter on "The Working Day," after having developed the concept of commodity exchange up through the exchange between capital and labor and after having demonstrated the antagonistic interests of capitalist and worker as buyer and seller, respectively, of labor power, Marx writes:

We see then that, leaving aside certain extremely elastic restrictions, the nature of commodity exchange itself imposes no limit to the working day, no limit to surplus labor. . . . There is an antimony, of right against right, both equally bearing the seal of the law of exchange. Between equal rights force decides. Hence, in the history of capitalist production, the establishment of a norm for the working day presents itself as a struggle over the limits of that day, a struggle between collective capital, i.e. the class of capitalists, and collective labor, i.e. the working class. (Marx 1976, 344)

The length of the working day and its division into necessary and surplus labor time is fundamental for Marx's theory of capital and forms the basis of his theory of surplus value. In his conception, struggles of labor and capital over the working day develop capitalist production while the freedom of labor from the domination of capital depends on shortening the working day. Yet, at precisely this point there is a break in the logical continuity of his argument (Dunayevskaya 1958, 90–91). The division of the working day into necessary and surplus labor time can only be determined historically. It depends upon the contingent balance of class forces and outcomes of class struggles, which cannot be determined theoretically. Thus, at the core of Marx's theory, he recognizes irreducibly contingent and indeterminate relations that are shaped by real historical struggles beyond the purview of theoretical reasoning and "objective laws of development." (Interestingly, at the end of the chapter, the discussion of struggles over the working day is linked to the end of slavery and the development of the railroad. But these comments remain merely hints of a history that remains unwritten.)

From this perspective, the categories of Marx's theory are neither descriptive of "real" social relations, nor are they arbitrary heuristic models. Still less are they normative statements about the "true nature" of capitalism. His theory neither describes nor predicts the actual course of historical development. Rather, it provides a cognitive structure that organizes and governs inquiry and allows us to arrange and order concepts, to contextualize categories, to construct data, and to formulate analyses in order to reconstruct historical processes. It is a point of departure, not a point of arrival for historical analysis. As Gramsci argues: "Reality is rich in bizarre combinations, and it is the theoretician who must . . . out of this confusion . . . 'translate' into theoretical language the elements of historical life; not, on the contrary, reality which must present itself according to an abstract scheme" (in Merrington 1968, 149).

TOWARD A THEORETICAL HISTORY

Marx's purpose in writing *Capital* is to theoretically delineate the inner structure of the capital–wage labor relation concealed beneath the commodity form. He conceives of this relation as historically specific and presents the *logical* relations between categories as "the key to understanding of *historical* development" (Rosdolsky 1974, 65, my emphasis). But his rational abstractions are intended as *mirror images* of the historical processes of capitalist development, not as the history itself. The movement (from simple to complex, abstract to concrete) in Marx's text toward wage labor as the fullest expression of the capital relation is a movement toward the *logical synthesis* of a general theory of capital. It provides a perspective from which to reconstruct historical processes, but it does not itself provide a historical account. To allow the theoretical narrative of *Capital* to provide the script for the historical narrative is to confound a general theoretical abstraction with history. It is to ignore broader and more complex historical processes of capitalist development and reproduce the exclusions made in the process of abstraction. Indeed, Marx himself cautions that it is "necessary to correct the idealistic manner of presentation, which makes it seem as if it were merely a matter of conceptual determinations and the dialectic of these concepts" (Marx 1973, 151). Later in the text, he adds that "much more important for us is that our method indicates the points where historical investigation must enter in, or where bourgeois economy as a merely historical form of the production process points beyond itself to earlier historical modes of production" (Marx 1973, 460).

Once we recognize the significance of Marx's method of abstraction and, as a result, distinguish his theory of capital from historical accounts of capitalist development, we are able to overcome the theoretical fragmentation that has characterized the treatments of slavery discussed above. The problem is not to simply add slavery to an already given and completed concept of capital. It is, rather, to rethink the totality of relations of capital in a way that is inclusive of slavery and diverse non-waged relations. (Perhaps it is worth recalling here Lukàcs' admonition that the core of Marxism is not the results of his research or one or another of his theses, but his method [Lukàcs 1960, 18].) Such rethinking requires inverting the order of procedure. Instead of moving from history toward higher levels of theoretical specification and synthesis, it entails going *against the grain of Marx's classical theoretical presentation* in order to reincorporate into the field of analysis those "historical contingencies and disturbing accidents" that were eliminated in the process of abstraction. By moving from "rational abstractions" toward engagement, appropriation, and theoretical reconstruction of diverse historical relations excluded by the logic of Marx's presentation, we may comprehend the historical complexity of world capitalist development.

The social relations of commodity production themselves may be taken as the focal point and anchor for such an approach. The commodity relation forms the nexus of the material and the social of production and exchange. Through it, these concepts are conceptually and practically linked. It establishes the inner coherence of these relations and allows the reconstruction of the world economy as a unified, structured, contradictorily evolving totality. From this perspective, production appears as an intrinsically social and historical process. Social relations are not regarded as external and contingent to categories of economic analysis, but rather are taken to be constitutive of specific, historical conditions of production. Production can only take place within and through definite social relations. Material production and the social form of its organization are two inseparable aspects of human productive activity. Thus, the relation between material production (the relation of human beings to nature) and social relations of production (the relations between human beings) cannot be regarded as external and contingent. Rather, it is an internal and necessary relation. It is internal because each aspect exists only in and through the other; thus, it is necessary in the sense that the material and the social are inherently interconnected, and within this connectedness neither is reducible to the other (Sayer, 1987, esp. chapters 1–2).

In this approach, totality is not understood as the sum of, or attempt to account for, all possible facts and relations. Rather it is posited as an open-ended theoretical construct (Kosík 1976) that entails a process of progressive abstraction and reconstruction through which concepts are formed and reformed in an effort to specify relations in a comprehensive field of knowledge. In *Capital*, Marx is concerned with the theoretical movement from the world market to the wage labor form and capitalist production. This construct treats slavery and similar relations as external and contingent to the logic of the formal development of the capital relation. In so doing it excludes from consideration the division of labor and the historical relation of diverse forms of labor that are expressed through the world market. In order to move beyond the limitations of the wage-centered totality of *Capital*, the approach developed here turns to the more abstract and general conception of totality as the unity of production, distribution, exchange, and consumption presented by Marx in the *Grundrisse* (Marx 1973, 85–101).

Such an understanding of totality opens the way for us to overcome the dualistic opposition of market vs. production, precapitalist vs. capitalist, and so forth, that limited the approaches discussed earlier. Here we may conceive of production, distribution, exchange, and consumption as a unified field of relational concepts linked by the commodity form. Each term is defined through its relation with the others. Production and exchange, for example, appear here as general and abstract relations. However, in practice, any particular instances of production or exchange are necessarily organized through some specific social form. Further, from this perspective, such particular instances presume historically given relations of production, distribution, exchange, and consumption that can affect the course of their development. Thus, specific forms of social production or exchange are not regarded as autonomous units with their own history but as formed through their relation to the larger political economic whole.

This analytically open framework enables us to avoid "violent abstractions" and instead focus on particular relations as themselves outcomes of complex historical processes. Through it, we may integrate slavery and other forms of unwaged labor into the totality of political economic relations. This approach does not treat wage labor and slave labor as external to one another, neither does it eliminate the differences between them and assimilate both into a homogeneous conception of capital. Rather, it allows us to posit a definite historical relationship between wage and slave labor, not as an "integrated duality," but as a "contradictory unity" (Franco 1976, 10–11), and to systematically interrogate the historical interrelation of forms of labor within the division of labor through diverse modes of interaction. Here slavery and capitalism are seen not as mutually exclusive categories or as simply coincident with one another. Slave relations are not conceived as separate from or prior to the world market and international division of labor. They are not regarded as capitalist because they entail production for the market or as non-capitalist because they are not the waged form of labor. Rather, slave labor is treated as part of the organization of social labor on a world scale. It constitutes a specific form of commodity production that is related to other such forms through the world market and international division of labor. In turn, the world market and division of labor remain the ongoing conditions of the reproduction of slave relations. This broad conception of totality enables us to reconstruct the historically formed world division of labor as a relation among specific material processes and social forms of labor in particular places, integrated by the world market, changing with regard to one another over time and in space.

Such a theoretical-historical approach allows us to move away from unproductively general definitions and to grasp the relation of slavery and capitalism as itself a complex historical process. Capitalism, as a definite historical phenomenon, is not identified simply with production for the market or confined to the wage form. Although the market and wage labor may be regarded as essential in their different ways to determining—theoretically and historically—the capitalist character of the world economy, when viewed in isolation from historical process they remain abstract, static, and unchanging categories. In contrast, from the perspective proposed here, these relations and processes of commodity production and exchange are treated as simultaneous and mutually formative. Each form of labor retains its specificity and imposes its own conditions on social production. It is not a question of which relations seen in isolation are capitalist and which are not. Within the evolution of this totality, the categories of analysis move with respect to one another. They are relational and historically specific rather than universally valid. Rather than having a single fixed meaning, each illuminates the others, and their specific contents and meanings derive from the ensemble of relations of the world economy. They therefore represent real social processes whose interrelationships and significance vary over time in accordance with the development of the ensemble of social relations. Both the capitalist character of slavery and the slave character of capitalism emerge from the historically evolving relations among the various forms of production and exchange within this totality (Kosík 1976, 1–35; Sayer 1987, 1–14).

Conceived in this way, the historical hierarchy among forms of labor is not, and cannot be, the same as the theoretical hierarchy. Even as the wage labor–capital relation forms the theoretical pivot of Marx's analysis, this relation cannot be presumed to be the "prime mover" of historical capitalism. At any particular point in time, whether from the perspective of any single form or the ensemble of forms, relations among forms of production, of exchange, of distribution, and of consumption are historically given, and they substantively affect the course of historical development. By integrating diverse relations into a unified analytical field, the approach presented here allows us to interrogate their systemic interrelation and interaction. From the perspective of this unified conceptual field, we may apprehend the course of historical development of both individual slave formations and the world economy as a whole through the ongoing interplay of structure and contingency across multiple analytical levels. At one such level, a relation may appear as a contingent relation; and at another as a given structural condition of social action. By moving from one such level to another, this approach discloses the complex, multidimensional, structured totality of relations forming the capitalist world economy. We may then theoretically reconstruct the historical development of specific local slave regimes as outcomes of world economic processes and differentiate such regimes from one another by their position within the political economic whole. The specificity of particular slave regimes at once contributes to and discloses the spatial and temporal heterogeneity of the capitalist world economy. In this way, slavery reveals the constant asymmetry, unevenness, and tension between particular local histories and the diverse but unified temporal rhythms and spatial extensions of world economic processes.

Chapter Two

World of Capital, Worlds of Labor

A Global Perspective

Since the late 1940s a series of debates centered on the works of Maurice Dobb (1947) and Paul Sweezy (in Hilton 1976); André Gunder Frank (1967) and Ernesto Laclau (1971); and Immanuel Wallerstein (1974, 1979) and Robert Brenner (1977) provided a fundamental point of reference for much scholarship on capitalism, slavery, and development. Nonetheless, from today's vantage point, perhaps the most striking feature of the debate is that over the course of fifty years, its terms have been reasserted ever more forcefully despite dramatic shifts in purpose, subject matter, and intellectual context. From one round of the discussion to the next, the focus of inquiry has shifted from the origins of European capitalism, to the nature of underdevelopment, to the historical formation of capitalism as a world economy. Yet, on each occasion, the problems have been formulated within the same theoretical terms, and the same options for interpretation and analysis have been presented. In general, the debates have crystallized around two broad perspectives. The first emphasizes the importance of the market and the transnational character of capitalist development. In this perspective, capitalism is identified with production for the market, and diverse waged and unwaged forms of labor may be regarded as capitalist. The second, grounded in Marxist historical materialism emphasizes the specificity of social relations of production linked to the particularity of national experiences. This approach identifies capitalism strictly with the social organization of production by means of wage labor. At each juncture, these positions and the theoretical premises associated with them have shaped discussion independent of the ostensible subject matter. Indeed, it is arguable that the persistent contraposition of market to production relations has provided the essential continuity of

32

these controversies. Such categorical thinking creates what Giovanni Arrighi (1998) calls "non-debates" in which the "participants" inevitably talk past one another because there is no point of contact between the conceptual frameworks they employ.

These debates have reached an impasse. The very repetition of their terms suggests their failure to provide an adequate means to comprehend the complexity of capitalist development on a global scale. Neither one approach nor the other is able to incorporate into a unified analytical framework complex historical combinations of *both* wage *and* nonwage relations of production together with the world market. Nonetheless, these influential polemics continue to define the terms of discussion. Over the decades they have generated a series of binomial oppositions—internal vs. external; mode of production vs. world market; capitalist vs. precapitalist; wage labor vs. unwaged labor; dependency vs. development; structure vs. agency—that at once shaped and limited understandings of capitalism and slavery. These oppositions have locked theoretical comprehension of both capitalism and slavery into a restrictive logic of either/or. Historical interpretations of capitalism have oscillated between wage labor and world market as their organizing pole. Those who identified capitalism with wage labor regarded slavery as a precapitalist or noncapitalist relation; those who emphasized production for the world market as the common grounding of capital treated slavery as capitalist but were unable to account for the specificity of slave relations of production.

The binomial oppositions generated in the course of these debates are the result of what Derek Sayer (1987) terms "violent abstractions," which oppose production to market and capitalism to slavery as if each of these terms represented a closed, distinct, and fully integrated reality. Whichever concept is chosen, a single feature, taken in isolation, is treated as the defining characteristic of capitalism. The historical complexities of capitalist development are reduced to a single dimension which defines its essence as a system. The privileged category, be it wage labor or market, is presumed to possess a universal validity and is used to form an a priori model through which historical narratives of capitalist development are constructed. This privileged category is taken to define a realm of necessity where the "laws of motion" of the system operate. This realm is identified with the "real history" of the system; in contrast, processes that lie outside of it are regarded as contingent and secondary. Beyond creating the grounds for arbitrary decisions in the classification of relations and ordering of causal sequences, these abstract and partial approaches result in an impoverished conception of historical temporality. Despite their claims to account for historical change, none of these approaches succeeds in treating relations in their own temporal and spatial dimensions.

The cornerstone of these controversies has been Dobb's study of the historical development of capitalism from the decline of feudalism through the Second World War, focusing on England as the classic case (Dobb 1947). In particular, Dobb's treatment of the transition from feudalism to capitalism attracted the attention of scholars. Dobb organizes his account around the historical emergence of the capital–wage labor relation as the outcome of crisis and breakdown created by contradictions within feudalism. He was concerned to demonstrate that the decline of feudalism was not caused by the rise of the capitalist mode of production. Rather, while the disintegration of feudalism created the conditions for the emergence of capital–wage labor as the dominant political economic relation, it was the result of struggles between lord and serf over rents.

Dobb's historical interpretation hinges upon his conceptualization of capitalism. Following conventional understandings of Marx's historical materialism, he construes capitalism as a particular mode of production. For him, the concept of mode of production refers not only to the state of technique (productive forces) but also to the way the means of production are owned and to the relations among men that result from their connections with the process of production (social relations of production). From this perspective, capitalism is distinguished from other modes of production by the purchase and sale of labor-power as a commodity on the market. Its historical prerequisite was the concentration of the means of production in the hands of a minority class and the emergence of a propertyless class for whom the sale of labor-power was the only source of livelihood (Dobb 1947, 7).

In accordance with this formulation, Dobb's account of the transition from feudalism to capitalism emphasizes not trade and the growth of markets but the transformation of the social relations of production. In his view, the need of feudal overlords for revenue in the context of the low level of development of productive forces caused the "crisis of feudalism." A seigneurial reaction that sought to extract greater surplus from the peasantry provoked peasant resistance in the form of flight and rebellion. Peasant class struggle in combination with demographic decline and labor shortage resulted in the commutation of feudal dues. The appearance of rents in kind or money rents modified the dependence of the petty mode of production upon feudal overlordship and eventually enabled the small producer "to shake loose" from feudal exploitation (Hilton 1976, 59). In this interpretation, trade is not inconsequential, but it is clearly assigned a secondary role. According to Dobb, "trade exercised its influence to the extent that it accentuated the internal conflicts within the old mode of production" (Hilton 1976, 60).

In Dobb's view, to the degree that the petty mode of production (where producer is in possession of his means of production as an individual produc-

ing unit [Hilton 1976, 58]) secures independent action and social differentiation develops within it, it creates, on the one hand, propertyless and abundant
labor (for Dobb, a decisive factor) and, on the other hand, a "kulak" yeo-
manry who hire the labor of others (Hilton 1976, 59–65). In this way, according to Dobb, the realignment of the petty mode of production within
feudalism creates the conditions that allow the emergence of a capitalist class
employing wage labor and the transformation of productive forces that establishes the domination of capital in the direct process of production. Here,
class relations are defined by the relations of the direct producers to the process of production, and class is regarded as the decisive conceptual key for
historical analysis (Dobb 1947, 7). Once the wage labor–capital relation is
established, it alone is taken to determine the course of capitalist development; other forms are relegated to a secondary position without the capacity
to initiate historical change. (Characteristically, Dobb regards England as the
classic site of capitalism and treats Marx's *Capital* as a direct and unmediated
statement of the "laws" of English development. It is perhaps worth noting
here that these controversies evolved in the context of concern with strategies
for national development and the problem of "socialism in one country.")

Among the critics, Paul Sweezy was most influential in shaping the terms
of the debate, particularly through his emphasis on the role of long-distance
trade in dissolving European feudalism (Hilton 1976, 33–56, 108). Sweezy
argues that it was not the internal struggle between lord and serf, but what he
construed as the external influence of commerce and of the rise of towns that
was necessary to break down the system of serfdom. In his view, by the four-
teenth century a system of production for the market emerged alongside feudal production for use and eroded the feudal system. However, he does not
equate these processes with the rise of capitalism, which he believes to have
taken place two hundred years later and identifies with the emergence of the
capital–wage labor relation. Once the transition is completed, he, too, regards
capitalism as the historical unfolding of the wage labor–capital relation.
Thus, Sweezy and Dobb share the same conception of capitalism and agree
over the chronology of the transition, but differ with regard to the mechanisms of transition, the processes of class formation, and the role of class in
historical transformation. Sweezy emphasizes the role of the market and trade
in eroding feudal relations, while Dobb's account is grounded in the transformation of class relations in the immediate process of production (Hilton 1976).

During the 1960s, the theoretical issues raised in the first debate were
revisited in a new context. André Gunder Frank challenged the identification
of capitalism with the capital–wage labor relation. Instead, he emphasized the
appropriation of surplus through the relation between metropolis and satellite
in determining the capitalist character of Latin American and Third World

underdevelopment, despite the prevalence there of nonwage relations of production (Frank 1967). In response, Ernesto Laclau reasserted the Marxist identification of capitalism with the relation between capital and wage labor. He emphasized the autonomy of distinct modes of production understood as national phenomena and distinguished between capitalism as a mode of production (wage labor and capital), subject to its own autonomous "laws of development," and capitalism as a system resulting from the "articulation" of capitalist and noncapitalist modes (Laclau 1971).

Beginning in the 1970s, Immanuel Wallerstein transformed the dependency position by conceptualizing capitalism as a world system—a historical whole—rather than as a series of dyadic metropolis-satellite relations. He conceived of capitalism as a global division of labor organized through a singular world market and a system of multiple states. In his view, this world system emerges in the sixteenth century and remains the organizing structure of economic, political and cultural life (Wallerstein 1974). He explicitly breaks the temporal-spatial frameworks in which the arguments were cast and puts forth a fully global conception of capitalism as a historical system. Nonetheless, he fails to treat adequately the specificity of particular forms of social production, as I shall argue below. Rather, he regards diverse social relations of production as uniformly capitalist since the formation of the world market in the sixteenth century and treats their specific characteristics as contingencies of secondary importance to the market-based division of labor. Robert Brenner sharply criticized Wallerstein, along with Frank and Sweezy, as "circulationists" who overestimated the role of the market in capitalist development and, for that reason, misapprehended the nature of capitalism and the processes of change within it. Brenner, in contrast, called attention to contingent class struggles in determining the transition to capitalism (Brenner 1977). For Brenner, too, this transition was achieved with the establishment of the capital–wage labor relation as the exclusively capitalist form of production. Thus, his response to Wallerstein's work remains grounded in a national conception of capitalism and tied to the wage labor form. He thereby reproduces the fundamental opposition rather than engaging Wallerstein on the new terrain.

The Wallerstein–Brenner debate is not only the most recent expression of these debates, but in certain respects, it represents their fullest and most systematic development. The remainder of this chapter examines the methodological assumptions and procedures of Wallerstein and Brenner in greater detail in order to formulate an alternative to the dualistic approaches that have characterized these attempts to comprehend the diverse forms of labor in the capitalist world economy.

IMMANUEL WALLERSTEIN: CLASS IN
THE MODERN WORLD SYSTEM

During the 1970s Immanuel Wallerstein posited a theoretical conception of capitalism as a world-system that emphasizes the importance of unwaged forms of labor and the social-historical complexity of modern capitalism. He argues that capitalism is defined precisely by the coexistence and systematic interdependence of a multiplicity of forms of labor, both waged and unwaged, that comprise the modern-world system. All these labor forms are integral to the system and the production of surplus value. (In contrast to Marxist writers, Wallerstein does not distinguish between "surplus," "surplus product," and "surplus value." These terms remain interchangeable within his conceptual framework.) The character of the system derives from the relation among them, and the processes of class formation occur on a world scale.

Social class is conceptualized within the framework of Wallerstein's capitalist world-system. This is regarded as a historically distinct system composed of a singular world market and multiple state structures. The market is the structure "within which calculations of maximum profitability are made and which therefore determine over the long run the amount of productive activity, the degree of specialization, the modes of payment for labor, goods, and services, and the utility of technological innovation." The state structures, on the other hand, "serve primarily to distort the 'free' workings of the capitalist market so as to increase the prospects of one or several groups for profit within it" (Wallerstein 1979, 222–223). From this perspective, the market defines the capitalist character of production. The interaction of market and states here shape the axial division of labor (core, semiperiphery, and periphery) that integrates diverse forms of production into the unified and unifying structure of the world economy and provides the conditions for class and class formation.

Within this framework, classes are defined on the basis of whether they appropriate surplus value. Wallerstein views class relations as a structural polarity between bourgeois (those who receive surplus value they do not themselves create and use some of it to accumulate capital) and proletarians (those who yield part of the value they have created to others) on a world scale (Wallerstein 1979, 285–286). Wallerstein uses the proportion of surplus value appropriated or retained and the form of remuneration to labor in order to distinguish further between different "modes of labor control" in the capitalist world economy. In his view, the producer may keep all, part, or none of the surplus. If some portion of it is transferred to (appropriated by) someone else, the producer may receive no remuneration or be remunerated in goods, money, or some combination of the two. On the basis of these *logical possibilities,* he constructs a typology of modes of labor control to which various historical forms of production relations—wage labor, petty production, peasant production, tenant farming, sharecropping, slavery, and peonage—are assigned (Wallerstein 1979, 289). Thus, Wallerstein at once accounts for the multiple forms of class relations that characterize the capitalist world economy and maintains the essential polarity between bourgeois and proletarian.

In Wallerstein's conception, the market structure maximizes the production of surplus value and creates conditions of exploitation and class structure that characterize *the world economy as a whole.* The structural polarity between bourgeois and proletarian is mediated and given its particular forms by the workings on a world scale of the antimonies economy/polity and supply/demand (Wallerstein 1979, 275–276). World class structure emerges from the contradictory need of capital(ists) to at once maximize the appropriation of surplus and realize profit through the sale of the product (Wallerstein 1979, 277). Wallerstein argues that although wage labor is suitable for tasks requiring a high degree of supervision, it is a relatively expensive form of labor organization for labor processes that can be supervised simply. Consequently, it is not the desired option for those who appropriate surplus value and has never been the exclusive, nor even the predominant, form of labor organization in the world economy. Indeed, Wallerstein attributes the expansion of wage labor in the world economy, not to its productive efficiency, but to the system's need to increase effective demand over the long run by returning a portion of the surplus to the producer in the form of wages. In contrast, he contends that coercive forms of labor control maximize the expropriation of surplus value by pushing toward zero the share going to labor. The ideal arrangement for this, in his view, is one of the many varieties of so-called quasi-feudal relations in which the cash-crop sector or industry is controlled by an enterprise (Wallerstein 1979, 277). Under these conditions, capitalists can, according to Wallerstein, most effectively reduce the return to labor the "biological" minimum while adjusting surplus production to market conditions (Wallerstein 1979, 277).

The contradictory need of the system to at once maintain effective demand and maximize surplus appropriation works through market and state structures to differentiate and unevenly distribute the various forms of labor control through space (core, semiperiphery, periphery) and time (cycles of expansion and contraction) (Wallerstein 1979, 278–279, 290–291). There are systemic differences in kinds of bourgeois and proletarian in core and periphery. Core states contain a higher percentage nationally of the bourgeoisie than peripheral states. Skilled, waged labor is concentrated in the core, while forms of coerced labor are more prevalent in the periphery (Wallerstein 1979, 293). Through processes of unequal exchange, surplus flows from the periphery to the core, as strong states of the core are able to divert a disproportionate share of the surplus to the bourgeois located within their borders (Wallerstein 1979, 292–293).

Thus, this conception treats the capitalist world economy as a historical and geographical whole and attempts to identify the mechanisms which integrate it into a single system. While insisting on the historical uniqueness of the world market and therefore the capitalist world system, Wallerstein offers a comprehensive account of capitalism and of class relations within the world economy. In contrast to Dobb and other Marxists, he eliminates wage labor as the defining condition of the proletariat and of capitalism and emphasizes instead the multiplicity of forms of labor relations within the system. In his conception, the bourgeois-proletarian relation (capitalism) is not identified exclusively with wage labor, nor is it confined to national societies. Rather, it encompasses a variety of modes of labor control—wage labor and self-employment, tenancy and sharecropping, slavery and other forms of coerced cash-crop production—unevenly distributed among core, semiperiphery, periphery, and integrated through the world market. The persistence of non-wage relations is not seen simply as "resistance" by feudal (semifeudal, or quasifeudal) groups to the advance of capitalism, but instead is regarded as a defining structural feature of the system. In this view, the world economy is regarded as capitalist, at least from the sixteenth century onward, and the nonwage labor relations that characterize peripheral and semiperipheral social formations are treated as integral parts of the system. *Relations of production are the relations of the whole system* (Wallerstein 1979, 127). The expansion of the system entails the differential incorporation of various forms of "labor control" and not the generalization of wage labor.

ROBERT BRENNER: CLASS STRUGGLE
AND THE TRANSITION TO CAPITALISM

In an influential article published in 1977, Robert Brenner sharply criticized Wallerstein's conception of capitalist development and social class. For purposes of exposition, I shall not focus on Brenner's historical essays (Aston and Philpin, 1985) but rather on the 1977 essay, which continues and constructs the debate about the transition to capitalism and makes his methodological and theoretical assumptions more explicit. In this essay, Brenner contends that Wallerstein, like Sweezy and Frank before him, displaces class relations from their proper position in the analysis of economic development and underdevelopment. In Brenner's view, by equating capitalism with a trade-based division of labor such "neo-Smithian" approaches fail to account for either the way in which specific class structures determine the course of economic development or the way in which class structures themselves emerge. Instead, classes are treated as technical adaptations to market requirements. Differences between forms of class relations are de-emphasized, and diverse forms of class relations are treated as uniformly capitalist. Consequently, Brenner contends that Wallerstein is unable to analyze the qualitatively distinct processes of capitalist development and class formation.

In contrast, Brenner, like Dobb and Laclau, emphasizes the primacy of the social relations of production in determining both the character of a given mode of production and the contingent outcomes of class struggles in determining the transition from one mode to another. Instead of presuming a universal response by producers to the pressures of the capitalist market, Brenner's perspective draws attention to the "differential limitations and potentialities imposed by different class structures on differentially placed exploiters and producers responding to such market forces—and, further, the different sorts of interests or goals to which such exploiters and producers might attempt to subordinate exchange" (Brenner 1977, 38). From this perspective, capitalism is identified exclusively by the capital–wage labor relation. This economic relationship is constituted through the free laborer's sale of her or his labor power. It requires as its necessary preconditions the separation of the direct producer from possession of means of production and the emancipation of laborers from any direct relation of domination (such as slavery or serfdom). On the other hand, if the social relations of production are not characterized by free wage labor, then the mode of production is not capitalist, even if its products are destined for the world market.

By emphasizing the specificity of particular forms of class relations, Brenner calls attention to the qualitative difference between capitalist (wage labor) and pre- or noncapitalist (nonwage) modes of production and the distinctive processes of capitalist development. He argues that only the capital–wage labor relation generalizes commodity production. The commodification of labor-power alone allows systematic development of productive forces through technological innovation and increasing productivity of labor (relative surplus product/labor), which, for Brenner, is the decisive characteristic of capitalism. Thus, in his view, the class structure of the (national) economy as a whole determines the character of capitalist economic development by compelling individual component "units" to increase their production, develop their forces of production, and increase the productivity of labor in order to secure their reproduction. In contrast, he contends that even where trade is widespread, precapitalist (nonwage) economies can develop only within definite limits because the class structure of production neither requires nor permits systematic increases in productive forces and labor productivity as the condition of their reproduction (Brenner 1977, 32–33).

This emphasis on the specificity of the capital–wage labor relation leads Brenner to dissociate capitalist development from underdevelopment as separate and distinguishable processes (Brenner 1977, 60–61). According to this view, the market is regarded as external to the prevailing relations of direct production. Surplus transfer (unequal exchange) accounts for neither development in the core nor underdevelopment in the periphery. Rather, economic development is a qualitative process, which requires not merely the accumulation of wealth in general, but the development of the productivity of labor of the direct producers of the means of production and means of subsistence. The capital–wage labor relation is privileged as both the source and the site of capitalist economic development. On the other hand, peripheral social formations characterized by nonwage labor are regarded as distinct precapitalist (or noncapitalist) modes of production that coexist with capitalist modes in the world capitalist system. But they are outside of the decisive capital–wage labor relation and are externally "articulated" to it. The particular pattern of their development is determined by the internal structure of class relations.

Furthermore, Brenner's emphasis on the specificity of the capital–wage labor relation raises the question of the historical origins of capitalism. From his perspective, the origins of capitalism are to be found not with the expansion of the world market and the rise of a world division of labor in the sixteenth century but rather with the emergence "of the property/surplus extraction (class system) of free wage labor—the historical process by which labor power and the means of production become commodities." In contrast to more economistic conceptions, Brenner stresses that the historical formation of class relations of capitalist production cannot be understood as the product of ruling-class selection of optimal methods of labor control under the pressures of a competitive world market. Rather, he contends capitalist class relations in Europe result from the "process of 'self-transformation' of class relations from serfdom to free wage labor—that is, of course, the class struggles by which this transformation took place" (Brenner 1977, 38). In his analysis, the contingent outcomes of these struggles, above all in agriculture, created the uniquely successful conditions for the development of capitalism in Western Europe: "A class system, a property system, a system of surplus extraction, in which the methods the extractors were obliged to use to increase their surplus corresponded to an unprecedented, though enormously imperfect, degree to the needs of development of the productive forces" (Brenner 1977, 67). (However, once contingent class struggles have created the conditions for the development of capitalism, the capital–wage labor relation appears, in Brenner's view, to carry within itself the telos of its subsequent development. In his view, once the capital–wage labor became predominant in English agriculture during the seventeenth century, the class structure compelled capitalist landowners to introduce technical innovations in agriculture and increase relative surplus labor "dramatically" in order to expand their surplus and accumulate capital. The consequence was continually increasing agricultural productivity, a growing home market, and a "symbiotic relation" between agriculture and industry that culminated in the industrial revolution of the eighteenth century [Brenner 1977, 77–78].)

Brenner's approach emphasizes the specific character of social relations of production in determining economic development and underdevelopment. Class relations are either characterized by nonwage labor and are regarded as precapitalist or noncapitalist, or identified with wage labor and are viewed as capitalist. In this interpretation, the market is of secondary importance. It is regarded as external to the prevailing relations of direct production. Thus, according to this view, we can, on the one hand, speak of the historic emergence of the capitalist mode of production only with the triumph of the wage labor relation (within a given national arena), while, on the other hand, we should regard peripheral social formations as distinct precapitalist modes of production that coexist with capitalist modes of production in the world capitalist system.

CRITIQUE: THEORETICAL DUALISM

The perspectives under consideration here appear to present two distinct and generally opposed conceptions of class, capital, and world economy. Dobb, Laclau, and Brenner emphasize the immediate relations of production in defining social classes and the capital–wage labor relation as the defining feature of capitalism. In contrast, Frank and Wallerstein call attention to the diversity of forms of social labor producing for the world market as the fundamental characteristic of the capitalist world economy. (In this regard, Sweezy seems to occupy an intermediate position. Although he emphasizes the role of the market and trade in the transition from feudalism to capitalism, his conception of capitalism is closer to the first formulation than the second.) There is an underlying unity beneath these apparent differences, however. Common to both views is the independence of their concepts from historical process. Each approach presented here takes a single feature seen in isolation, the wage form or the market, and treats it as if it were the sole defining characteristic of capitalism. These theoretically key concepts thereby assume a universal validity independent of the historical relations that they are intended to represent. In each case, these abstracted and partial concepts form a priori models through which the respective historical narratives of capitalist development, underdevelopment, and class formation are reconstructed. Each reconstruction creates a privileged realm of systemic necessity which is at once the source and arena of the "laws of motion'" of the system, while relations and processes outside of this realm are treated as contingent and secondary. Thus, the theory and the history of capitalist development and class formation are collapsed into one another. The privileged concept becomes identical with the "real history" of the system. The complexities of capitalist development are thereby reduced to a single dimension which comes to define its essence as a historical system. These two theoretical perspectives are thus opposed to one another within a shared set of assumptions, their respective interpretations are mirror images of one another.

In its attempt to understand capitalism as a unified historical whole, Wallerstein's world-system theory emphasizes the market as the connecting link between geographically bounded categories of core, semiperiphery, and periphery. Through integration into the market and division of labor, diverse forms of class relations—wage laborers, petty commodity producers, tenant farmers, sharecroppers, peons, slaves—are subsumed under the heading "proletarian" and subjected to a universal logic of profit calculation. In this perspective, what classes have in common takes precedence over what differentiates them. Each form of class relation is equated with every other as production for the market. Production for the market becomes the lowest common denominator to which all forms of social labor are reduced.

This perspective offers no theory of social relations, and we are unable to theoretically reconstitute historical class relations. The category "proletarian" is reduced to the most general and therefore the most abstract determinant of class—the appropriation of surplus product—and is imposed from without upon the most diverse social relations. Classes are defined in relation to the products of labor rather than by their relation to one another in the processes of social production and reproduction. It is as if people's relations to things rather than to one another were decisive. We are left with concepts that apply to things that are the products of human social relations rather than to the social relations themselves; or conversely, social relations themselves appear as things. The structural polarity of bourgeois and proletarian overrides the specific character of particular forms of class relations. Class is treated as an essential relation independent of the specific forms which particular relations may take: differences which distinguish one form of class relation from another are regarded as secondary and contingent. Instead, historical class relations are classified into a series of logical types which are functionally related to the universal requirements of a static and unchanging market structure. The specific development of distinct forms of social labor and class relations is eliminated as subject matter, as are the historical relationships among such forms; moreover, the differences between distinct forms of class relations—indeed, change itself—are reduced to a merely quantitative dimension.

This failure to come to grips with the problem of historical specificity of class relations undermines the insights of the world economy perspective. As presently constituted, it is unable either to distinguish between different forms of class relations or to comprehend the relations between these different forms in the historical development of the capitalist world economy. The fundamental categories of class (as well as, e.g., those of core, semi-periphery, periphery, etc.) are taken as given rather than theoretically reconstructed from the elements that constitute them in specific historical circumstances. Both market and production are understood independently from the global web of relations that sustain and support them. The relation between them is functional, not historical. Specific forms of class relations and particular local histories are reduced to their positions within a predetermined whole. The result is a historical system without a history, a choreography of events within a static and immutable framework. It is as if the capitalist world economy had existed virtually full blown from the sixteenth century onward. In consequence, not only does the market appear as the dynamic force of historical development, but it simultaneously remains an ahistorical abstraction—"not only the teleological outcome of history . . . [but] also its starting point" (Merrington 1976, 174)—which is itself not explained.

On the other hand, Brenner's historical materialist approach emphasizes the autonomy of separate, geographically bounded modes of production. It is based upon Marx's theoretical claims of the primacy of production over exchange, a perception of the historical specificity of different forms of social relations of production, and the importance of the internal development of each form of class relations as the source of fundamental change. From this perspective, production is understood simply as the combination of human labor with the instruments and materials of production. These elements are regarded as attributes of each independent form of class or production relations (wage labor, slavery, serfdom, etc.); that is, each such form possesses or contains its own integral "production" processes and each structures the relations among these elements under specific social conditions. What distinguishes one form from another is the manner in which these elements are socially organized. These "primary" relations of production form the necessary starting point of analysis, and all understandings of the development of the "society" in question derive from them.

However, if scholars writing from this perspective regard production as determinant, they fail to distinguish adequately between the concept of production and empirical instances of production. (To put it otherwise, this position confounds the conditions for theoretical reflection and the results of such reflection.) It is one thing for Marx to present a general theoretical argument for the primacy of production over other political economic relations. It is quite another matter to treat historically given instances of production as if they coincide with and directly express the general theoretical category "production." To do so is to confuse the general and the particular. It is to treat the latter in isolation from the complex ensemble of social relations and material processes of which it is a part. In consequence of such confusion, this approach presumes, without any theoretical justification, that social relations of production, above all capitalist relations, are exclusively the attribute of a given national or local "society" (i.e., that the general category is an attribute of the particular instance) or that such historically given class or production relations are to be regarded as invariably prior to market relations (and to the state, ideology, etc.) and as universally determinant (i.e., the particular operates as if universal). Such misplaced concreteness slips easily into a linear causality that attributes a priori causal primacy to production relations and eliminates the need for the theoretical reconstruction of historical processes.

This conception of class relations thus operates on a distinction, taken to be analytically decisive, between what is internal and what is external. It treats each form of production relations as a closed entity, possessing a stable and self-contained internal structure subject to autonomous laws and having a fixed and singular external boundary demarcating it from other such units. It regards each form as discrete and analytically independent and considers it in terms of its own "internal" characteristics. One such form is related to another as if to an external object.

Such a procedure loses sight of the global dimensions and systemic character of such relations. Each immediate local form of production is examined in its particularity, in isolation from the wider range of relations constituting it (Corrigan 1977, 437). Commodity production is artificially separated from commodity circulation. Geopolitical spaces and temporalities are taken as given or are derived directly from the conception of production. The wage labor form alone is regarded as authentically capitalist, and capitalism is identified exclusively with its empirical presence. In contrast, nonwage forms of labor are treated as inherently noncapitalist, while market relations are at best derivative and secondary, at worst inconsequential.

This approach remains abstract and fails to adequately conceptualize the interrelation between various forms of production and reproduction of social labor in the world economy. By granting analytical priority to what it construes as primary production relations, this approach necessarily constructs the world economy as a fragmented and heterogeneous ensemble with no systemic unity. It conjoins isolated and autonomous individual forms of production and class relations with one another to create a pluralistic conception. Capitalist and pre- or noncapitalist class relations coexist within a composite of linear historical spaces and temporalities: modern, not yet modern, and never to become modern (Corrigan 1977, 441). Emphasis on the apparently distinctive "internal" characteristics of these relations privileges the peculiarity of prevailing local forms and contingent local outcomes. The world economy appears here as no more than the sum of its parts and serves merely as the general backdrop against which the "primary" individual units play their roles.

Thus, within the premises of this perspective, world-scale processes of class formation are distorted or excluded from consideration altogether. Production relations are fragmented. Ostensibly "primary" class relations, the justification for the approach, remain abstract and partial in the sense that some aspects of class formation are emphasized but not others. Markets are viewed in isolation from production relations and seen as simply the realm of abstract exchange. The historical interrelation and interdependence of diverse forms of class relations on a world scale is eliminated as theoretical subject matter.

Consequently, both approaches fail to develop an adequate methodology for reconstituting the processes of capitalist development and class formation in their historical complexity *as world process*. Instead, the theoretical strategy pursued by each generates the continual (and unresolvable within the theoretical claims and methodological conditions of each argument) juxtaposition of production and exchange, wage and nonwage labor, capitalist and precapitalist, and world and national/local which has shaped their respective understandings of the character and role of class relations in modern capitalism.

THEORETICAL RECONSTRUCTION:
WORLD ECONOMY AND CLASS

An alternative to this dualism, and a more productive theoretical approach, would emphasize the nonidentity of theoretical categories with historical narratives of capitalist development and class formation. The approaches discussed above treat concepts of production and exchange as if they coincide with social processes and thereby exhaust historical reality. I suggest that such concepts be seen as points of departure in the process of cognition of a reality yet to be known. From this perspective, neither production nor exchange may be privileged as the singular authentic domain of social-historical development. Rather, if we treat both categories as analytical abstractions, that is, as the means of comprehending historical phenomena, it becomes possible—and necessary—to reconstruct theoretically their changing historical interrelation and interaction. Here, the concept at once serves as the means to describe, evaluate, order, and interpret particular phenomena more adequately and to explicate the complex, differentiated historical structure and coherence of the political economic whole. It thereby enables us to disclose the dense historical interconnectedness of specific relations and processes of capitalist development through multiple temporal and spatial frameworks. Such an approach broadens the range of interpretive possibilities and indicates new dimensions of the organization of labor and class formation on a world scale.

In contrast to the conventional Marxist conception of production as simply the socially organized combination of human labor, instruments, and materials, production may be theoretically constructed as a general historical relation that presupposes and includes within its concept distribution, exchange, and consumption. (Although this line of thought in Marx's work has been less influential, it opens rich possibilities for historical reconstruction and interpretation.) Taken together, these relations form an interrelated and mutually dependent theoretical whole, "distinctions within a unity." Each of these terms requires the others and is defined through its relation to them. Their interrelation delineates the processes of social economy (Marx 1973, 83–100). As analytical abstractions, these broad categories are intended to isolate the common features of all social production. But, taken by themselves, they yield no "general laws" and tell us little about specific historical conditions of production (Marx 1973, 83–88). Nonetheless, this approach is methodologically productive. It establishes the relational character of the concepts and allows more adequate historical reconstruction of political economic processes.

In this formulation, these categories and the relations they represent appear neither as isolated and separable fragments nor as undifferentiated particulars subsumed under a single dominant general category (whether production or exchange). Production and exchange are no longer conceived as discrete entities that are divorced from their broader contexts and separated from and opposed to one another as external objects, nor are they treated as identical. Rather, production and exchange may be understood as relations that presuppose, condition, and are formative of one another as distinct parts of a whole. If we conceive of the social economy in this way, the relevant unit of analysis is defined by the extent of the interrelated processes of production, distribution, exchange, and consumption. As a general category, production is defined through its relation to the other moments of this process; its coherence, scope, and significance are defined within this conceptual field. If production is to be treated as determinant, it is determinant with regard to the totality of these relations.

By emphasizing the interrelation of production and exchange, this more abstract and general conception of the totality of political economic relations provides a framework that allows us to theoretically reconstruct the historical formation and reformation of the modern world economy as a unity of diverse elements. The creation of a world market beginning in the sixteenth century may be understood as the establishment of a unified network of commodity production and exchange, varying in scope and degree of intensity, on a world scale—a distinct historical social economy. Systematic and sustained exchange of commodities on a world scale implies and requires the organization of commodity production and relations, direct or indirect, among producers, i.e., social labor, on a world scale. Production is an attribute and constitutive element of the world economy as a social historical whole. But, of course, there is no general and undifferentiated production, only particular branches of production and individual producers whose activities and relations are organized through distinct social forms. Thus, in the modern world economy the production and exchange of commodities unite multiple forms of labor and diverse groups of producers, and, at the same time, they establish specific conditions of material and social interdependence among them. Production as a general systemic relation is realized and expressed through the division of labor on a world scale. (From this point of view, the sixteenth century is decisive for the formation of the modern capitalist world economy because of the conquest of the Americas, the remaking of the world division of labor, and the invention of racial slavery as a revolutionary new form of commodity production.)

Within such a framework, the market appears neither as a secondary element outside of particular "primary" production relations nor as an abstract universal over and above particular production relations. Rather, it is understood as a constituent element of global production relations. By providing the systemic link between definite groups of buyers and sellers, and producers and consumers, the market establishes the interrelation and interdependence of various forms of social labor across national boundaries. Exchange continues and completes commodity production and is the condition of renewed production for both particular units and the system as a whole. Of course, distribution, exchange, and consumption themselves entail distinct labor processes (production!) conducted through specific social forms, and various aspects of theses processes are subject to state or private appropriation as well as diverse types of formal organization outside of the exchange relation

(Weber 1978, 63–126). Therefore the market may be viewed as a substantive, historically formed, social and political relation that integrates the diverse relations of production forming the division of labor. Commodity exchange renders "abstract" both waged and unwaged labor and equates the various forms of social labor and material processes of production with one another. Thus, the market contributes to the inner coherence and "systemic" unity of this historical social economy. It thereby delineates the parameters of the system as a whole and gives it spatial expression as the world economy.

This approach allows us to understand production and exchange—world market and division of labor—not as discrete and separate entities, but as mutually interdependent relations: as moments of an ongoing process of social production and reproduction on a world. Each conditions the other. The expansion of the world market requires an increase in the volume and variety of commodities to be exchanged. It encourages the development of new points of production to be integrated into the division of labor and stimulates the transformation of labor and labor processes. In turn, such large-scale, specialized commodity production is only possible with the social and political organization of adequate trading networks. These networks must be capable of coordinating the movement of goods, money, and information, often across great distances and over periods of long duration; they must be able to reduce the costs of exchange, that is, transaction and transportation costs; they must provide stable and regular markets for specific quantities and types of merchandise; and they must establish social conventions and institutions that guarantee exchange. The rationalization of exchange and the development of trade and the world market create conditions for expanding the scale of production and encourage greater specialization and efficiency of labor (Torras 1993, 198–202). They thus promote the deepening of the division of labor, greater material and social interdependence, and increasing subordination of labor to commodity production.

These interdependent relations of production and exchange—the division of labor and world market—at once define the unit of analysis and the most general relations of the capitalist world economy. At this stage of theoretical reconstruction, however, they do not yet adequately disclose the structure of the world economy as a whole. They remain abstractions that presuppose as yet unspecified relations among the various forms of social labor integrated into the world economy and the structures that mediate their interrelation. Different productive relations—master and slave, lord and serf, and bourgeois and proletarian—organize and structure the labor process in distinctive ways. As scholars writing in the Marxist tradition have long argued, each such form specifies a particular relation to nature, particular modes of surplus production and appropriation, and particular class relations and conflicts. Specific forms of social relations of production thus come to define distinctive patterns of social-economic development (Marx 1976, 325; Wolf 1982, 73–76). Attention to the specificity of forms of social production allows us to comprehend the world economy not simply as the sum of its parts or as an abstraction over and above them, but as distinct relations among particular social forms and material processes of production, integrated with one another through definite modes of exchange and political power—as a structured and differentiated whole changing over time. Conversely, the totality of relations as a whole defines labor. Specific forms of commodity production presume exchange relations and are constituted through them within a distinct division of labor. Each such form of labor is subject to complex, multiple determinations and mediations.

This approach enables us to account for the systemic interrelation and interdependence of diverse material processes and social forms of production and to avoid the difficulties entailed in conjoining separate entities. Specific production relations appear as constituent parts of a global system of labor, not as empirically distinct, mutually exclusive labor systems (McMichael 1991, 10; Tomich 1990). Each form of labor, whether waged or unwaged, is defined through its relation to the others. Similarly, the market may now be understood as the concrete historical mediation between specific forms of social production and political organization. Within this theoretically constructed historical economy, specific forms of production, exchange, and political power shape one another and are understood in relation to one another. Taken together, these diverse yet interdependent relations form an integrated whole, a totality which is the outcome of their mutual interaction. By establishing the specific relations among these various forms of material and social production, social interaction and political power, all of which vary through time and in relation to one another, it becomes possible to reconstruct the development of the world economy as a concrete historical entity.

From this perspective it is possible to reevaluate the role of the capital–wage labor relation in the historical formation of the world economy. Both Marx and Weber have called attention to decisive features of this relation as a general theoretical category. With the commodification of labor power, the relation between land, labor, and capital is organized through market relations. Production for the purpose of exchange may be conducted through purchase and sale of its constituent elements. Labor power, instruments of labor, and raw materials all take the form of commodities: each can be related to the others through its value. This relation gives meaning to concepts of labor cost, labor time, and labor productivity. Exact calculation in time and money becomes the basis for the organization and systematic transformation of the labor process. The labor supply can be rationally adjusted to production requirements through the labor market. These conditions facilitate technological change, socialization of labor, and division of labor within the productive unit (Marx 1976, 439–639; Weber 1978, 90–116, esp. 137–138, 160–164.)

From the perspective presented here, however, the importance of the capital–wage labor relation is not that it is itself coterminous with capital as a historical relation. It is neither the most frequent form of production nor the teleological end point of the evolution of all production in the world economy (McMichael 1991). Rather, its significance is determined by its position within the interdependent network of relations of production and exchange— its relation to other forms of labor. The formation of the capital–wage labor relation as a historical social relation presupposes, among other things, the growth of markets, the expansion of commodity production either through the transformation of existing forms of nonwage production or the creation of new ones, the concentration of wealth, and the dispossession of peasantries and independent artisans. Where wage labor could be established on a sufficient scale, its productive superiority transformed commodity circuits throughout the world economy. Its competitive advantage over other forms of production allowed it to become the key form of labor and organizing pivot of the world economy, altering the conditions of labor elsewhere and establishing a new global hierarchy of labor.

Here Polanyi's account of the formation of a "market society" in nineteenth-century Britain is extremely suggestive. Polanyi links the formation of land, labor, and capital markets in Britain—that is, the creation of a self-regulating market society and liberal state—with the transformation of global commodity and money circuits and the creation of a world market based on free trade (Polanyi 1957, 33–134). While he is most concerned with the subordination of land, labor, and money to the market economy within Britain, it must be remembered that Britain was at the confluence of world trade. Its strategic position in the world division of labor, hence its relation to various forms of unwaged labor throughout the world economy, contributed to the emergence of a "market society" and the capital–wage labor relation in Britain and imparted world historical significance to their subsequent development. (Interestingly, even in the period before the Industrial Revolution, it was precisely in the leading world commodity circuits of the day—tobacco, sugar, shipbuilding, and maritime transport—that the confrontation between capital and labor resulted in the regularization of the wage relation as a means of imposing effective labor discipline on workers [Linebaugh 1992, 153–183, 371–441.]) Viewed in this light, Polanyi's account prompts consideration of how the consolidation of a market society and the capital–wage labor relation in Britain imposed new conditions and rhythms on production and exchange in the world economy as a whole. The wage labor regime and industrial production resulted in the demand for new products, the expansion of markets, and increased velocity of circulation. Free trade, the gold standard, and the "self-regulating market" (in conjunction with the reorganization of the interstate system and the rise of British hegemony) reorganized and reintegrated production and exchange on a world scale.

Under these circumstances, the world division of labor was at once expanded, diversified, and more tightly integrated, and the various forms of unwaged labor within the world economy were subjected to new conditions. The creation of markets for new products, the expansion of old ones, and new technologies of production and transport increased the sheer scale of the demand for labor. The integration of markets and increased velocity of circulation put pressure on labor productivity and required producers to valorize production in new ways. These systemic changes produced specific effects on particular forms of labor, both waged and unwaged, and altered relations between classes in ways contingent upon local conditions and their position within the division of labor. In a complex movement of global pressure and local response—engendered and conditioned by a variety of political and social conflicts with contingent local outcomes—new zones of production, forms of labor, groups of laborers, and products were created while old ones stagnated or were transformed (Tomich 1988, 1991, 1994; Trouillot 1988; Samuel 1977). The scale and intensity of commodity-producing labor was increased throughout the world economy. Cheap food products and industrial raw materials produced by unwaged labor became the condition of the renewal on an expanding scale of the capital–wage labor relation (Wolf 1982, 310–353; Hobsbawm 1968, 134–153).

Wage labor and capital in Britain may thus be seen as the crucial productive node of the nineteenth-century world economy, tying together global commodity circuits through the national market society while the restructured free trade world market subordinated producers everywhere to new conditions of valorization. Although forms of unwaged labor may have remained unchanged—slavery, serfdom, peonage, sharecropping, and independent commodity production—their role, composition, and significance in the development of the world economy were redefined through the capacity of the capital–wage labor relation to transform the particular constellation of relations of production and exchange forming the world economy and to recast the division of labor and world market around itself. The predominance of the capital–wage labor relation thereby established a new hierarchy among forms of labor within the world economy and marked a decisive step of its historical evolution.

Attention to the specific forms of production relations and their interrelation allows us to explicate the structure of the world economy as a whole. However, within the premises of the argument presented here, it would be fundamentally distorting to treat *particular historically given* production relations—for example, wage labor in England or slavery in Brazil—as if they were analytically prior to the totality of relations of production and exchange composing world market and division of labor and form in themselves the "real material basis" of social development, as conventional Marxist approaches would have it. Rather, any particular instance of production presupposes the existence of *already historically given* relations of production, distribution, exchange, and consumption. Such particular class relations and forms of labor are themselves formed within the division of labor and world market—that is, within the social-historical whole. Rather than independent entities that simply exchange commodities with one another, they represent interdependent processes of social production.

The world economy develops by means of the incorporation of distinctive geographical zones and natural environments. These environments are transformed by selective material processes of production organized through specific forms of social relations of production. Although each form of social labor embodies distinctive patterns of political economic organization and conditions of production, the particular organization of labor is, in each instance, constituted in relation to other material processes and social forms of production within the division of labor. Through the market and the division of labor, each interacts with the others. Although the character, scope, and intensity of interaction may vary, at every stage in their historical evolution particular production relations are structurally conditioned and constrained by the other relations comprising the whole. The nature and composition of production processes and class relations within each particular form incorporate the relation of this particular form to the others and to the world economy as a whole. Each represents a distinctive position and constellation of material processes and social relations within the division of labor at a given point in its development.

Thus, systemic processes produce specific and irreducible "local faces" (Tomich 1990; Mintz 1977, 1978). Each individual form is simultaneously constitutive of the global system and a particular manifestation of its processes. Its course of development is dependent upon its position within the division of labor (that is, its relation to forms of production elsewhere, or to changes in exchange, distribution, or consumption). Differences in the demand for specific goods and the material conditions of their production, differences in the social conditions of labor (levels of production costs, productivity, etc.), and the capacity of states and enterprises to organize circuits of production and exchange at once profoundly shape the fate of individual production zones and the scope and complexity of the division of labor.

From this perspective, specific forms of production relations cannot be presumed to form discrete, coherent units that develop autonomously from their own unique "inner processes." Rather than seeing each form of class relation or national economy as an internally stable and externally bounded unit that is brought into relation with other such units, particular class relations and social conflicts may be better understood as the product of multiple and diverse yet interrelated relations and processes of varying intensity, extent, and duration. Viewed from the vantage point of the world economy, particular relations of production appear as points of convergence and concentration within the broader political economic network. Each represents a contingent, "unstable equilibrium" of processes that are spatially and temporally uneven, overlapping, and noncoincident with one another in the range of their effect. Consequently, particular class boundaries appear to be inherently plural, heterogeneous and unstable, the product of the interaction of multiple relations and processes operating simultaneously across varying spatial and temporal scales. Rich, many-sided, and historically dense and complex concentrations of diverse elements, they are not comprehensible in terms of their apparently "intrinsic" characteristics, but rather through their relation to the whole.

CONCLUSION

This emphasis on the historical formation of production processes and on the specificity of relations of production permits a more historically and sociologically adequate understanding of processes of world economy and world class formation. Such a perspective requires us to address the formation over time and in space of the social-political frameworks through which commodity production and exchange occur in order to account for their specific character within the unifying whole. It thereby enables us to theoretically reconstruct at once the historical unity and interdependence of specific forms of social labor and of particular political economic units through the division of labor and world market and the world economy as the concrete relation of diverse forms of social relations of production, exchange, and power—a structured, historical whole.

By calling attention to production and exchange as general, systemic, yet abstract relations, the approach presented here allows diverse forms of social labor to be theoretically integrated into a conception of a world-scale political economy without artificially separating general from particular, production from exchange, and global from local. It draws attention to the material and social interdependence of diverse relations and processes united through the division of labor and world market (Tomich 1990). If the *object* of analysis is particular class relations, the appropriate *unit* of analysis is the totality of relations forming the historical world economy. This perspective permits the disclosure of the complex, uneven, and contingent processes within the totality of interdependent relations that form particular class relations as a historical outcome. Such a reconstruction of the historically specific character of particular relations also contributes to an understanding of the unity and diversity of the multiple forms of waged and unwaged labor constituting the world economy. By seeing the whole as the unity of global and local, this perspective seeks to avoid the reification of world, national, or regional units and, consequently, either the construction of false necessity or the premature emphasis on local agency or particularity. Rather, relations are seen as at once necessary and contingent: necessary because of the systemic unity imposed by the interdependence of forms of commodity production and exchange and political power; and contingent because the particular character of those forms is always the product of specific, complex, uneven historical processes within the relational network. Comprehension of given relations, whether of the world economy as a whole or its particular forms, is the result of theoretically informed inquiry that is capable of reconstructing these relations and processes in their historical complexity.

Following the logic of the approach presented here, production (and similarly distribution, exchange, consumption, indeed the "whole" itself) remains an abstract and general category unless and until we are able to theoretically specify and historically reconstruct its various material processes (extraction, cultivation, manufacture, transport and communications, and information) and social forms (the varieties of waged and unwaged labor) in their relation to one another through the division of labor and mediating structures of market and state. Our knowledge of these relations only becomes concrete as we establish their historical interrelation and interdependence, that is, establish the social economic system as a historical, not an abstract entity. Therefore, the problem, from this perspective, is to develop methodological procedures and analytical frameworks that concretize theoretical categories, not to create abstract models (McMichael 1991, 15). Here the role of theory is to reconstruct this social economic whole in its historical complexity by specifying relations, establishing their historical interconnections and contexts, and ordering narrative accounts. Its purpose is neither to discover repetitive causal regularities nor to reveal paradigmatic or exceptional cases, but rather to identify significant difference within a spatially and temporally unified historical whole.

Chapter Three

The "Second Slavery"

Bonded Labor and the Transformation of the Nineteenth-Century World Economy

The abolition of the slave trade and slavery in the Western Hemisphere are certainly among the most significant and dramatic occurrences of the nineteenth century. By means as diverse as legislation, revolution, and civil war, slavery and the slave trade were eradicated in a sequence of events beginning with the Haitian Revolution in 1791 and extending to slave emancipation in Brazil in 1888. Indeed, the strength and effectiveness of anti-slavery thought and action contributed importantly to the nineteenth century's self-consciousness as a period of the growth of human freedom and moral and material progress (see, for example, Davis 1984). During this period, slavery came to be understood as the antithesis of the emergent forms of polity, moral sensibility, and economic activity: it formed the negative standard against which the new forms of freedom were defined. In the elaboration of political economy, for example, the stark contrast between the African slave and the free worker of Europe and North America was used to illuminate what was distinctive about capitalist property relations, wage labor, and industrial production (Smith 1976, 90, 413; Marx 1976, 1031–1034). Slavery was not treated as simply one form of human labor among others; rather, it came to be conceived as the polar opposite of free (wage) labor. It was viewed as the epitome of archaic, backward, and inefficient production and was generally presumed to be incompatible with the emerging modern world, while free (wage) labor was regarded as the universal outcome of the historical processes of capitalist development.

The presumption that slavery is incompatible with the modern world has persisted into the twentieth century. Within this framework, scholarly debate has focused on whether material or moral factors were more important in its demise. Whichever interpretation is favored, the abolition of slavery generally has been understood in one of two ways. One view, which emphasizes the role of Britain as harbinger of a modern political, economic, and ideological order, is akin to a type of domino theory. Once Great Britain abolished the slave trade, the fate of African slavery in the Americas was sealed, and forces were set in motion that slowly, unevenly, but inevitably dismantled the peculiar institution throughout the hemisphere. (It should be noted that in such accounts the revolution in Saint Domingue and the founding of Haiti are apparently aberrations that cannot be assimilated into the narrative and are ignored [see Trouillot 1995, 70–107]). The other view emphasizes the national histories of the various slave societies of the Americas. In this perspective, the "internal" contradictions of slavery become heightened, and in case after case, slave relations give way to a higher form of economic rationality. Both interpretations assume the singularity of slavery. Slavery is seen or presumed to be essentially the same phenomenon everywhere, and different slave systems are distinguished from one another only by their economic, cultural, and political contexts. As a result, the abolition of slavery, whether considered in its international connection or in its various national arenas, is regarded as a unilinear transition from archaic to modern forms of economy. It is this assumption of the singularity of slavery that I wish to examine here.

My purpose in this chapter is to call attention to the changing character of slavery in the nineteenth century world economy. (It should be noted that I do not propose to avoid explaining the causes of slave emancipation which remain diverse and conjunctural.) This chapter demonstrates the formation and reformation of slave relations within historical processes of the capitalist world economy. If slavery was ultimately abolished everywhere in the hemisphere, the "anti-slavery century" was nonetheless the apogee of its development. Beneath the apparent uniformity of nineteenth-century slave emancipation, we find complex and differentiated trajectories and outcomes that are traceable to the position of particular slave systems within the world economy. At the end of the eighteenth century, the Caribbean sugar industry, particularly the British and French colonial empires, was at the center of slave production in the world economy. Slavery in non-sugar areas was moribund. Rice, indigo, and tobacco were of secondary importance in the North American slave colonies, Brazil was at the end of its "gold cycle," and in the Spanish Empire, with the exception of Cuba, slavery was marginal. Yet, during the course of the nineteenth century, slavery expanded on a massive scale precisely in these relatively backward areas in order to supply the growing world demand for cotton, coffee, and sugar. At the same time, the former centers of slave production declined. This second cycle of slavery was initiated by the rise of British hegemony and declined with the challenges to it as U.S. economic and political preeminence grew in the Western Hemisphere and the depressions of the 1870s and 1880s triggered crises of colonial commodity markets. Examination of these concomitant processes of decline and expansion at once emphasizes the complex ways that slavery is imbricated in world economic processes and the intrinsic and irreducible unevenness of capitalist development.

BRITISH HEGEMONY AND THE NEW INTERNATIONAL DIVISION OF LABOR

The changes in the world economy during the first half of the nineteenth century fundamentally altered the parameters and conditions of production in the periphery. These changes included not only the spatial redistribution and quantitative increase in the production of tropical products but also the qualitative restructuring of the social relations and processes organizing the world market. Previously, the relations between core and periphery had been constituted by competing colonial empires. Each metropolitan power maintained an exclusive sphere of production in its colonies. The division of labor between metropolis and colony and the nature and direction of commodity flows were defined through politically enforced monopolies, privileges, and restrictions determined in the metropolis. Each metropolis reserved for itself the produce of its own colonies, monopolized colonial shipping, and used the colonies as a sheltered market for its industry. By means of these mercantilist policies, rival nation-states forcibly expanded their markets, stimulated production, and promoted the accumulation of national wealth. This system expressed not only the limits of commodity production and exchange but also the weak integration of the world market during this period. Within the framework of this market structure, world production of tropical staples grew steadily but slowly, and colonial producers were relatively insulated from direct competition with one another by their reliance on the political conditions of their monopoly of the metropolitan market.

However, this form of the organization of the world economy broke down between 1780 and 1815, and the emergence of British economic and political hegemony signaled the beginning of the structural transformation of the world market. The market was no longer constituted through the direct political domination over the sources of colonial production. Rather, the key to power under the emerging conditions of world economy was economic control over the flow of commodities. The nexus of direct colonial control was broken, and the system of imperial preference broke down. Increasingly a more or less self-regulating market, the political conditions for which were maintained and established by the power of the British state, became the mediation between producers and consumers, and supply, demand, and price appeared as the determinants of the division of labor and flow of commodities on the world market (McMichael 1984, 1–31).

This restructuring of the world market was underpinned by processes of industrialization, urbanization, and population growth. While the rate of economic advance during the first half of the nineteenth century was slow compared with that of the second half, the advance of industrialization in Europe and North America changed the pattern of demand in the world market over the course of this entire period. Modern industry required new raw materials on an unprecedented scope and scale, while the growth of population and development of predominantly urban middle and working classes in Europe was associated with new patterns of consumption that increased Europe's dependency on peripheral producers for foodstuffs. While its relative importance declined, in absolute terms sugar remained a key item of world trade. Alongside it, cotton and coffee assumed new commercial importance. The production and consumption of these articles increased on a massive scale over the course of the century and their importance grew. European and North American capital extended the area of supply of these materials and established a global system of transport based on the railroad and steamship to carry them, while, increasingly, peripheral regions specialized in their production. New poles of economic attraction were created between core and periphery that did not coincide with the old colonial boundaries. World trade and crop cultivation increased dramatically though unevenly throughout the century, and world rather than local prices increasingly dominated the trade in agricultural staples and raw materials (Hobsbawm 1968, 128; Woodruff 1971, 657–658; McMichael 1984, 12–13).

The chief agent and beneficiary of this transformation was Great Britain. With the collapse of France and its colonial empire after 1815, there was no power that could rival Britain in the international arena, and a process of reintegration of the world market began under the hegemony of British capital. Britain's position was not due simply to technological superiority. Rather, British commercial, financial, and maritime supremacy sustained its industrial development; and, in turn, Britain's productive advantage over its rivals widened, and its control over the market was strengthened. The control of international finance by London and the creation of the new financial institutions of the City represented new levels of integration of the world economy and new channels for economic domination. Britain emerged as the keystone of international trade. World production and consumption were progressively shaped around the conditions imposed by the requirements of British capital accumulation and integrated into its rhythms and cycles.

Although the thrust of British economic activity toward the periphery became more pronounced after 1857, British economic development became increasingly dependent upon trade with the periphery, especially Latin America and India, for industrial raw materials, foodstuffs, and, to a lesser extent, as an outlet for manufactured goods and the investment of accumulated surpluses during the first half of the century as well. British imports increased fourfold between 1780 and 1850. The amount of raw cotton used by British industry increased nearly fivefold between 1800 and 1830, and by 1831 it supplanted sugar as the country's leading import. On the other hand, the growth of cotton manufactures in Britain depended not on domestic consumption but on markets in the periphery. Particularly important in this regard was Latin America. Brazil constituted the largest single market for British cotton exports during the first half of the century (Hobsbawm 1968, 58, 135, 138, 146–148; Woodruff 1971, 662–663).

To the extent that Britain came to control commerce outside the bounds of its own empire, it became less committed to formal colonialism as the means of defining the nature and direction of commodity flows and the division of labor between core and periphery. Instead, British commercial and industrial superiority enabled it to penetrate the markets of the other colonizing powers, and to establish trade with the periphery on the basis of complementarity—British manufactured goods (and other services such as capital, shipping, banking, and insurance) for peripheral raw materials and agricultural products. It was the world's largest consumer of products from the periphery and was the only purchaser that could absorb increased peripheral production. On the other side of the coin, it was the only country that could supply the credit, machinery, and manufactured goods required to support this expansion. The advance of British industry accentuated the relative differential between industrial and agricultural prices in the world economy and pushed Britain to develop cheap new sources of supply in the periphery in order to redress its unfavorable balance of trade. The result was growing European demand for tropical and sub-tropical food products, among them sugar, cotton, and coffee, and increased international specialization in production of food and raw materials. The dramatic fall in price of these commodities benefited Britain more than any other country (Hobsbawm 1968, 135, 138, 146–148).

The establishment of this division of labor between core and periphery was organized by the City of London whose position as the center of world trade was both instrument and expression of British hegemony. The extension of commodity production in the periphery and the expansion not only of British trade with the periphery but also of its rivals relied upon the financial power of London banks. As McMichael has argued, British loan capital extended the scope of the world market for all states. A system of multilateral trading emerged that depended upon sterling balances and the credit of London banks as well as the City's ability to settle trade balances among states indirectly. Bills of exchange drawn on London banks replaced transfer of precious metals in organizing international exchanges, and sterling balances were used to adjust the status of national currencies in world trade. The centralization of banking enabled Britain to maintain and extend world exchange and to achieve financial supremacy beyond its commercial and industrial supremacy (McMichael 1984, 12, 21–23, 26–27). The creation of these global exchange relations centered on Britain established a world division of labor dependent upon and responsive to an integrated world market. Within this new configuration the conditions of slave labor in the world economy were altered.

THE TRANSFORMATION OF
AMERICAN SLAVERY

The effect of these developments was not to destroy archaic forms of social organization and establish the general mobility of capital and labor in a universal free market. Rather, previously existing social relations were recast within the new constellation of political and economic forces. The prior interdependence of colonialism and slavery was broken up, and the conditions of existence, function, and significance of each were modified. The rise of British hegemony and the industrial revolution in Britain restructured the world division of labor and stimulated the material expansion of the world economy. These developments not only created the conditions for the destruction of slavery within the British Empire but also encouraged the expansion and intensification of slavery outside of it. This "second slavery" developed not as a historical premise of productive capital, but presupposing its existence and as a condition for its reproduction. The systemic meaning and character of slavery was transformed. The emerging centers of slave production were now increasingly integrated into industrial production and driven by capital's "boundless thirst for wealth."

The British West Indies were the initial beneficiaries of the rise of British hegemony and the destruction of the French colonial sugar industry. Between 1791 and 1815, sugar production in the British Caribbean rose more rapidly than at any other time in its history. (See chapter 4.) The old colonies increased their output and new sugar territories were added to the empire. However, the impact of the transformation of the sugar market was felt differently among the various British colonies. The small islands of the British Lesser Antilles, exploited intensively since the seventeenth and eighteenth centuries expanded rapidly during these years. However, by the late 1820s, they reached the physical and technical limits of expansion and went into a period of decline. In Jamaica, on the other hand, there was room for territorial expansion and new investment. However, this expansion was into the inland valleys of the island, and expensive overland transportation raised the price of the Jamaican product. Slave production in the British West Indies had been geared to the pre-industrial organization of the world economy and was dependent upon now outmoded monopolies. The productivity of slave labor could not be increased, and new supplies of slaves and land were not available. Despite the gains made during this period, the expansion and intensification of sugar production pushed the older colonies to their limit, and they were surpassed by newer producers in an expanding market.

The alternative was to start slave production in new areas. Britain further expanded her sugar cultivation by bringing the islands conquered in the Seven Year's War—Grenada and the Grenadines, Saint Vincent, Trinidad, and Tobago—under cultivation as well as the territories of Berbice, Demerara, and Essequibo newly acquired from the Netherlands. However, if these new areas of slave production were maintained within the old colonial nexus of monopoly and restriction, surplus production in the less productive older colonies would be subsidized within anomalous social relations. Whereas, if a labor force could be guaranteed by other means in the new production areas they would still prosper, and the market mechanism of accumulation and expanded reproduction of the world economy would be freed.

With the centralization of world trade in its hands, there was no need for Britain to secure its own labor supply for tropical and semi-tropical goods. Its concern was increasingly for cheap commodities without regard to the form of labor that produced them. The slave as productive labor took precedence over the slave as commodity. These structural shifts in the world economy contributed to the efficacy of the anti-slavery movement in Britain. However, the movement against the slave trade was not simply a function of economic factors, but added another dimension to the processes leading to the destruction of slavery and forced different paths of development on British and non-British colonies. The abolition of the slave trade not only cut off the labor supply to the British slave colonies but, as Paula Beiguelman has indicated, destroyed the commodity market most intimately linked to the slave form (Beiguelman 1978, 71–80). British efforts to suppress the slave trade internationally formed a counterpoint to the expansion of slavery in Cuba, the United States, and Brazil during the nineteenth century. Slavery in these areas developed in the face of the restriction and ultimately the elimination of the slave trade as well as against a mature, widespread, and successful abolitionist movement.

The interplay of market forces and the anti-slavery movement pushed Britain toward a policy of free trade and undercut the competitive position of its West Indian colonies. By 1815, British expansion in the Caribbean came to an end. With the exception of Jamaica and Guiana, British Caribbean sugar production had reached its saturation point. British West Indian planters were faced with rising costs and the inability to expand production. The abolition of the slave trade had cut off their labor supply, while British slave emancipation disrupted the production in both the decadent and the vital slave colonies alike. The high price of British West Indian sugar and the protective tariffs it required restricted British domestic consumption and seriously weakened Britain's position in the re-export market. As cheaper American sugar invaded European markets, re-exports of British West Indian sugar had to be subsidized by the government by means of drawbacks and export bounties in order to make them competitive with sugar from countries that were often substantial customers for British manufactures. The British West Indian sugar colonies found themselves unable to compete in an expanding world economy. Their position was undercut not by British industry but by the more efficient production in the new American slave zones and elsewhere in the periphery.

The very processes that contributed to the destruction of slavery within the British Empire resulted in the intensification of slave production elsewhere in the hemisphere. The demand for cotton, coffee, and sugar reached unprecedented proportions during the nineteenth century, and the production of these crops revitalized slavery in Cuba, the United States, and Brazil as part of this emergent capitalist international division of labor. This is reflected in the scale and nature of slave production itself. Vast expanses of land were opened up, and millions of slaves set to work producing these crops. New industrial technology—notably the railroad, steamship, and steam mills—transformed the labor process in the new slave frontiers. Behind this expansion was the power of British capital and state organizing the world market and international division of labor. In the first half of the nineteenth century, London provided what Jenks has aptly described as a "credit bridge" to the United States, Brazil, and the Spanish colonies in order to stimulate production and trade (Jenks 1971, 67; McMichael 1984, 22–23). By themselves or in conjunction with foreign, especially North American, banks and merchant houses, London financial institutions provided capital through credit and direct investment for the development of plantations and the railroads and banks supporting them. The development of these new plantation zones lowered costs and increased the scale of production as well as providing outlets for surplus British capital in one form or another. British credit also expanded world trade and increased the demand for new crops outside of Britain. For example, merchants and bankers in New York, Boston, and Philadelphia could use the trade surplus from cotton exports to draw bills on London banks in order to finance purchases of not only British manufactures but also significant amounts of Brazilian coffee and West Indian sugar. While these activities helped build up American finance, commerce, and industry, such multilateral trading extended British financial power, increased the volume of commodities in circulation, developed cheap sources of supply, and secured markets for British manufactures throughout the world economy. It was within this complex of world production and exchange that the "second slavery" emerged.

Cuban sugar production increased sharply in scale after the British occupation of Havana (1762), which brought with it increased imports of slaves. However, it catapulted forward from the 1790s onward aided by the destruction of export production in Saint Domingue and the decline of the British West Indian sugar industry. By 1830, Cuba emerged as the world's largest producer with an output of 104,971 metric tons. World demand continued to grow at an accelerating rate, and Cuban production more than kept pace with it. By 1848, the 260,463 metric tons produced accounted for nearly one-quarter of the world's supply (Moreno Fraginals 1978, I, 46–47, 67–71, 95–102, 167–255; II, 93–97, 106–174; III, 35–36; Scott 1985, 10; Guerra y Sánchez 1964, 40–45, 52–53; Knight 1970, 14–18, 40–41).

This expansion of production in Cuba was accompanied by and dependent upon a dramatic increase in the slave labor force. In Cuba, slave imports rose drastically, and the demographic composition of the island was transformed despite British attempts to put an end to the slave trade. Hubert Aimes estimates that 400,000 slaves were imported into Cuba between 1762 and 1838. Cuba's slave population went from 85,900 in 1792 to 199,100 in 1817, and in the latter year over 32,000 slaves were imported. By 1827 the slave population in Cuba reached 286,900, and in 1841 it stood at 436,500 and accounted for more than 43 percent of the total population. The slave trade continued to supply Cuba with fresh manpower until the middle 1860s, and the slave population in 1862 was some 368,550 (Curtin 1969, 34; Knight 1970, 10–11, 22–23, 41; Scott 1985, 87).

The development of the sugar industry was centered in the western part of the island. Sugar cultivation spread south and west of Havana displacing coffee and tobacco producers and spreading onto new lands. New and ever-larger plantations were established at a frenetic pace and old ones increased their capacity. The number of *ingenios* increased almost fourfold between 1800 and 1857. During the initial stages of expansion the multiplication of traditional production units accounted for much of the increase in total production. However, steam power made an early appearance, and the methods of sugar manufacture in Cuba were transformed by the application of modern industrial techniques. According to Knight, in 1827 only 2.5 percent of the 1,000 *ingenios* in Cuba were steam powered. But by 1860, 70.8 percent of the 1,365 *ingenios* used steam. Railroads opened new lands and, in contrast to the situation in Jamaica, permitted profitable exploitation of the interior by the sugar industry. In 1837, thirteen years after the first steam-driven railway began to operate in England, the first railroad in Latin America or the Caribbean was completed between Havana and Güines. This line, created to serve the sugar industry, was only 51 miles long, but it was successful and soon railroads were in operation in all sugar growing areas of the island. Shipping costs were reduced drastically, and land use was maximized (Guerra y Sánchez 1964, 66; Knight 1970, 32–33, 35–36, 38; Scott 1985, 21–24).

Cubans enjoyed the technological edge of latecomers. Though they were few in number, the appearance of mechanized sugar mills represented a qualitative transformation in the conditions of sugar production. The Cuban sugar mill developed on a giant scale, and the technology of sugar production there attained the most advanced level known under slavery. Steam-powered mills and the vacuum pan increased the capacity of the more advanced plantations and produced more and higher-quality sugar. On large estates small rail lines were introduced, often using animal-drawn equipment, to transport cane to the mills from the fields, for transportation within the factories and to the wharves. These developments broke the fixed ratio between land, labor, and mill capacity that had limited the development of the old *ingenio*. With the introduction of steam-driven machinery, it was no longer necessary to limit the acreage under cane. The use of rail transport within estates allowed a greater area to be planted which provided the increased supply of cane required by modern refining techniques. The scale of production increased, and sugar mills could grow in size. The capital requirements for founding an *ingenio* increased enormously. With the introduction of estate railways, there was bitter competition for land and labor. Small producers were squeezed out, and a monocultural economy emerged that was dominated by large planters who could afford the increased costs of the new mechanized mills. The foundations were established for Cuba's position as the world's sugar bowl (Knight 1970, 18–19, 30–40; Guerra y Sánchez 1964, 54, 66; Moreno Fraginals 1978, I, 167–255; II, 93–97, 106–174; III, 34–36; Scott 1985, 20–21).

Similarly the growing industrial demand for cotton, the new industrial raw material par excellence, revived slavery in the United States. Between 1780 and the mid-nineteenth century, annual cotton consumption by British mills increased from 2,000 to 250,000 tons. This demand was met through the development of a zone of supply in the American South. Cotton had played a relatively unimportant role in colonial North American agriculture, and supplies of cotton to Britain were of little commercial significance before the 1790s. In the year 1793, the first year of the cotton gin, 487,000 pounds were sent to England. Cotton exports reached 62,186,081 pounds by 1811, the eve of the war with England. From the close of the War of 1812 to 1859 the amount of cotton produced in the United States increase by over thirtyfold from less than 150,000 bales to 4,541,000 bales. Cotton became the leading American export commodity, By 1860, it accounted for more than half the nation's total exports of $400 million, and had attained an unprecedented position in the American economy (Cohn 1956, 88; Gray 1958, II, 691; Scherer 1969, 125–126, 142–146; Furtado 1968, 112–113; Crawford 1924 126, 129–131, 137–139).

The growing demand for cotton opened a vast territory of virgin land to commercial agriculture and the profitable use of slaves. The invention of the cotton gin by Whitney enabled short staple cotton that could be grown in frost areas to be grown on a commercial scale. Up until the Civil War cotton cultivation pushed rapidly into the fertile lands of Alabama, Mississippi, Louisiana, Arkansas, Texas, and Florida. To keep pace with growing world demand, less fertile lands in the Piedmont were abandoned in favor of the ideal climate and soil conditions of the lower South. This migration was less an escape from soil exhaustion than, as Wright argues, "a rational process of geographical expansion and relocation." Indian lands were occupied and the plantation system revived by vast tracts of new land as the cotton kingdom shifted its center from the Upper South to the new, fertile lands of the Gulf States. The steamboat and railroad facilitated the development of cotton culture in the Lower South. The steamboat brought modern transportation methods to the navigable rivers and coastal waters, and from 1845 to 1860 the South built more miles of railroad than the New England and the Middle Atlantic States combined. This extensive water and rail transportation network opened new lands to cotton cultivation, linked the South to the markets for its goods, and reduced the cost of Southern living by providing a plentiful supply of Western foodstuffs. By 1850, the "Cotton Belt" extended for more than a thousand miles from South Carolina to the region near San Antonio and dominated world production (Cohn 1956, 90, 95, 108–109; Wright 1978, 13, 15–17, 325; Gray 1958, II, 691; Scherer 1969, 202–204, 336–339).

Slave labor provided sufficient cheap manpower to support this expansion. Slavery and cotton marched hand in hand across the map of the South. The slave population of the South increased from about one million at the beginning of the century to four million on the eve of the Civil War. Gray estimates that slave imports into the United States between 1800 and 1860 amounted to about 320,000 slaves, of whom some 270,000 were smuggled in after the U.S. abolition of the slave trade in 1808. The majority of the labor supply was thus provided by the remarkable natural increase of North American slaves unique among New World slave populations and the regional shift of slaves from the North and Upper South to the Cotton Belt. Nevertheless, the availability of slave labor curbed the expansion of the cotton industry. The demand for slave labor drove the price of a good field hand from $200 in 1790 to $2,000 in 1860. The cotton plantation did not require the heavy capitalization of the sugar estate, but these high slave prices favored the larger productive units. Big planters of the Gulf States could absorb these high prices. They not only had larger, more productive estates on more fertile land and easier access to credit on better terms, but they worked large gangs of slaves and could more easily reproduce their labor force without recourse to market. They were thus able to increase their advantage at the expense of small planters. The cotton industry absorbed almost the entire increase in the slave population, and the vast majority of slaves were concentrated in the Cotton Belt by the eve of the Civil War (Cohn 1956, 90–91, 116–117; Scherer 1969, 149–150, 199; Gray 1958, II, 691; Furtado 1968, 124, 127–128n).

Coffee was also transformed into an article of mass consumption during the nineteenth century, and Brazil emerged as the new center of world production. The progress of coffee cultivation in Brazil was slow until it began to be exported as a result of short supply and high prices caused by the Haitian revolution. But by the decade 1821–1831, coffee was already Brazil's third leading export after sugar and cotton and accounted for 18 percent of exports by value. Between 1837 and 1878, Brazil's annual coffee exports climbed dramatically from one million to four million sacks, and by 1881, coffee represented more than 60 percent of Brazil's exports by value (Prado 1981, 157–159; Furtado 1963, 121–124).

The development of the coffee plantation in Brazil relied upon the intense utilization of slave labor. The equipment used was simpler than in sugar manufacture and, more often than not, of local manufacture. Costs were low, and if there was sufficient land, the availability of labor was the only obstacle to its growth. Curtin estimates slave imports to Brazil during the nineteenth century at 1,145,000. However, the high rate of slave mortality reduced the impact of new Africans on the economy. Beyond this, the coffee economy had available to it, first, the underutilized slave manpower reservoir in the former mining region, and, later, transfers of manpower from the sugar industry in the Northeast. In 1823, the provinces of Rio de Janeiro, Minas Gerais, and São Paulo had a slave population of about 386,000 while Bahia, Pernambuco, and Maranhão, sugar and cotton regions of the Northeast and North, had approximately 484,000. In the next fifty years the development of the coffee industry reversed this situation. Bahia, Pernambuco, and Maranhão had about 346,000 slaves while the coffee provinces of Rio de Janeiro, Minas Gerais, and São Paulo counted over 800,000 (Curtin 1969, 234–237; Furtado 1963, 124,127–128n).

The initial expansion of coffee cultivation in Brazil was concentrated in the Paraíba Valley, which remained its center until the third quarter of the nineteenth century. Close to Rio de Janeiro, this area enjoyed a relatively abundant supply of manpower because of the decline of the nearby mining economy, while abundant mule convoys provided easy transport to the nearby port. However, as the boom continued, the railroad aided in pushing coffee cultivation further inland. The Estrada de Ferro Central do Brasil (Dom Pedro Segundo), built by the Brazilian government, but with the aid of British loans and by a British contractor, opened the further reaches of the Paraíba Valley, parts of Minas Gerais, and finally the Oeste Paulista to coffee cultivation. The effect of this line on the economy of the Paraíba Valley was not long lasting because the valley had almost reached its peak of productivity by the time the railway was constructed. But it served to prolong its prosperity by lessening the cost of transport, and also it contributed to the intensification of coffee production in the upper Paraíba Valley in the province of São Paulo (Furtado 1963, 123–124; Prado Júnior 1981, 161–162; Graham 1968, 52–54).

Land speculation and speculative agricultural practices pushed coffee cultivation south and west into the state of São Paulo. The Oeste Paulista (geographically the east and northeast of the province of São Paulo, but in terms of the spread of coffee to the west of the Paraíba Valley) enjoys natural advantages and greater ease of transport and communication over Paraíba Valley. The irregular and varied terrain of the Paraíba Valley and the dispersion of hillsides with proper exposure to sun and shelter from wind scattered the coffee estates in small nuclei separate from one another. Credit and manpower were in relatively short supply as well, and plantations did not exceed a few tens of thousands of plants at most. In the new region of São Paulo, the unbroken terrain was covered with a uniform and uninterrupted "sea of coffee" that covered the landscape as far as the eye could see. Large estates began to form with greater frequency in these new zones of the Oeste Paulista. From early on plantations were formed with hundreds of thousands of plants, and by the end of the century, estates with more than a million plants began to appear. The scale of production and domination of resources by the big estates and the size of the investment required made these new lands less accessible to small and medium producers. In contrast to the backward techniques that characterized the earlier coffee production in the Paraíba Valley, the Oeste Paulista produced on a greater scale and with greater technical sophistication. These large coffee plantations utilized elaborate modern equipment for processing the coffee and even smaller planters sent their coffee to the towns to be processed mechanically. These large plantations could extend the area under cultivation and use privately owned railroads instead of oxcarts to haul the coffee to the center of the plantation for processing. The railroad made the exploitation of Oeste Paulista possible, and the railroad in turn depended on coffee. A new network of rail lines centering on the São Paulo–Santos axis lowered freight costs and linked producers with the rapidly growing world demand for coffee. Further, the railroad opened up the vast coffee lands to the west of Campinas and thus ensured the region's prosperity into the twentieth century (Graham 1968, 45–46, 66–67, 71–72; Prado Júnior 1981, 164–166).

CONCLUSION

This chapter argues that slave labor and its abolition cannot be seen as a linear evolutionary process, but as complex, multiple, and qualitatively different relations within the global processes of accumulation and division of labor. For the purposes of this discussion, two qualitatively distinct relations of slavery and processes of slave development—each with different roles and meanings—in the nineteenth century world economy can be distinguished. The first was constituted by a specific set of socio-historical processes and played a particular role in the formation of the world economy from the sixteenth through the eighteenth centuries. These relations were either destroyed or radically reconstituted by the nineteenth century transformation of the world economy. The second was created by and within the historical processes and ensemble of social relations specific to the nineteenth century world economy itself. The second slavery consolidated a new international division of labor and provided important industrial raw materials and foodstuffs for industrializing core powers. Far from being a moribund institution during the nineteenth century, slavery demonstrated its adaptability and vitality.

Implicit in these two processes of the development of slavery are two processes of emancipation. A full account of the history of the destruction of slavery during the nineteenth century would have to take into consideration a variety of political, social, and ideological factors, not least of which would be the actions of the enslaved themselves. Nevertheless, the transformation of the world economy made the conditions of the existence of slave labor more vulnerable and volatile than previously. Price competition in an expanding world market and the growth of wage labor made the productivity of labor more important. The new zones of slave production no longer monopolized the production of particular commodities but had to compete with other forms of labor organization elsewhere in the world economy as the spectrum of forms of labor control was expanded and a global hierarchy of labor was created. Slave producers had to compete with one another and with other peripheral producers, and their position in the international relations of production were determined by the price of staples. At the same time, price differentials were evened out by industrial production and the integrated world market, and world prices were established. The relations between core and periphery were determined by the opposition of industrial prices versus primary goods prices, and high cost versus cheap labor. Further, the systemic meaning of slavery was transformed with the emergence of the capital–wage labor relation during the nineteenth century. The products of slave labor entered directly into the consumption of the European wage working class on an increasing scale. They were important as a means of maintaining the exchange relation between wage labor and capital and also contributed directly to lowering the cost of reproducing the labor power of wage labor. As the capital–wage labor relation became widely established, a systemic imperative to increase surplus value by reducing the value of labor power emerged which required slave producers to provide cheaper and cheaper goods for working class consumption.

At the same time as British hegemony created an integrated world market, the conditions for the production and reproduction of the social relations of capital became "national": The conditions imposed by the international division of labor occasioned a variety of political responses on the part of the planter classes of Cuba, the American South, and Brazil. Unlike their colonial predecessors, they developed varying degrees and modes of national self-consciousness through which they attempted to consolidate their position in the world economy. The conditions imposed by the international division of labor occasioned a variety of political responses on their part, including at times anti-colonialism, anti-slavery, and even attempts to establish an independent national state. Further, slaveholders had to be entrepreneurs concerned with the productivity of labor. While the Civil War and emancipation truncated the "natural evolution" of slavery in the United States, the search for greater productivity and shortage of labor following suppression of slave trade led the Cuban and Brazilian planter classes to experiment with new forms of labor organization and new sources of labor. Slavery in these areas was complemented by other forms of labor control—indentured labor, wage labor, and peasant labor. The development of these other forms of labor control are conventionally seen as evidence of the dissolution of slavery, but slaves remained the strategic fulcrum of the labor process and other forms were complementary to it. These mixed forms of plantation labor are a testimony to the resiliency and adaptability of slave labor. Such experiences were characteristic of the second slavery and aided planters in Cuba and Brazil in negotiating the transition to post-slave production more successfully than their predecessors.

Part Two

The Global in the Local

Chapter Four

World Slavery and Caribbean Capitalism

The Cuban Sugar Industry, 1760–1868

This chapter explores the relation of capitalism and slavery by considering the history of the Cuban sugar complex as part of the historical formation of the capitalist world economy. It treats slavery as one of the multiple forms of social labor organized by and constitutive of world capitalism, and emphasizes the continual reconstitution of slave relations across the space of the Americas over the course of four hundred years. Consequently, it treats Cuban slavery as a particular constellation of slave production formed under specific historical conditions of world economy and views slavery as the particular form of capitalist development that occurred in Cuba.

The development of the Cuban sugar industry between 1760 and 1868 was remarkable. Cuba was only a minor producer in 1760 despite ideal soil and climate conditions for the cultivation of sugar cane. Sugar was grown primarily for domestic consumption rather than for export, and Cuba accounted for an insignificant portion of world output. Yet, by 1868, Cuba supplied nearly 30 percent of the world sugar market that itself had increased tenfold over the same period (Guerra y Sánchez 1964, 40–43; Moreno Fraginals 1978, I, 42; III, 35–36). It possessed the largest and most technically advanced sugar mills in the world. At mid-century, the slave population reached nearly half a million, the great majority of whom were employed in the production and marketing of sugar.

The origins of the transformation of sugar production and slave labor in Cuba are to be found in the social, economic, and political transformations of the world economy between 1760 and 1860. During this "long wave" of economic expansion, slavery was established on a massive scale in previously marginal areas of the world economy in order to supply the growing demand for sugar, cotton, and coffee; at the same time the former centers of slave production declined. There were, paradoxically, perhaps more slaves producing more commodities of greater value for the world market during the first half of the nineteenth century than at any other time in the history of the colonization of the Americas. While cotton and coffee were relative newcomers to world trade, sugar had been central to European expansion in the Americas for nearly two hundred years. Nonetheless, both the unprecedented increase in the amount of sugar produced and the dramatic transformation of the processes of its manufacture, transport, marketing, finance, distribution, and consumption during the first half of the nineteenth century redefined the role and character of sugar in the world economy. Perhaps the clearest expression of these changes was the development of slavery in Cuba. If the Industrial Revolution, the independence of Britain's North American colonies, and the French Revolution may be regarded as opening the historical period of modernity, they nonetheless initiated and sustained the expansion and intensification of an "archaic" form of servile labor. As the example of the Cuban sugar plantation illustrates, the new economic and political conditions prevailing in the world economy shaped the distinctive character of this "second slavery," while, in their turn, reconstituted slave relations extended and deepened the world scale division of labor by expanding specialization in primary products.

By locating slavery within definite temporal-spatial parameters of the evolving world division of labor, I find the approach presented here goes beyond ideal typical conceptions of capitalism and slavery. Such conceptualizations treat these relations as if they were conceptually and practically independent of one another. They exclude from consideration both the unity and the heterogeneity of the historical field in which these relations operate and from which they derive their meaning. The external juxtaposition of such isolated and partial categories produces abstract and one-sided models of causality, if not teleological conceptions of historical change. Nowhere has this procedure been more evident than in treatments of slavery and technological change. The prevailing opposition of capitalism and slavery has created deterministic arguments in favor of their incompatibility. This chapter addresses the problem of technological determinism in accounts of the end of slavery by means of a critical assessment of the historical Manuel Moreno Fraginals' *The Sugarmill* (1976), the authoritative character of which compels our attention. It rejects the either/or logic of internal/external; premodern/modern; global/local that such conceptualizations such as that of Moreno Fraginals generate. Instead, it adopts a logic of both/and in order to integrate into a unified and comprehensive conceptual field the diverse relations of production, exchange, and political power constituting the capitalist world economy. This approach enables us to consider the simultaneity and historical complexity of social relations, that is, Cuba as at once slave *and* capitalist and to demonstrate the changing character of slave relations in the nineteenth century through the theoretical reconstruction of the local history of the Cuban sugar complex within world economic processes.

Thus, instead of undertaking to apply abstract and general categories to the interpretation of specific processes, in this chapter I emphasize the need to adopt theoretical perspectives and methodological procedures that take as their premise the historical unity and specificity of the capitalist world economy. Only in this way does it become possible to comprehend the complexity of slave relations—the ways in which they are both continually formed and reformed within the processes of the world economy and contain within themselves conditions of modern economy and polity. Similarly, such an approach permits the world economy itself to be understood as the unity of diverse relations and processes, the modernity of which is defined not by the ever-increasing dominion of a homogeneous and one-dimensional rationality, but by its inherent complexity and historical unevenness.

THE TRANSFORMATION OF THE
WORLD MARKET, 1760–1860

The dramatic development of sugar and slavery in Cuba was inseparable from the expansion and structural transformation of the world market. Although the rate of economic advance between 1760 and 1860 was slow compared with that of the second half of the nineteenth century, industrialization, urbanization, and the growth of population in Europe and North America changed the pattern of demand in the world market. Modern industry required new raw materials on an unprecedented scale. At the same time, the growth of population and development of predominantly urban middle and working classes in Europe was associated with new patterns of consumption that deepened Europe's dependency on peripheral producers for foodstuffs. The result was increased European demand for tropical and sub-tropical products. European and North American capital extended the area of supply of these materials and established a global system of transport based on the railroad and steamship to carry them, while peripheral regions specialized in the production of food and raw materials for export. New patterns of supply and demand were created that no longer coincided with old colonial boundaries. Economic control over the flow of goods assumed greater importance than political control over the sources of production. Increasingly world-scale markets mediated between producers and consumers, and supply, demand, and price appeared as the determinants of the division of labor and of the flow of commodities within the world economy (Hobsbawm 1968, 128; Woodruff 1971, vol. 4, part 2, 657–658; McMichael 1984, 12–13).

The chief agent and beneficiary of this transformation was Great Britain. With the defeat of France in the Napoleonic Wars, Britain emerged as the single dominant economic and political power in the European world economy. Under its hegemony there began a process of reintegration of the world market and a redefinition of the role and significance of colonialism and slave labor. To the extent that Britain came to control commerce outside the bounds of its own empire, it became less committed to formal colonialism as the means of defining the nature and direction of commodity flows and the division of labor between core and periphery. Instead, British commercial and industrial superiority enabled it to penetrate the markets of the other colonizing powers and to establish trade with the periphery on the basis of complementarity—British manufactured goods (and other services such as capital, shipping, banking, and insurance) for peripheral raw materials and agricultural products. Britain was the world's largest consumer of products from the periphery and was the only purchaser that could absorb the increased peripheral production. On the other side of the coin, it was the only country that could supply the credit, machinery, and manufactured goods required to support this expansion. The advance of British industry accentuated the relative differential between industrial and agricultural prices in the world economy and pushed Britain to develop cheap new sources of supply in the periphery in order to redress its unfavorable balance of trade. British shipping and credit also expanded world trade and increased the demand for new crops outside of Britain. The development of such multilateral trading extended British financial power, increased the volume of commodities in circulation, developed cheap sources of supply, and secured markets for British manufactures throughout the world economy. World trade and crop cultivation increased dramatically, if unevenly, and world rather than local prices increasingly dominated the trade in agricultural staples and raw materials (Hobsbawm 1968, 135, 138, 146–148).

However, the effect of these developments was not to destroy archaic forms of social organization and establish the general mobility of capital and labor in a universal free market. Instead, the very success of Britain in establishing its hold on the world market provoked a protectionist response on the part of its rivals. The second-rank European powers sought to protect their "national economies" from British economic power and from competition in the world market through high duties or outright prohibition of trade. As Britain undermined old colonial empires, rival powers were forced into greater reliance on their colonies and tried to strengthen their control over them. At the same time, colonial producers were increasingly brought into competition with one another as world demand and production grew. Those in a strong competitive position had to struggle against the limitations of the colonial policies of their own metropolitan centers and against protectionism in general. Those in a weak position of course demanded that colonial policy and market preferences be used to protect them from world competition (Labrousse 1954, 40). But for all of them, the ongoing processes of market integration, expansion, and competition compelled, directly or indirectly, productive efficiency—or their collapse as producers.

These changes created new conditions for slave labor internationally. To the degree that Britain was able to exercise influence over world production through its control of the market, it was able to develop a flexible global economic and political strategy utilizing a variety of forms and sources of labor, ranging from slaves to tenants, sharecroppers, and peasants, and from indentured laborers to free wage laborers (Beiguelman 1973, 3–8). Slave labor lost its privileged status for Britain: the particular social form of labor became less important than its cheapness. In contrast, rival producers were made more dependent on slave labor by the expansion of demand, the competitive nature of the market, and the lack of alternative sources of labor. The very processes that contributed to the destruction of slavery within the British Empire resulted in the intensification of slave production elsewhere in the hemisphere. As part of the emerging international division of labor, slavery developed on a massive scale in Cuba, Brazil, and the United States during the course of the nineteenth century. The rapid development of these new zones of exploitation brought with it changed economic and political conditions for slave labor. Production in the new areas was premised upon a competitive and expanding market and an industrializing world economy. The scale and nature of slave production were altered. Vast expanses of land were brought under cultivation, and millions of slaves were set to work producing sugar, coffee, and cotton. New industrial technology—notably the railroad, steamship, and the steam engine—transformed the labor process in the new slave frontiers. The development of these new plantation zones lowered costs, increased the scale of production, and provided outlets for surplus British capital in one form or another. This structural transformation of the world market was the condition for the development of the sugar plantation and slave labor in Cuba during the first half of the nineteenth century.

THE SUGAR PLANTATION IN CUBA

World sugar production and consumption increased steadily from 1760 to 1868, while the period of war and revolution between 1776 and 1815 dramatically altered the political organization of markets. The Haitian Revolution (1791–1803) not only destroyed the world's richest colony and the source of nearly half the world's sugar but signaled the end of French imperial ambitions in the Americas. With the collapse of France and its colonial empire, there was no power that could rival Britain in the international arena, and a process of reintegration of the world market began under the hegemony of British capital. Under the aegis of British capital, the growth of world sugar production and consumption accelerated after 1815. Sugar was transformed from a luxury good into an article of mass consumption (Mintz 1985). Sugar prices soared, and producers rushed to fill the void. The unparalleled expansion of the world sugar market during the first half of the nineteenth century stimulated the development of new producing areas and hastened the decadence of old ones.

The British West Indies were initially in the best position to take advantage of the destruction of the French colonial sugar industry and the consolidation of British hegemony. Between 1791 and 1815, sugar production in the British Caribbean rose more rapidly than at any other time in its history. The old colonies increased their output and new sugar territories were added to the empire. However, the interplay of market forces and the anti-slavery movement pushed Britain toward a policy of free trade and undercut the competitive position of its West Indian colonies. While the slave trade was abolished in 1807, British expansion in the Caribbean came to an end by 1815. In the smaller islands of the British Caribbean, sugar production reached its saturation point by the late 1820s. In Jamaica, Trinidad, and Guiana, where expansion was still at least technically feasible, economic and political restructuring restricted the development of the sugar industry. In Jamaica, new investment and territorial expansion were only possible in the inland valleys where high transportation costs raised the price of sugar. The progress of the sugar industry in the Crown colony of Trinidad was retarded by the struggle between pro- and anti-slavery forces in Parliament over land and labor policies: it never developed to its full potential. In contrast, sugar monoculture grew rapidly in Guiana between 1814 and 1833, but its further development was limited as British slave emancipation disrupted production in the declining and vital colonies alike. Short of land and labor and unable to take full advantage of the technical advances in sugar manufacture, the British West Indian sugar colonies found themselves unable to compete in the expanding world economy. Their position was undercut not by British industry but by more efficient production in the new sugar regions. Sugar production increased dramatically in Cuba and Brazil after the Napoleonic Wars, and by mid-century, India, Java, Mauritius, Bourbon [Réunion], and Louisiana as well as the European beet sugar industry could also be counted among the world's major producers.

Over the long term, Cuba gained most from the crisis of world sugar production triggered by the Haitian Revolution. The initial stimulus to the Cuban sugar industry had been provided by the introduction of 5,000 slaves by the British during the occupation of Havana in 1762. Despite the subsequent restrictions of Spanish commercial policy, sugar production increased steadily as the Cuban planter class won both trade concessions and the right to import more slaves. Between 1764 and 1792, 59,000 slaves were brought to Cuba, almost equal the number imported during the previous 250 years.

Increased imports of slaves permitted the expansion of the sugar industry and the construction of more sugar mills. However, from the 1790s onward, Cuban sugar production catapulted forward aided by the destruction of export production in Saint Domingue, and by the decline of the British West Indian sugar industry. The fall of Saint Domingue encouraged the ambitions of the Cuban planter class, and the aggressive creole sugarocracy was prepared to take maximum advantage of the opportunity offered to them. New and larger plantations were established at a frenetic pace, and old ones increased their capacity. In the diocese of Havana alone, the number of sugar mills jumped from 237 in 1792 to 416 in 1806. The average output per mill more than doubled during this period, and the first generation of giant Cuban mills appeared, each of which produced over 300 metric tons of sugar and had over 300 slaves. Cuba's slave population went from 85,900 in 1792 to 199,100 in 1817, and in the latter year over 32,000 slaves were imported (Moreno Fraginals 1978, I, 46–47, 67–71, 95–102; II, 96–97; Curtin 1969, 34; Bauer 1970, 403–405). In 1791, Cuba exported 16,731 metric tons of sugar. This increased to 32,586 metric tons in 1799 and reached 45,396 metric tons by 1815 (Marrero 1983–1986, II, 149, 151). However, the Haitian Revolution also inspired the fear of slave rebellion, and increased repressiveness formed the counterpoint to the development of the Cuban sugar industry. The massive Spanish military presence, justified at least in part by the possibility of slave revolt, and the taxation necessary to support it weighed on the development of Cuban society and shaped Cuban politics with regard to Spain during the nineteenth century (Paquette 1988).

Cuban sugar production increased rapidly and continuously in the years after the Napoleonic Wars. By 1820, sugar was established as the dominant sector of the Cuban economy. In 1827, Cuban output reached 76,669 metric tons and surpassed Jamaica's peak year. By 1830, Cuba emerged as the world's largest producer with an output of 104,971 metric tons. World demand continued to grow at an accelerating rate, and Cuban production more than kept pace with it. In 1840, Cuba produced 161,248 metric tons, a little more than 19 percent of the world sugar market. Its output nearly doubled over the next decade. The 294,952 metric tons produced in 1850 accounted for nearly one-quarter of the world's supply. By 1868, the Cuban sugar crop more than doubled again. Production climbed to 720,250 metric tons, and Cuba supplied nearly 30 percent of the world market (Moreno Fraginals 1978, I, 46–47, 67–71, 95–102, 167–255; II, 93–97, 106–174; III, 35–36; Scott 1985, 10; Guerra y Sánchez 1964, 40–45, 52–53; Knight 1970, 14–18, 40–41).

This expansion of sugar production in Cuba was accompanied by and dependent upon a dramatic increase in its slave labor force. Slave imports rose drastically, and the demographic composition of the island was transformed. Hubert Aimes (1967, 269) estimates that 400,000 slaves were imported into Cuba between 1762 and 1838. The Anglo–Spanish treaty of 1835 attempted to outlaw the traffic in slaves to Cuba, but it had little practical effect. Illegal trade continued to supply Cuba with fresh manpower until the middle 1860s. Some 387,000 African slaves were imported between 1835 and 1864. In 1827, the slave population reached 286,900; by 1841, it stood at 436,500 and accounted for more than 43 percent of the total population. However, it fell to 363,288 by 1868. Between 1853 and 1874, some 125,00 Chinese contract laborers were imported as the illegal slave trade died out (Curtin 1969, 34; Knight 1970, 10–11, 22–23, 41, 53; Scott 1985, 87). (These figures suggest that in contrast to the British and French Caribbean where the introduction of Asian indentured labor was a response to the ability of the freed population to successfully struggle over the conditions of labor after emancipation, in Cuba it was a response to an absolute shortage of labor within an expanding plantation system.)

This dramatic expansion of sugar production aggravated the Cuban oligarchy's relations with Spain. The metropolis was unable to provide adequate markets for Cuban sugar, and, by 1818, the colony secured the right to virtual free trade. It was thus able to profit greatly from the expanding world demand for sugar and especially from the shortage of supply following slave emancipation in the British colonies. Cuba exported its products not only to Spain but also to the United States, Britain, Germany, France, Russia, and the Low Countries. It developed important commercial relations with Great Britain and, above all, with the United States. By 1830, the United States emerged as Cuba's major trading partner. As a consequence of its independence from Britain and the Haitian Revolution, the United States had been cut off from its former access to both the British West Indies and Saint Domingue; Cuba provided a dynamic alternative both as a source of supply of sugar and its by-products and as a market for North American goods. The United States had the world's fastest growing population and was the second largest consumer of sugar in the world after Britain. Perhaps more importantly, it consumed much more sugar than it produced. The gap was nearly 500 million pounds in 1855. Cuba was by far the major source of supply. By 1865, 65 percent of Cuban sugar was exported to the United States. Conversely, only Britain and France exceeded Cuba in the total value of trade with the United States (Knight 1970, 43–45; Paquette 1988, 186–187).

These close links between the United States and Cuba were a significant exception to Britain's ability to dominate the markets of peripheral countries through its industrial and commercial superiority. The United States was not only the major consumer of Cuban sugar, but increasingly a supplier of lumber, foodstuffs, and, significantly, industrial goods to Cuba. However, this trade was linked to and dependent upon the emergent system of multilateral trading organized around the hegemony of British capital. The trade surpluses that permitted the importation of Cuban sugar to the United States were the result of North American cotton exports to Britain, and trade between the United States and Cuba was often organized through bills of exchange drawn on London and through the credit drawn on London banks (Paquette 1988, 186–187; Jenks 1973, 67; McMichael 1984, 22–23).

Throughout the nineteenth century, the world sugar market increased enormously. There were more countries producing more sugar, both cane and beet, than ever before, and the price of sugar fell steadily. Without a preferential market of its own, Cuba was forced to compete against protected sugar in the highly competitive "free" sugar markets of the United States and continental Europe. In order to maintain their position in these markets, Cuban planters were under constant pressure to expand their output, increase the efficiency of their operations, and lower the costs of their product (Marrero 1983–1986, II, 179–180; Zanetti Lecuona and García Alvarez, 1987, 23–24). They were able to respond successfully to these demands precisely because Cuba was still a "sugar frontier" through most of the nineteenth century. The unprecedented expansion of the Cuban sugar industry was due to the ability of Cuban planters to increase the area under cultivation, establish new plantations and concentrate labor, and incorporate scientific advances into production processes in combinations and on a scale that were not possible in the older Caribbean slave colonies. The availability of fresh land and labor, especially in the context of a rapidly expanding world market, made possible the remarkable evolution of the Cuban sugar mill from trapiche to mechanized mill. Land and labor could be combined with the mill and refinery in new proportions as the capacity of the latter developed. Indeed, technical innovation was arguably the condition for the expansion of sugar and slavery in Cuba.

The development of the Cuban sugar industry was centered in the western part of the island. Sugar cultivation spread south and east of Havana, displacing coffee and tobacco producers and extending onto new lands. The number of *ingenios* increased almost fourfold between 1800 and 1857. During the initial stages of expansion, the multiplication of traditional production units accounted for much of the increase in total output, although even at this early stage the scale of operations was often considerably larger than elsewhere in the Caribbean. However, steam power made an early appearance, and beginning in the 1830s, the application of modern industrial techniques developed by the European beet sugar industry transformed the methods of sugar manufacture in Cuba. Knight estimates that in 1827 only 2.5 percent of the 1,000 *ingenios* in Cuba were steam powered. But according to Moreno Fraginals, in 1860 there were 359 animal powered with an average production capacity of 113 tons; 889 semi-mechanized mills using steam engines with an average production capacity of 411 tons; and 64 mechanized mills using steam power and more advanced processing technology, with an average production capacity of 1,176 tons. The mechanized mills were few in number, yet they accounted for about 15 percent of the island's sugar crop. Although this remarkable concentration is responsible for a relatively small fraction of the total output, the appearance of mechanized sugar mills signaled a qualitative transformation in the conditions of sugar production. They both represented the culmination of the development of the previous decades and were the forerunners of the modern *centrales* that were to be established later under quite different conditions. The trajectory of the Cuban slave plantation is marked by a distinctive pattern of technological innovation and socio-economic dynamism absent from other Caribbean slave societies (Moreno Fraginals 1978, I, 170–173; Scott 1985, 20–21).

Cubans enjoyed the technological edge of latecomers. The Cuban sugar mill developed on a giant scale, and the technology of sugar production there attained the most advanced level known under slavery. Steam-powered grinding mills, the vacuum pan, and the centrifuge established precise and scientific controls over what had previously been artisanal processes of sugar making. As a result of their adoption, the quantity of sugarcane that could be processed was augmented and the amount and quality of sugar obtained from it were increased. On large estates small rail lines were introduced, often using animal-drawn equipment, to transport canes to the mills from the fields and for transportation within the factories and to the wharves. These developments broke the fixed ratio between land, labor, and mill capacity that had limited the development of the old *ingenio*. With the introduction of steam-driven machinery, it was no longer necessary to limit the acreage under cane. The use of rail transport within estates allowed a greater area to be planted, which provided the increased supply of cane required by modern refining techniques. The optimal size of a large sugar estate rose nearly tenfold, to two or three thousand tons from the previous three or four hundred tons. The capital requirements for founding an *ingenio* increased enormously. Especially following the introduction of estate railways, there was bitter competition for land and labor. Small producers were squeezed out, and a monocultural economy emerged that was dominated by large planters who could afford the increased costs of the new mechanized mills. There was a steady process of land concentration in conjunction with the adoption of steam power and new manufacturing techniques. The average size of a sugar estate in western Cuba in 1762 was between 300 and 400 acres. By 1860 it had reached 1,432 acres (Daubrée 1841, 29–30; Marrero 1983–1986, II, 153, 158–159; Knight 1970, 18–19, 30–40; Guerra y Sánchez 1964, 54, 66; Moreno Fraginals 1978, I, 167–255; II, 93–97, 106–174; III, 34–36; Scott 1985, 20–21; Paquette 1988, 51–52).

However, distance and the lack of internal transport limited the land that could be exploited for sugar cane cultivation and raised its price. Overland transport was slow, difficult, and costly. Enormous trains of oxcarts were required to carry sugar to market. The high volume and low price of sugar made land transport over long distances impractical. Thus, the establishment of new plantations was initially limited to the regions around maritime or river ports, particularly Havana, in order to facilitate transportation (Guerra y Sánchez 1964, 54; Marrero 1983–1986, II, 169–170; Knight 1970, 40). These difficulties made planters look for novel, if not audacious, solutions to the transportation problem. In 1837, thirteen years after the first steam-driven railway began to operate in England, the first railroad in Latin America or the Caribbean was completed between Havana and Güines. This line, built with English financing and North American technology, was created to serve the sugar industry. It was only 51 miles long, but it was successful. Soon railroads were in operation in all sugar-growing areas of the island. Between 1837 and 1851, the railroad "followed" sugar and facilitated the geographic expansion of the sugar industry. It connected productive centers to nearby ports of embarkment and stimulated the development of regional ports such as Matanzas, Cárdenas, Cienfuegos (Zanetti Lecuona and García Alvarez 1987, 61–62; Bergad 1989, 95). In the 1850s there were 618 kilometers of railroads in operation in Cuba and 1,281 kilometers by 1860. These were concentrated in the sugar zone in the western part of the island (from Havana to San Antonio and Batabanó to the west and Sagua la Grande and Cienfuegos to the east). In addition, steamships began to be employed for the coastal trade by 1818. In 1851 the telegraph was introduced to Cuba and a network was established that covered the entire island. By 1867, a submarine cable connected Cuba with Florida (Marrero, 1983–1986, III, 154–159, 191, 209, 212–213; Zanetti Lecuona and García Alvarez 1987, 6, 61–62).

The railroad and the sugar industry developed in the closest interdependence. On the one hand, the railroads were built to serve the sugar industry, and on the other, sugar provided most of their profits. The rail network opened new lands and permitted the profitable exploitation of the rich soils of the interior of the island. Sugar replaced coffee and tobacco. Shipping costs were reduced drastically, and land use was maximized. Enormous quantities of sugar were moved rapidly to ports for overseas shipment, and heavy supplies, such as machinery for the *ingenios*, could be carried distances inland. New, larger, and technically more advanced sugar mills could be established on virgin lands. In the course of this process, slavery was extended, expanded, and intensified. Increasing production and lowering costs, in part due to the railroad, allowed the Cuban planters to prosper in the growing world sugar market despite falling prices. Conversely, after the construction of the Havana-Güines line, Cuban planters and merchants financed the building of new railroads from the profits of sugar production and slave labor. More than 25,000,000 pesos were raised in Cuba for this purpose between 1835 and 1855 (Guerra y Sánchez 1964, 66; Knight 1970, 32–33, 35–36, 38–39; Scott, 1985, 21–24; Marrero, 1983–1986, III, 191–193).

The accessibility of fresh land, particularly in the interior of the island, enabled Cuba to take maximum advantage of the scientific advances of the nineteenth century. Between 1837 and 1851, the center of gravity of the Cuban sugar industry followed the railroad eastward from Havana toward present-day Matanzas and the Santa Clara provinces. In these new territories, ever larger plantations were founded as the lands of the interior were cleared. In 1827, Matanzas had 111 sugar mills producing an average of 183.9 metric tons of sugar (compared with 231 sugar mills with an average output of 183.7 metric tons for Havana, the largest sugar zone during that period). The number of mills in Matanzas climbed to 351 averaging 300 metric tons by 1846, while Havana stagnated. Finally, in 1860, Matanzas counted 401 sugar mills, each producing an average of 603 metric tons annually. The new plantations incorporated not only the steam engine but also the latest refining technology available from the European beet sugar industry. By 1860, Matanzas had forty-four of the island's sixty-four fully mechanized mills, followed by Santa Clara with ten. With the highest number of steam-powered mills and the largest number of mills with vacuum pans, Matanzas had the largest total output and the largest average output on the island. Matanzas' share of the island's sugar crop went from 25 percent in 1827 to 55 percent by mid-century. Further, these central sugar zones had the largest concentration of slaves and the most slaves per sugar mill of any region on the island (Zanetti Lecuona and García Alvarez 1987, 18–19; Scott 1985, 21–24; Marrero 1983–1986, II, 168, 187, 198–202, 229–230, 248–249, 279).

This transformation of the Cuban sugar industry rested upon the labor of African slaves. As sugar production grew, slavery was extended and expanded. While the shortage of labor and the political advance of emancipation led the Cuban planter class to experiment with new forms of labor organization and new sources of labor, slavery remained an economically and socially viable labor system. As both Scott and Bergad argue, the technological transformation of the Cuban sugar industry increased the output per slave (Bergad 1989, 96–97, 109; Scott 1985, 24–37). For most slaves the old drudgery intensified as a result of the changes. Others performed tasks as technically sophisticated as those of any factory operative. The slaves' ability to successfully adapt to the new conditions sustained the Cuban sugar complex in new conditions of modern world economy.

Yet, perhaps more important than the viability and profitability of slave labor is the question of the transformation of the systemic meaning and character of slavery. The transformation of the world economy made the conditions of the existence of slave labor more vulnerable and volatile than previously. Price competition in an expanding world market and the growth of wage labor made the productivity of labor more important. The new zones of slave production no longer monopolized the production of particular commodities. On the contrary, they had to compete with other forms of labor organization elsewhere in the world economy as the spectrum of forms of labor control was expanded and a global hierarchy of labor was created. Slave producers had to compete with one another and with other peripheral producers, and their position in the international relations of production were determined by the price of staples. At the same time, price differentials were evened out by industrial production and the integrated world market, and world prices were established. The relations between core and periphery were determined by the opposition of industrial prices versus primary goods prices and high cost versus cheap labor. The systemic meaning of slavery was further transformed with the emergence of the capital–wage labor relation during the nineteenth century. The products of slave labor entered directly into the consumption of the European wage working class on an increasing scale. They were important on two counts: as a means of maintaining the exchange relation between wage labor and capital and as a direct contribution to lowering the cost of reproducing the labor power of wage labor. As the capital–wage labor relation became widely established, a systemic imperative to increase surplus value by reducing the value of labor power emerged, which required slave producers to provide cheaper and cheaper goods for working class consumption.

CUBAN SLAVERY IN THE WORLD OF
CAPITAL: THE REPRESENTATION
OF SLAVE LABOR

The development of the sugar industry and of slavery in Cuba between 1760 and 1868 coincides with not just the expansion of the world market but its transformation and articulation with new political forms of the organization of states, new social forms for organizing labor, and new technical means for producing and transporting goods. Yet the question of how slavery is to be understood within this process remains to be elaborated. I would like to address this problem through a brief examination of Manuel Moreno Fraginal's treatment of slavery in his classic work *The Sugarmill*. (Manuel Moreno Fraginals, *The Sugarmill: The Socioeconomic Complex of Sugar in Cuba, 1760–1860*, trans. Cedric Belfrage. [Monthly Review, 1976] is a translation of the 1964 Cuban edition. An expanded version appeared as *El ingenio. Complejo económico social cubano del azúcar*, 3 vols. [La Habana: Editorial de Ciencias Sociales, 1978].) While documenting the technical transformations of the Cuban sugar industry during the nineteenth century, Moreno forcefully makes the argument for the incompatibility of slave labor and technological innovation in the sugar industry. In this interpretation, slaves are viewed as incapable of attaining the minimal technical level required to operate complicated machinery, and the introduction of free wage workers is regarded as necessary to modernize production (Moreno Fraginals 1976, esp. 40–41, 112–113, 144). If I am critical of Moreno's representation of slavery, it is nonetheless necessary to recognize the fundamental importance of his work. His careful and detailed reconstruction of technical and social aspects of the slave labor process opens the way for a deeper understanding of both the history of Cuba and of New World slavery in general. Yet, at the same time, the complexity and sophistication of his description of the plantation labor process on the Cuban *ingenio* is vitiated by the static juxtaposition of slavery and capitalism that informs his analysis.

Moreno's interpretation of slavery in Cuba rests upon the construction of a conceptual opposition in which capitalism represents all that is modern and slavery represents all that is archaic. Slave labor on the sugar plantation is identified with unqualified manual labor. The slave is regarded as capable of only primitive tasks "to be performed by brute physical strength and by the quantity rather than the quality and technological state of labor" leaving little or no opportunity for technical improvement (Moreno Fraginals, 1976, 31). In contrast, capitalism joins wage labor and technological innovation in a spiraling growth of technical efficiency. Within this analytical framework, the distinctive character of nineteenth-century Cuban slavery results from the impact of the world market on this backward form of labor:

The relatively patriarchal type of slavery, maintained as long as production was limited by the special conditions of the period, was replaced by intensive exploitation
of the Negro. Now it was no longer a matter of extracting a certain quantity of useful
products from him, but of producing surplus value for its own sake. But Marx has
clearly shown how in modern colonies the application of cooperation rests on a
regime of despotism and servitude which is almost always a slave regime. In this it
differs from the capitalist form, which from the outset presupposes the existence of
free wage-workers who sell their labor to capital. We are dealing with a quantitative
change in an agricultural industry, where the relatively large labor force revolution-
izes the objective conditions of the work process, although the system as such does
not change. Its form is that of a production mechanism whose parts are human
beings. The operation retains its manual character, depending on the strength, skill,
speed, and assurance of the individual worker in handling his implement. . . . Two
essential premises of the capitalist system were present in the new sugar enterprises:
the production and circulation of commodities. But the fundamental base was lack-
ing: the wage-worker. Thus we have the slave system, but slavery for the production
of commodities destined for the world market. It differed from the capitalist production system not only in the form in which the killing hours of work were imposed,
but also in the impossibility of constantly revolutionizing production methods, an
inherent part of capitalism. (Moreno Fraginals 1976, 18)

Thus, slavery, the world market, capitalism, and wage labor are shown to
coexist and reciprocally influence one another. But they are conceived as separate terms. The relation between them remains external. They influence one
another, but only from the outside. Thus, "production for the market"
imposes "the essential laws of the capitalist system" on slavery, but slavery
retains and is defined by its "inherent" characteristics (Moreno Fraginals
1976, 131). Quantitative expansion is counterposed to qualitative transformation. Change within the Cuban slave economy is marked by the impossibility
of revolutionizing the means of production—a property of the capitalist
"other."

The consequences of this external opposition between stagnating slavery
and forms of capitalist modernity are most evident in Moreno's treatment of
technological innovation in the Cuban sugar mills. The mill and refinery, the
great bottlenecks of nineteenth-century sugar manufacture, had most innovations concentrated in them. The introduction of the steam-powered grinding
mill and the vacuum pan radically transformed the manufacturing process.
However, Moreno regards slaves as incapable of operating such devices.
Instead, they required the establishment of autonomous cells of wage workers
within the slave plantation.

The most important effect [of the vacuum pan] was on the labor system. The new
apparatus was too complicated for slaves, and Derosne trained free workers to operate it. Thus what had previously happened with the grinding mill now happened with

the vacuum apparatus: another free-labor cell emerged within the sugar mill's slave establishment. The slave neither ran the Derosne apparatus nor tested its temperatures nor watched the safety valves. He continued his old routine, operating the whole process up to the machine and after the machine, while that particular sector of the production line was barred to him. (Moreno Fraginals 1976, 112, cf. also 103, 106)

In Moreno's view, the effect of the machinery was to multiply the traditional tasks of the slaves and intensify their exploitation, while the new, technologically advanced sectors became the exclusive province of cells of free wage laborers, in this instance, Chinese laborers who performed the tasks of the mill and refinery and made possible "the jump from manufacture to big industry" (Moreno Fraginals 1976, 103, 106, 112, 141–142).

In this interpretation, slavery is no longer treated relationally. Backwardness becomes an attribute not of the slave relation, but of the enslaved. The incompatibility of slave labor and modern technology, congealed in the physical person of the slave, becomes almost absolute. Conversely, wage labor and technological transformation are projected as teleological outcomes of historical development. Technological advance virtually extrudes free wage labor as a necessary relation and requires wage laborers to be inserted into the production process.

The steam engine and the vacuum pan, which were being experimented with in Europe in 1812, started a sugar-industry revolution which left Cuba no alternative but to establish a cell of wage-workers within the mill's slave corps. . . . Everyone agreed that industrialization with slaves was impossible. It was not a question of lowering costs: free workers were a matter of survival, the only way to make the leap from manufacture to big industry. . . . Producers now felt the urgent need of labor which would be cheap but of a minimal technical level unattainable by slaves. The Industrial Revolution meant the changeover to the wage-worker. . . . Steam-powered mills started a process which led in the end to the abolition of slavery. (Moreno Fraginals 1976, 134–135, 112–113, 106)

The external opposition between archaic and modern here becomes transformed into a technological determinism which finds its complement in a biological or cultural opposition between Africans and Chinese.

Such a one-sided interpretation both misreads the historical evidence and misunderstands the relation between slavery and technological change. Against this technological determinism, Rebecca Scott has documented for Cuba the high number of skilled slaves performing technically advanced jobs and the dependence of the largest and most mechanized plantations on slave labor (Scott 1985, 3–41, 84–110). That slaves commonly operated such devices should not be surprising. The proponents of the new technology emphasized its simplicity and its role in imposing a new labor discipline. The purpose of the new machinery was precisely to do away with the complicated manual labor entailed in sugar manufacture and to simplify the activities of the worker. Their operation required no specialized knowledge or skill. Derosne, describing an early version of his refining system that combined clarifiers, carbon filters, and flat-bottomed copper swing kettles, contends that "any Negro boiler, in one operation, may be taught to use it, without fear or possibility of anything going wrong" (Daubrée 1841, 27; Derosne 1833, 12; Derosne and Cail 1844, 15–16, 23–24).

The relationship between technological innovation and slave labor was posed most sharply by the vacuum pan. It was the most complex and sophisticated apparatus introduced into the colonies and the one most responsible for revolutionizing the methods of sugar manufacture. Describing their system of vacuum pan evaporation, Derosne and Cail write:

> Combining the machines with care, the operations have been facilitated and made independent of the workers' lack of attention in such a way that today the worker is subject to the machine itself and is unable to incur the faults that bore witness to his incapacity in the old system. And for the very reason that with the new processes the worker is relieved of every laborious operation, more sustained attention can be demanded of him. (Derosne and Cail 1844, 15–16, 21–22)

This system substituted mechanical power and the conscious and systematic application of scientific principles for the skill, dexterity, and strength of the worker. It may have been more complex than the implements previously used in its place, but the work performed by the individual slaves became simpler and less physically demanding. The purpose of this new machine was the suppression of manual labor both in terms of the difficulty and complexity of the tasks and of the number of workers required to perform them. As manual labor was reduced or eliminated, the skills and subjective judgment of the slave craftsmen were appropriated as the property of the machine. The vacuum pan fused the technical supervision of the process of material production and social discipline over the activity of the workers. The instrument of labor, freed from control by the worker and transformed into a self-activating mechanism, became the repository of control over both the material process of production and the social process of production.

The vacuum pan required a small group of specialized workers—generally an engineer and one or two mechanics or boilermakers—for its operation. Persons with necessary technical qualifications, generally not to be found among the colonial population, slave or free, had to be brought from abroad. To focus on the failure of slaves to occupy these positions misses the larger point of the transformation of the labor process and the shifting locus of control over it. Beyond the technical staff, "the main part of the manufacture is only composed of very ordinary labor, as much within the scope of the Negroes as the present manufacture." Far from exerting pressure to transform the social relations of production throughout the other sectors of the labor process, this isolated nucleus of free workers was dependent upon slave labor and constrained by its presence. The slaves adapted themselves to this new work regime so successfully that the extent to which the technical staff entered into its routine operation beyond the most general supervision may also be questioned. In Bourbon, where pioneering efforts were made with the vacuum pan on the plantation of A. Vincent beginning in 1838, "All the workers . . . are Negroes, and, nevertheless, they have not had the least difficulty in habituating themselves to the management of the machines." On the estate of Vila-Urrutia in Cuba, where Derosne's vacuum pan was producing 12,000 kilograms of crystallized sugar a day in 1843, Derosne and Cail report: "The factory had no other white worker than the sugar master. All the rest of the personnel was composed of Negroes, who have mastered their work very quickly" (Daubrée 1841, 34, 51–52, 76; Derosne and Cail 1844, 8, 15–16, 21–24).

Yet, factual error is less interesting here than the conceptual framework that produced it. Moreno presents the colonial economy not as a contradictory unity, but as an integrated duality (Franco 1976, 11). The connectedness of Cuban slavery and transformation of the world economy is de-emphasized. Instead, slavery and capitalism are regarded as two distinct and conceptually and practically autonomous categories. These two terms are conjoined to construct the complexity and heterogeneity of the historical processes under consideration. There is no historical synthesis. Instead, their simple coexistence defines the spatial and temporal boundaries of nineteenth-century Cuban history. Within this duality, the slave relation is treated as if it were a local phenomenon that is situated in Cuba and impinged upon from the outside by a capitalist world market, which in turn is spatially conceptualized as "somewhere else." Slavery is inserted into the processes of modernity as a static and inert category. The resulting historiographical account produces a linear narrative of the development of all slave societies articulated externally with the world market. Thus, for example, slavery in Barbados in the sixteenth century, Jamaica and Saint Domingue in the eighteenth century, and Cuba in the nineteenth century are equated with one another and are seen to exist within a single, homogeneous temporal frame. Their external contexts vary, but the same "laws" of slave production are mechanically repeated.

Such a view simply eliminates from consideration the ways in which the opposed elements of capitalist modernity and slave labor are constitutive of one another. Slavery in Cuba was created by and within the historical processes and ensemble of social relations specific to the transformation of the nineteenth-century world economy. Productive capital, an integrated world market, technological innovation, and the emergence of a wage working class in Europe and North America were the conditions for the formation and expansion of slavery in Cuba, while Cuban slavery consolidated a new world division of labor and provided needed industrial raw materials and foodstuffs for industrializing core powers. The specific historical trajectory of slavery and plantation agriculture in Cuba is the particular outcome of a unitary, though uneven, world process. Slavery is thus recreated within a new socioeconomic complex of forces and imbued with new content and character.

CONCLUSION

The perspective presented here constructs the distinct way in which land, labor, and technology in Cuba were constituted within specific historical processes of the evolving capitalist world economy. Technological development had dynamic consequences for Cuba. In Cuba, the availability of land—essential to the extensive pattern of exploitation of the Cuban sugar industry—was blocked by the difficulties of transport. Nevertheless, this limit—instead of being simply destructive and leading to a regression—led to the surpassing of the previous order: it resulted in a new social-economic form on which an accelerated rhythm was imposed with the introduction of the railroad, the integration of the island's sugar economy into the world-scale circuits of capital, and the expansion and intensification of slave labor.

To the degree that Moreno ignores the world historical character of Cuban slavery, he obscures what is distinctive about its local history. The apparent continuity of the history of slavery and slave emancipation and its seemingly singular relationship to capitalist development conceal the complex, multiple, and qualitatively different relations and processes constituting slavery in Cuba within the world processes of capital accumulation and division of labor. Despite the apparent similarities, the sugar plantation and slave labor in Cuba are not the same as in Barbados, Saint Domingue, or Jamaica. The latter represent a cycle of slave production that precedes industrial capital and the integration of world markets characteristic of the nineteenth century, whereas the organization of land, labor and technology in Cuba presupposes the integration of world markets and capital circuits increasingly centered in industrialized production. The nexus of market and productive processes in these two socio-economic situations results in sharply contrasting temporal differences. In Cuba, a structural change in historical time itself took place.

(One may speak of the "denaturalization of historical time" which can be grasped from the perspective of technology and industry [Koselleck 1985, 96].) The development of the sugar industry in Cuba was characterized by movement, acceleration, and openness to new social-economic arrangements within and new spaces without. In this context, specific rhythms, sequences, and periods appear within a plurality of temporal strata, of variable extension and duration that interact in the same historical dimension of modernity, and which can only be understood in relation to one another.

Chapter Five

Spaces of Slavery

Times of Freedom—Rethinking Caribbean History in World Perspective

The Caribbean region presents the observer with the problem of simultaneously understanding diversity and unity. On the one hand, it appears as an archipelago of distinctive island societies that, whether considered individually or taken together, present an almost bewildering variety and complexity of peoples, languages, cultural forms, social groups, economic activities, and political organization. At the same time, colonialism, the sugar plantation, and racial slavery and coerced labor have imposed a common matrix on its development and have shaped its historical unity as a region. They ground it in broader networks of economic, social, political, and cultural relations as they mark it with profound inequalities of wealth and power. From this perspective, the islands of the Caribbean appear as subordinate parts of a larger system rather than as independent societies. Their destiny has been formed elsewhere. As colonialism, the plantation, and slavery integrate the region into broader spatial fields, so they shape its distinctive temporality. In the Caribbean, indigenous populations and their cultures were effectively destroyed or eliminated. Both colonizers and colonized were immigrants from elsewhere (though, of course, under very different conditions). The historical evolution of the region was formed within the historical processes of capitalist modernity even as it contributed significantly to the making of a modern world. Thus, in the Caribbean nothing is traditional, and tradition itself is an active response to distinctly modern forms of domination and exploitation (James 1963).

At first glance, colonialism, the sugar plantation, and slavery appear to create a serial pattern, the seemingly monotonous repetition of "sugar islands," each like the other. But in important ways they have contributed to the region's diversity. The succession of colonial empires—Spanish, Dutch, English, and French—has shaped the Caribbean's institutional and distinctive linguistic heritage. In the African slave trade, the importation of Asian indentured labor, and the subsequent internal migrations caused by the singular demand for plantation labor, is to be found the source of much of the region's ethnic diversity. Slavery and coerced labor, too, are subject to important variation, both in their organizational forms and in the polyvalent cultural and political processes through which the enslaved in different times and places adapted to and resisted the conditions forced upon them (Gilroy 1993).

Yet, on further reflection, even this approach is insufficient to grasp the region's diversity. The history of the Caribbean is not simply a grand narrative of colonialism, the sugar plantation, and slavery. It is, as one of its greatest thinkers reminds us, a history of counterpoints (Ortiz 1991). If the sugar plantation, slavery and coerced labor, and colonialism (and the manifold forms of resistance to them) form the dominant motifs, their counterpoints appear in the cultivation of tobacco, coffee, bananas, or provision crops; in the existence of multiple types of smallholding peasantries (whether these form prior to, exist alongside of, or emerge within or precipitate from regimes of plantation slavery can be sociologically, historically, and politically decisive [Mintz 1979]); and in the assertion of diverse racial, ethnic, class, and national identities. Motif and counterpoint coexist, compete, and develop through complex forms of interdependence and conflict that move within and between islands as they draw on wider Atlantic and world sources.

Viewed in this light, the Caribbean appears as a rich, multi-layered, multi-textured sediment of world history—an intricate pattern of diverse spaces, groups, and activities formed within distinct historical temporalities, ultimately unified through the plural spatial and temporal dimensions of the world economy. To understand the historical trajectory of individual social formations or of the entire region requires conceptualizing over historical time its specific spaces, their interrelations and interactions, and their simultaneous embeddedness in larger spatial-temporal frameworks, not only of particular imperial systems, but of the world economy as a whole. This article contributes to such an approach by treating time and space as constitutive elements of Caribbean history. Through a critical examination of the historiographical debate between Eric Williams and Seymour Drescher, it seeks to establish the specificity of sugar and slavery in the British West Indies within the temporal rhythms and spatial recompositions of world capitalism. By thus treating particular historical sequences within "world time and space," it discloses the temporal-spatial complexity of the dominant motifs of Caribbean history at a crucial moment in their evolution. It thereby suggests a theoretical framework for incorporating plural temporal and spatial relations into causal models and interpretative accounts and develops an approach to Caribbean history sensitive at once to temporal-spatial difference and to the interrelation and unity of diverse processes.

THE LIMITS OF HISTORIOGRAPHY

Since its publication in 1944, Eric Williams' *Capitalism and Slavery* has been a foundational text of Caribbean history. Perhaps an important reason for its enduring influence is Williams' effort to place the history of the Caribbean and of racial slavery squarely in the framework of capitalist development and the Industrial Revolution in Britain. In a frankly materialist attack on idealist interpretations of abolition and slave emancipation, Williams sought to disclose the economic processes and interests undergirding slavery and abolition in the British West Indies. In its barest essentials, the Williams' thesis is that "slavery created capitalism in Britain and capitalism destroyed slavery." Williams was not the first to comment upon the relation between the abolition of slavery in the British West Indies and the rise of industrial capitalism in Britain. He built upon two very different works: Lowell Ragatz' *The Fall of the Planter Class in the British West Indies* (1971) and C.L.R. James' *The Black Jacobins* (1963). Nonetheless, he systematically and thoroughly addressed the problem with a combination of rigorous scholarship, polemical thrust, and West Indian anti-colonial perspective. Williams' historical interpretation valorizes the role of slavery in the construction of modern capitalism, while his account of underdevelopment represents the nationalist and developmentalist aspirations of newly independent Caribbean peoples and presents a frontal challenge to the self-congratulation of the imperial center. The book and its thesis proved controversial when presented as a doctoral dissertation in history at Oxford (Williams 1971; Oxaal 1968). Animated by movements against economic exploitation and racial domination in both the Third World and the metropolitan centers and given additional force and appeal by Williams' position as first prime minister of Trinidad and Tobago, it continued to be at the center of international academic and political discussions, above all through the 1960s and 1970s.

By the 1970s, however, the impasse of anti-colonial nationalism and developmentalism altered the position of Williams' work in intellectual and political debates. At the same time, the tide of academic opinion began to turn against the "Williams thesis" particularly after the advent of the "New Economic History." Equipped with micro-chip technology and neo-classical economic theory, a new generation of scholars set out to process large quantities of data and produce a scientific history based on fact and free of ideological distortion. The most successful and influential critique of Williams is that of Seymour Drescher, *Econocide* (1977). While not himself a New Economic Historian, Drescher systematically challenged Williams' argument about the decline of the West Indian slave economy and its relation to the abolition of the slave trade through a rigorous empirical examination of prevailing economic conditions. He contends that the slave trade was abolished during a period of prosperity both for the West Indies and the slave trade and that there are no demonstrable links between the abolitionist movement and interests promoting capitalist development. After discounting economic processes and motives, Drescher points to the effectiveness of abolitionism in mounting a mass social and political movement in order to account for its success in undoing a prosperous sector of the imperial economy.

The interpretations of West Indian slavery and its abolition offered by both Williams and Drescher imply conceptions of time and space that profoundly condition their causal accounts and limit their capacity to address complex historical phenomena. Both authors construct historical narratives by establishing sequences of cause and effect that link one event to another. The causes and consequences of social change are treated as residing in the linear relation between particular events or sequences of events. Such an approach presumes that all historical phenomena may be apprehended as discrete events and that such events coexist within a single temporal plane.

Although both conceptual frameworks emphasize the construction of causal sequences over time, space plays a secondary and passive role in them. It is regarded neither as the product of social relations nor as constitutive of them. Rather, space is taken as given and is treated simply as the medium in which causal sequences occur. Both authors treat existing political units as units of analysis and regard them as closed and independent of one another. Such units organize the relation of causal sequences. Both authors presume that causal chains of events either occur within these units or are formed from the interaction between them. Thus, Britain and the West Indian slave colonies are conceived as distinct and independent social systems. Capitalism and the Industrial Revolution are seen as distinctively British phenomena, whereas slavery is confined to Britain's West Indian colonies. The relations between them are narrated as cause and effect interactions between two independent entities. The links between these systems are external and secondary to primary internal characteristics. Thus, trade, prices, colonial policy, etc., are taken as the form of the relation between metropolis and colony. The problem becomes one of charting the movements of such "relations" (i.e., the profitability of slavery) as a measure of prosperity or decline.

Such an approach removes from consideration the relational character of metropolis and colony, markets and production, slavery and wage labor, and the division and integration of labor across national boundaries. Time and space appear neither as constitutive of nor constituted by social relations, but as homogeneous empty fields across which causal chains form. The focus shifts subtly toward acting agencies, their interests and motives, which appear at one end or the other of such causal chains. The field of relations in which metropolis and colony are reproduced and agencies are formed recedes from view; social relations then appear as the products of social action (Hopkins 1982b, 149–152). Thus, instead of inquiring into linkages, interdependence, and the mutual formation and reformation of social relations, political units and agencies through multiple spatial and temporal scales, both authors treat relations of capitalism and slavery as if they were integral political economic systems located in the particular property of distinct spatial entities, themselves conceived abstractly and presumed to be given. Capitalism and slavery appear in the work of both authors as singular and repeatable relations distinguished only by their varying contexts. Consequently, neither author is able to adequately gauge the breadth and depth of processes transforming the role and meaning of slavery in the Americas.

ERIC WILLIAMS: THE TELEOLOGY OF CAPITALIST DEVELOPMENT

In *Capitalism and Slavery*, Eric Williams (1966) frames the decline of slavery in the British West Indies within a transition from mercantile capitalism to industrial capitalism over a period of fifty to sixty years. In his conception, the fate of West Indian slavery is tied to that of monopoly. The West Indian colonies, as mercantilism and monopoly more generally, represented a brake on expanding industrial capitalism in Britain that had to be removed. With the deployment of water and steam power and the industrialization of cotton, iron, and coal between 1783 and 1833, the potential productivity of British industry expanded greatly. In this new industrial order, the old colonial system was inadequate. By the 1830s and 1840s, the British West Indies could no longer meet either the production or consumption requirements of the new industrial economy. The sugar colonies had diminished in importance both as a source of tropical products and as a market for British goods, while the colonial monopoly of the domestic market kept the price of sugar high (Williams 1966, 131). In Williams' view, the fate of West Indian slavery was sealed. It was not only seen as "a vicious social system," but it was unprofitable as well. Its opponents included not just the humanitarians, but also the capitalists. The attack on slavery was subsumed within the more general attack on mercantilism and monopoly. The new industrial interests were ready to dismantle the West Indian sugar empire and slave labor in favor of free trade and anti-imperialism.

Williams distinguishes three stages in the attack on the West Indian monopoly: 1) The attack on the slave trade (abolished in 1807); 2) the attack on slavery itself (abolished in 1838); and 3) the attack on the colonial sugar preference (abolished in 1846). However, the narrative strategy employed in *Capitalism and Slavery* reverses the chronological order of these events. Williams begins his account with the abolition of the Corn Laws (and sugar duties) and the establishment of free trade in 1846. He then works backward in reverse order to treat in succession slave emancipation in the British West Indies during the 1830s and the abolition of the slave trade in 1807 (Williams 1966, 135–153). By structuring the argument in this way, Williams constructs a linear progression of events marking the passage from mercantilism to industrial capitalism that presents free trade as the end point of this stage of historical development (and virtually the inevitable outcome of industrialization). The abolition of the slave trade, slave emancipation, and the declining status of the West Indian colonies within the empire are construed as being of a piece with the abolition of the Corn Laws, the end of Mercantilism, and the emergence of Free Trade. Each event is treated as if it were a step on the road to laissez-faire. Each carries within itself the elements of this transition, which at once provide its cause and its purpose. The causal character of each is determined by the given outcome.

In constructing this causal narrative, Williams fails to make an analytical distinction between events (social action) and social-economic structures. Instead of identifying the specific structural features and distinctive temporalities of a transition from mercantilism to industrial capitalism, he locates the transformation in a linear sequence of particular events whose end point—the establishment of free trade—signals the shift to a new form of social economic organization. The teleological character of this formulation collapses structure and event into a single temporal plane. As a result, the relations between events and structural elements appear as synchronous, fluid, and transparent.

Here the telos constructs the agents, the agents then construct the telos. The teleological framework of the argument determines the role of all actors and actions, and all meanings and motives derive from it. Certain groups are privileged over others as historical agents. Diversity of interest and purpose among groups who otherwise may be seen to interact (or not) within common structural fields are collapsed into a single dominant causal strand. Thus, industrial capitalists are viewed as purposive creators of the free market and are therefore against slavery, whereas anti-slavery partisans mask economic interest in humanitarian rhetoric. Because structural transformation is treated as the result of an event sequence whose direction and outcome are already determined, motive is invoked to account for historical change. Social actors and their actions are understood in terms of interests and motives and appear capable of directly and intentionally constructing a capitalist social-economic order. Structural transformations are viewed as the immediate result of individual or class motive. Actors (at least those whose interests and motives coincide with the historical telos) produce the world they desire.

This procedure eliminates complexity from historical understanding. Particular historical events and processes of abolition and emancipation (but also of industrialization, the development of the free market and class formation) lose their specificity and autonomy and are subordinated to a general choreography of capitalist development. They are decontextualized and interpreted in the light of subsequent developments and outcomes. Williams' emphasis on the importance of the *potential* productivity of British industry (Williams 1966, 126–134) abstracts from the slow and uncertain pace of early industrial development and the economic and social crises of the first half of the nineteenth century that arguably impeded its progress if they did not threaten its existence (Hobsbawm 1969). The 1780s are read in the light of the 1840s. The massive and continuous development of productive forces, the rise of the industrial bourgeoisie, the free market, and anti-colonial ideology are presumed to be the natural complements of industrialization from its outset. Historical development is equated with their progressive emergence. The driving force of industrialization and the industrial bourgeoisie find their inevitable outlet in the establishment of the free market.

This formulation unilaterally identifies capitalism with the development of industry, wage labor, and the free market in Britain. It treats British capitalism as the single dynamic source of change acting on the static and unchanging West Indian slave colonies as though it were an external cause. The progressive development of industrial capital systematically eliminates presumedly archaic forms of mercantilism and slavery and projects a universal and homogenous capitalist modernity (industry, free market, wage labor, and the domination of the industrial bourgeoisie). The complex ongoing interdependence and mutual formation of metropolis and colony, slavery and wage labor, agriculture and industry is thereby disrupted. Each term is reified and treated as a discrete entity independent of the others. Cause and effect are treated as external and unilinear relations between such distinct entities separated in time and space. In one epoch slavery creates capitalism. In the next, capitalism destroys slavery.

SEYMOUR DRESCHER: THE AUTONOMY
OF EVENTS AND *ECONOCIDE*

In *Econocide*, Seymour Drescher (1977) confines his critique of Williams'
theory of the decline of slavery to the movement for abolition of the slave
trade. He examines the relation between the events leading to the abolition of
the trade and economic conditions in the slave sector of the British economy.
He charges that Williams' case for a decline of the British West Indian slave
colonies prior to abolition is based upon scattered evidence. Drescher systematically examines the available data for the period between 1770 and 1820 in
order to test the decline thesis. He demonstrates that there was no decline;
instead, this was a period of expansion and prosperity for the West Indian
colonies. He argues that there is no correlation between either long- or short-
term economic trends and the abolition of the slave trade, and that abolition
does not fit either the laissez-faire or the mercantilist models of abolition proposed by Williams. In Drescher's view, decline for the period between 1770
and 1820 is a statistical illusion caused by ignoring the years 1783–1815
(Drescher 1977, 16). Rather than economic decline being the cause of abolition and emancipation, Drescher contends that decline followed abolition and
only became visible in the decade or two after 1806–1807. By the beginning
of the 1830s, however, Drescher admits that the West Indies were in decline
at least relatively.

The effectiveness of Drescher's critique derives not only from his challenge to the empirical validity of Williams' account of the decline of British
West Indian slavery. His focus on the abolition of the slave trade, chronologi-
cally the first step in the sequence leading to emancipation and free trade, at
once reverses the narrative order of Williams' argument and pulls the linch-
pin from it. By demonstrating the non-correlation of the abolition of the slave
trade with economic decline, Drescher at once unravels the causal structure
of Williams' argument and calls into question the entire relation between capitalism and slavery proposed by Williams. The transition from mercantilism
to industrial capitalism and free trade can no longer choreograph the events
resulting in abolition and emancipation: The market efficiency of the West
Indian slave economies appears rehabilitated. In place of economic causes,
Drescher points to the importance of the independent influence of the mass
abolition movement in Britain in contributing to the decline of the West
Indian slave economy.

Drescher's critique importantly gives reason to reconsider the teleological
linking of the rise of industrial capitalism, anti-slavery, and the free market
that characterizes Williams' interpretation. Nonetheless, the structure of his
own argument provides only a limited alternative interpretation. In his

account, the political event of the abolition of the slave trade is the point of reference for organizing causal sequences. He arranges the narrative structure of the argument in terms of economic conditions *before* and *after* abolition. Thus, rather than treating cyclical economic phenomena as temporally distinct and autonomous from events and describing them fully in their own terms, Drescher interprets them through their relation to a particular event or sequence of events. He reduces temporally diverse social-economic phenomena (i.e., both political-economic structures and events) to a single plane of event-history. Consequently, instead of examining the complex historical interrelation of events and structures within a plurality of social time, Drescher conceptualizes historical transformation as potentially endless chains of particular causal sequences of events within a homogeneous temporality.

The effect of this approach is to separate politics from economics and to treat each as a discrete and independent set of variables. When causality cannot be attributed to economic factors (i.e., when they cannot be seen as the starting point of a causal sequence), they are discarded in favor of the political movement for abolition which is then regarded as a singular cause of the decline slavery. The result is a one-sided approach that undermines Drescher's own insights. While he usefully establishes the causal dynamic of the abolitionist movement, he provides no way of integrating it into the larger picture except as a particular event that sets off a linear chain reaction. It is first separated from its social-historical context and then reinserted into the argument as an independent causal factor. There is no attempt to account for the movement's emergence or its effectiveness within its specific social historical context. From this perspective, one may attempt, at best, to assess the relative weight of individual causal factors or particular causal sequences, but each remains a distinctive phenomenon whose possible historical interrelation, interdependence, and mutual formation with others is outside the scope of investigation. Abolition and its consequences form one causal chain among innumerable causal strands. One such sequence may be placed alongside others, but this approach permits no possibility of linking such chains into a coherent whole.

Thus, Drescher emphasizes the autonomy of particular events and the importance of strict chronological sequence. He thereby produces an open-ended historical narrative that at once effectively challenges Williams' thesis on the decline of West Indian slavery on empirical grounds and undermines his interpretive framework. However, Drescher, too, reduces structural history to the history of events. He thus remains confined in a restrictive before and after chronology that decontextualizes the problem and is unable to provide a comprehensive alternative interpretation. Methodologically and conceptually his approach shares much with that of Williams. It simply inverts the terms of the latter's argument. Williams submerges the event in the context (a deterministic scheme in which the end determines the individual parts); Drescher decontextualizes the event and treats it as an independent cause. For Williams, decline causes abolition; for Drescher, abolition is a cause of decline.

EVENT AND STRUCTURE: THE PLURALITY OF SOCIAL TIME

The shortcomings of the approaches presented by Williams and Drescher point to the need both to develop conceptual frameworks capable of incorporating more complex conceptions of time, space, and historical causality and to interpret the history of sugar and slavery in the West Indies within broader and more diversified temporal and spatial fields. The concept of plural time, perhaps best known through the work of Fernand Braudel, opens the way for such an approach to these problems. In his classic essay "History and the Social Sciences" (1972), Braudel identifies three planes of historical time: the event, the *conjoncture*, and the *longue durée*. Each refers to distinct temporal dimensions of historical movement. They differ from one another, not only in terms of their temporal extension, but each has a distinct structure. Each must be apprehended at a different conceptual level, and each requires a different methodological approach. Typically, each requires a different mode of representation—narration for events and description, the *conjoncture*, and *longue durée*. (For purposes of exposition, I will treat *conjoncture* and *longue durée* together as structural time.)

According to Reinhart Kosselleck (1985), events have a discernable unity that can be narrated. As he argues: "A minimum of 'before' and 'after' constitutes the significant unity which makes an event out of incidents." Thus, events are at once rooted in and constrained by a temporal sequence that requires strict chronological accuracy in the arrangement of its constituent elements. This temporal sequence forms a "threshold of fragmentation" below which the event dissolves (Koselleck 1985, 106). In contrast, structures are conceived in a different temporal plane from events and are understood as having a different structure. They represent "temporal aspects of relations which do not enter the strict sequence of events" and call attention to phenomena of long- or medium-term duration, stability, and change. Structures are reproduced through concrete individual events which possess their own time, but such events only gain *structural expressiveness* within the framework of periods of long duration (Koselleck 1985, 109). They are not reducible to single events or to individual patterns or causal sequences of events. The minimum chronological determinants of "before" and "after" are less crucial to their description. Such structures transcend the space of experience and action of specific actors. They cannot be reduced to the experience or action of individual persons or determinable groups (Koselleck 1985, 107–108). They exist prior to event experience and endure beyond it. For any group of actors, structures are given, not as chronological antecedent, but as ongoing condition and constraint, and their ability to effect them is limited. Such structures do not change from day to day and are preconditions for action (Koselleck 1985, 107). Typically such structural phenomena are most adequately represented through description rather than narration, and methodologically they require functional determinants, rather than causal sequences grounded in individual or group action.

To admit the presence of long- and medium-term structures that are not readily accessible to human action or experience does not necessarily imply a teleological approach to historical studies (Sewell 1997, 247–248). Indeed, it may be argued that recognition of the plurality of social time creates the possibility of avoiding determinism. Structures form the field of possibility and constraint within which events occur. They may condition outcomes but do not necessarily determine them. Thus if, for example, we regard economic cycles as an attribute of a social system (that is, a historically formed network of relations), to say that the system develops cyclically, that one cycle builds from its predecessors and creates conditions for succeeding ones, is not to say that one cycle inevitably determines the next or that they are steps along a predetermined road. Rather, recognition of the temporal and spatial character of such structures enables us to interrogate the systemic dimensions of social relations and the conditions under which they are reproduced.

Recognition of the difference between events and structures enables us to more effectively examine their interrelation and the circumstances and limitations of events in effecting structural transformation. Koselleck argues that understanding the formation and alteration of structures through time and space grants them "a processual character, which can then enter into everyday experience." From this perspective, events may be seen as the presupposition of structural expression, and long-term structures appear as the conditions of possible events. Events may attain structural significance, and duration may be treated as an event. Narration and description may be combined, and the relation of event and structure may be arranged in various ways according to the questions at hand. Yet, however much they may be seen to condition one another, these temporal levels do not merge (Koselleck 1985, 108–111). To read the transformation of social relations as the result of endless strings of events precisely eliminates from consideration their structural features—their distinctive temporal rhythms and sequences and their spatial extension and contours.

WORLD TIME, LOCAL SPACES: REMAKING THE CARIBBEAN SUGAR INDUSTRY

The crux of Drescher's case is his empirical invalidation of Williams' claims about the economic decline of the British West Indian sugar colonies. He appropriately points to rising prices, profits, and production at the time of the abolition of the British slave trade in 1807 in order to critique the Williams' thesis. However, if one looks at the world sugar industry during the first half of the nineteenth century, Drescher's results are not surprising. Expansion was not a uniquely British phenomenon. Production and profits were going up in the British Empire because they were going up throughout the European world economy. The period of prosperity identified by Drescher for the British West Indies was part of the cyclical expansion and restructuring of world economy as a whole during the first half of the nineteenth century. Its full significance becomes apparent when it is viewed in the context of a process of longer duration and greater spatial extension.

The period 1792–1842 is conventionally identified in the literature on economic cycles as a Kondratieff wave, a fifty-year cycle that may be divided into a period of expansion (A-phase) lasting from 1792 to 1815 and a period of contraction (B-phase) lasting from 1815 until 1842 (Schumpeter 1934, 252, cited in Wallerstein 1980, 32n.). Immanuel Wallerstein has argued that such cyclical economic movements are a structural feature of the modern capitalist world-system (Wallerstein 1974, 67–129). Their existence may be taken as evidence of the unity of a world economy that transcends national boundaries and as an indicator of the temporal rhythm of its expansion and development. They impose common conditions on economic actors throughout the world economy as a whole. Periods of expansion and rising prices encourage broad participation in market activities, whereas contraction and falling prices exert pressure for greater efficiency and promote the concentration and centralization of economic activity. However, such common conditions evoke varied responses from actors mediated by differential natural endowments, technological infrastructures, forms of labor organization, and position within the division of labor, commodity circuits, and political structures of the world economy. Thus, systemic regularities result in the creation of difference and of distinctive local conditions within a unifying global framework.

The dramatic growth of world sugar production during the period 1792–1842 combined the long-term effects of the cycle of expansion restructuring the world economy with the short-term impact of the Haitian Revolution. (Let us recall here that on the eve of its revolution, the French colony of Saint Domingue produced as much sugar as all the British West Indies combined.) Between 1791 and 1815–1819, world sugar production increased by nearly 40 percent despite the disruption and uncertainties of war and revolution and the collapse of the sugar industry in Saint Domingue, which had been the world's largest producer. In the next phase of the cycle, between 1815–1819 and 1838–1842, world sugar production went up by a bit over 90 percent (Moreno Fraginals 1978, I, 40–42; II, 173).

This long-term cyclical movement was accompanied by the redistribution and reorganization of labor, the adoption of new varieties of cane and new processing technologies, and, most importantly, the creation of new zones of sugar production. On the other side of the coin, not only was there unprecedented growth of sugar consumption but also changing patterns of imperial dominance and the restructuring of market relations and commodity and financial flows. Britain increasingly became the commercial and financial intermediary for sugar producers and consumers the world over. Growing demand for sugar, the integration of markets, and greater velocity of circulation increased the sheer scale of the demand for labor, put pressure on labor productivity, and required sugar producers to valorize production in new ways. In a complex movement of global pressure and local response—engendering and conditioned by a variety of political and social conflicts with contingent local outcomes—new zones of production, forms of labor, and groups of laborers were created while old ones stagnated or were transformed (Tomich 1988, 1991, 1994; Trouillot 1988).

The effects of this long-term systemic cyclical trend was felt unevenly in space and time across the sugar zones of the world economy. The British West Indian colonies were initially in a position to profit disproportionately from the expansion of the world sugar market after 1791. Established sugar producers, with room for new investment and territorial expansion, the British West Indies were linked to the dominant maritime and commercial power of the period and the one with the most rapidly growing domestic sugar market. Further, they were less subject to disruption from war, revolution, and blockade than other Caribbean sugar colonies. Between 1791 and 1815 sugar production in the British Caribbean rose more rapidly than at any previous time in its history. The old colonies increased their output significantly, new sugar territories were added to the empire, and Britain maintained the predominant share of the sugar and slave trades. By 1815–1819, despite the abolition of the slave trade, the British colonies accounted for nearly half of the world's sugar supply (Deerr 1945, I, 193–202; Williams 1966, 150–151; Drescher 1977, 78–83; Moreno Fraginals 1978, II, 107–130).

However, after the mid-1820s, economic contraction resulted in differentiation among various producing areas. The small islands of the British Lesser Antilles (Barbados, Antigua, St. Kitts, St. Vincent, Grenada and the Grenadines, and Tobago), many of which had been intensely cultivated since the seventeenth century, reached the limits of their expansion. While they continued to produce high amounts of sugar relative to the pre-1791 period, they never again attained the pre-1815 level of production, and their share of still expanding world production progressively declined. Jamaica nearly doubled its sugar output between 1792 and 1805. By the latter year, it exported more sugar than Saint Domingue on the eve of the French Revolution. Jamaica did not sustain itself at this high level of production, but it remained the world's largest supplier until the late 1820s when its output began to drop and its place was taken by Cuba. Jamaican production, although still substantial, declined steadily thereafter until it was disrupted by slave emancipation in the 1830s (Deerr 1945, I, 193–202; Drescher 1977, 94–103; Moreno Fraginals 1978, II, 106, 156–165).

In contrast, British Guiana and Mauritius, two colonies acquired by Britain after the Napoleonic Wars, reveal a different pattern. Both were new sugar-producing regions that dramatically increased their production and were able to overcome the downturn following the decade of the 1820s. In Guiana, a sugar frontier with extensive lands, large grinding mills, and early adoption of new refining technology, production rose from 3,000 metric tons under the Dutch in 1791 to 16,521 metric tons in 1816 under the English. Its production more than tripled between 1814–1818 and 1829–1833, whereafter British slave emancipation (1834–1838) limited its further development. Similarly in Mauritius, a colony in the Indian Ocean acquired from France, production climbed steadily from 4,000 tons in 1816 to 38,483 tons in 1832 (Deerr 1945, I, 193–201; Moreno Fraginals 1978, II, 106, 156–165; Rodney 1981, 1–59; Adamson 1972, 22–28).

A similar pattern may be discerned outside of the British Empire. The colonies remaining to France, Guadeloupe, Martinique, Guiana, and Réunion in the Indian Ocean, revived quickly after 1815 and underwent rapid development until the late 1820s when, together, they produced more sugar than Saint Domingue in its heyday. However, they ceased to expand thereafter and required aid of protective tariffs to maintain the levels they had achieved (Tomich 1990, 41–53).

The Brazilian sugar industry, encouraged by favorable political and commercial conditions during the Napoleonic Wars, was also rejuvenated. In 1791, Brazil produced only 21,000 metric tons of sugar. By 1815–1819, this figure reached an estimated 75,000 metric tons per year, and, by 1822, climbed to over 100,000 metric tons. However, the technical conditions of Brazilian sugar manufacture did not change significantly from what they had been in the seventeenth century, and the lack of an adequate transportation network limited geographical expansion. Further, the relatively poor quality of Brazilian sugar hampered its competitiveness on the international market. Although Brazilian sugar production was increasing in absolute terms, its share of the world market was declining sharply, and by mid-century, its total output began to stagnate as well (Prado 1981, 84–89; Moreno Fraginals 1978, II, 147, 173; Petrone 1968).

Cuba was the most dramatically successful of the new sugar zones. Cuban sugar production catapulted forward beginning in the 1790s aided by refugees from Saint Domingue who provided technical expertise and at times even capital for the growth of the Cuban sugar industry. In 1791, Cuba exported 16,731 metric tons of sugar. This increased to 45,396 metric tons by 1815. Cuban sugar production increased rapidly and continuously in the years after the Napoleonic Wars. However, unlike older sugar-producing regions, the growth of the Cuban sugar industry continued unabated throughout the 1820s. By 1830, Cuba emerged as the world's largest producer with an output of 104,971 metric tons. By 1848, the 260,463 metric tons produced accounted for nearly one-quarter of the world's supply. (See chapter 3, "The 'Second Slavery.'" Moreno Fraginals 1978, I, 167–255; II, 93–97, 106–174; III, 35–36.)

Thus, the cyclical rhythm of the world economy imposed a pattern of development on the world sugar industry, a pattern whose effects were felt unevenly across time and space. The upswing of the economic cycle between 1791 and 1815–25 was a period of world-scale expansion of sugar production. Old sugar areas were rejuvenated and new ones created. (Over the short term, the vagaries of war, revolution and blockade, temporarily affected some areas, and the consequences of the Haitian Revolution probably prolonged this phase of the cycle.) The British West Indian colonies were the greatest beneficiaries of this phase of expansion and enjoyed a period of unprecedented growth and prosperity. However, after the mid-1820s, the speculative boom touched off by the Haitian Revolution came to an end, markets were regularized, and the full effects of the downturn were felt. The crucial years are those of the second half of the decade of the 1820s when this cyclical contraction produced different effects among new and old producing regions. The new sugar producing regions that emerged at the beginning of the cycle were able to supersede the downturn of the 1820s and continue to expand, while the older regions could not.

Thus, sugar production continued to increase in the British West Indies despite abolition of the slave trade as part of the pattern of global expansion. But if we look at the long-term movement, such expansion could not be easily sustained. The decline came fifteen to twenty years after the abolition of the British slave trade but preceded slave emancipation in the British West Indies. It affected British and non-British sugar regions alike. Sugar production rose precipitously in the British West Indian colonies between 1791 and 1815. After the downturn of the late 1820s, they continued to produce substantial amounts of sugar but could not keep pace with growing production and consumption on a world scale. Within the British Empire declining sugar production in the Lesser Antilles and Jamaica was offset by increases in Guiana, Mauritius, and Trinidad, but the British colonies' share of world production fell from nearly 50 percent in 1815–1819 to just under 25 percent in 1838–1842 (Deerr 1945, I, 193–201; Moreno Fraginals 1978, I, 40–42; II, 173).

The situation of the British West Indies was further aggravated by changes in sugar markets and sugar consumption during this period. By 1815, Britain had gained command of the Continental re-export market. British refiners, shippers, warehousemen, and commercial and financial interests were becoming involved in trading large quantities of sugar in markets that, from the British point of view, were unstable and less liable to political intervention. However, British West Indian sugar was unable to compete with cheaper Latin American and Caribbean sugars in the Continental market and had to be subsidized by means of drawbacks and export bounties. British West Indian re-exports dropped from about 100,000 tons in 1802 to 27,000 tons in 1827. Excluded from foreign markets, the West Indian colonies were increasingly dependent on the British domestic market and preferential duties. By the 1820s, the high cost of British West Indian sugar and the demand of Caribbean planters for protection from both foreign and British East Indian sugar restricted the growth of per capita British consumption, prejudiced the development of the British refining industry, and hindered the development of the East Indian colonies. Nonetheless, British domestic consumption nearly doubled between 1815 and 1840, going from about 100,000 tons per year to nearly 200,000 tons. By the beginning of the 1830s, the British West Indies were unable to supply British domestic consumption (Williams 1966, 133–154; Drescher 1977, 155–157; Moreno Fraginals 1978, II, 157–161; Ragatz 1971, 434–435).

OLD SUGAR ZONES AND NEW:
JAMAICA AND CUBA

The contrast between patterns of land tenure and sugar cultivation in Jamaica and Cuba suggests the different conditions obtained in old and new sugar zones and therefore the different capacity of each to respond to the changing world conditions. Jamaica was the centerpiece of the British West Indian sugar economy and the world's leading producer until the late 1820s when it was surpassed by Cuba. The distribution of plantations by size, amount of sugar cultivated, number of slaves, and output on each is unknown for Jamaica during this period. However, the pattern of sugar cultivation and spatial distribution of estates reveals something about the obstacles faced by the old sugar colonies after the mid-1820s.

Jamaica, was a plantation society par excellence (Higman 1988, 5). Estates were large. In 1830, 36 percent of the slaves lived on units of over 200 slaves. A core of plantations had occupied the prime sugar lands in the southern coastal lowlands, across the north coast, and into the Westmoreland plain since the mid-eighteenth century. The number of plantations increased in the latter part of the eighteenth century, but these were often located in regions with less favorable soil and climatic conditions or in the interior of the island where transportation costs here higher. Between 1792 and 1799, 84 new sugar estates were established, over half of them in the northern districts of St. Ann, Trelawny, and St. James. According to James Robertson's map, drawn in 1804 at the high point of Jamaican sugar production, there were 830 sugar estates in Jamaica. These had wind-, water-, or animal-powered mills and were densely concentrated on the northern and western coastal plains as well as the southern coastal lowlands. By 1832, the number of estates had dropped to about 670 (Higman 1976, 14). This decline began before emancipation and was especially pronounced in Portland, where climatic conditions were unfavorable, and among those estates that had been opened up in the interior of the island at the end of the eighteenth century. Those parishes that were affected least by emancipation were those that had been occupied longest (Higman 1988, 10–11; Higman 1976, 14; Drescher 1977, 93; Moreno Fraginals 1978, II, 107–130). Thus, in an established sugar colony like Jamaica, there may have been a considerable amount of land available in absolute terms, as Drescher contends, but outside of the historically established plantation zones much of it was marginal for sugar production.

Within the geographical core of plantation production, the built environment itself was an obstacle to the amelioration of the Jamaican sugar industry. The dense occupation of the soil and the existence of contiguous properties made it difficult for estates to expand or to create new properties in the established plantation zone. Because it is necessary to process sugar soon after the cane is cut, the extent of cultivation, the size of the labor force, and the capacity of mill and refinery have to be coordinated with one another. Increase in one or another sector yields limited results unless there are proportionate increases in the other sectors. On the Jamaican estates, production was organized on a scale adequate to eighteenth century technical conditions. However, landholdings were often extensive as planters frequently occupied more land than they could cultivate in order to limit competition. Thus, there might be room for internal expansion on individual properties, although it could be difficult to maintain the optimal proportions between the capacity of the slave gangs, the cane fields and the factory. Further, planters with capital already sunk in slaves and equipment might be reluctant to devaluate it by investing in new plant that could offer only marginal increases in output.

Thus, Jamaica represents a settled plantation zone in which the existing pattern of land tenure and cultivation inhibited possibilities for expansion and greater productivity. The historically formed production environment restricted not only exploitation of the soil, but also the redeployment of labor and adoption of new technologies. Individual attempts to ameliorate production in this environment could only elaborate and reinforce the existing pattern of relations.

Under these conditions, abolition of the slave trade did not result in an absolute shortage of labor, nor did it, by itself, prevent the expansion of an otherwise dynamic sugar industry. Rather, the technical and spatial organization of Jamaica's plantation zone and the cyclical downturn of the world economy restricted its capacity to absorb fresh imports of labor. However, abolition of the trade did limit the flexibility of Jamaican planters in maintaining the effectiveness of the labor force by acquiring more able workers to supplement the existing slave population. Drescher raises the possibility of a "hollow generation," a generation of slaves, after the abolition of the slave trade, that would need to be supported until the slave population could become self-sustaining without the importation of new slaves. Although such a strategy was certainly possible, it would have required protective legislation and a variety of measures that would have impeded the exploitation of the slave labor force. Further, even if demographic balance were achieved, it is questionable whether it would have altered Jamaica's position in the changing world division of labor.

Beyond the sheer availability of labor, the quality of labor and its adaptability to new labor regimes also need to be considered. If there was sufficient labor to increase sugar production in the British Caribbean during the first part of the nineteenth century, the demographic composition, social practices, and cultural forms of the labor force were changing. A population of increasingly creolized slaves—including higher proportions of women, children, and elderly accustomed to the plantation labor regime and able to resist it from within, with settled family life, provision grounds, and developed internal markets, capable of appropriating aspects of abolitionist ideologies—was able effectively to exert pressure on the slave system while still enslaved and limit the room for maneuver available to planters (Braithwaite 1971).

In contrast, Cuba was a sugar frontier in the 1790s. Slaves and land were available to Cuban planters. In Havana alone the slave population increased from 86,000 to 199,000 between 1792 and 1806. The number and scale of sugar mills increased, and the first generation of giant Cuban mills appeared, each with over 300 slaves and producing more than 300 metric tons of sugar (see chapter 3, "The 'Second Slavery.'" Moreno Fraginals 1978, I, 46–47, 67–71, 95–102; II, 96–97; Curtin 1969, 34). During the following decades, new and fertile sugar lands were cleared. In 1837, the construction of a railroad, the first in Latin America, began the opening of the fertile interior of the island to sugar cultivation. The land, slaves, and sugar factory could be combined under optimal conditions. This possibility was particularly important as new technologies—steam power, iron grinding mills, and later the vacuum pan and centrifuge—transformed the refining process and required greater quantities of cane to be effective. New sugar plantations could be established on a larger scale. Even before adoption of the vacuum pan and centrifuge, large Cuban sugar mills multiplied the use of older technologies to increase the scale of their operations and take advantage of technological advances. Thus, with the adoption of steam-powered horizontal iron grinding mills, Cuban planters often combined four, six, or even ten "Jamaica trains" to boil the increased quantity of cane juice (Moreno Fraginals 1978, I, 109). Further, Cuba not only produced more sugar than Jamaica, but after the more general adoption of the vacuum pan and centrifuge by the more progressive planters in the 1840s, it began to produce better sugar as well. (These new devices required a supply of cane beyond the capacity of most Jamaican estates in order to operate economically.) Thus, Cuba represented a sugar frontier in the 1820s. There, successful planters emerged who were able to establish new economies of scale, incorporate new technologies, and organize labor in ways that were not possible in the old sugar zones.

The contrast between Jamaica and Cuba at once illustrates the difference between old and new sugar zones and calls attention to the importance of processes creating spatial differentiation in the historical development of the world economy. Each zone represents a distinct spatial-technical configuration of sugar production and slave labor formed during a specific world economic conjuncture. The relative position of each in the world division of labor shaped its developmental possibilities. In Jamaica, the historically constructed environment inscribed the political economic space of the sugar industry and shaped its decline within the temporal conjuncture of the 1820s and 1830s. On the other hand, Cuba enjoyed a dynamism, an openness to change, and an ability to reconfigure space and accelerate time in ways not available to Jamaica. Within these contrasting frameworks, the very efforts of planters in each zone to ameliorate their production in response to changing world conditions could only widen the distance between them. Successful innovation in Cuba created new patterns and increased productivity. In Jamaica, even where there were attempts to innovate, old patterns were reinforced, and the sugar industry stagnated. With the advance of the Cuban sugar industry, the physical plant in Jamaica (including slaves) and the capital invested in it were devalued as well.

CAUSALITY, STRUCTURE, AND EVENT:
PLURAL TIMES AND WORLD SPACE

Viewed from the perspective of the cyclical restructuring of the world sugar industry during the first half of the nineteenth century, the question of decline of the British West Indies and the abolition of the British slave trade appears in a different light from that presented by either Williams or Drescher. Decline had less to do with the internal characteristics of the British West Indian sugar colonies viewed in isolation than with the reformation of the division of labor on a world scale. Between the abolition of the slave trade in 1807 and slave emancipation in the 1830s, the British West Indies maintained higher levels of sugar production than they had during the eighteenth century. However, the emergence of new sugar producing regions during this economic conjuncture transformed the conditions of sugar production and trade, and therefore the conditions of slave labor throughout the world economy. The British West Indies were the victims of new, more efficient zones of sugar production utilizing slavery and other forms of coerced labor and incorporating new technologies of production and transport within new spatial configurations.

From this perspective, Williams' larger substantive argument about the decline of the British West Indies may be sustained, but in a different form. The decline may be more adequately apprehended as a specific conjuncture of processes operating across plural temporal and spatial scales. Thus, it was not the Industrial Revolution and the rising bourgeoisie in Britain that unilaterally destroyed slavery in the British West Indies as Williams would have it. Nor did slavery represent an archaic form of labor that was rendered obsolete and pushed aside by more efficient and "modern" forms of production and exchange. Rather, the social relations of slave labor in the British West Indies developed fully within a specific, historically constituted spatial-temporal framework of sugar production. The possibilities for their further reproduction were exhausted by the political and economic restructuring of the world economy during the first half of the nineteenth century. However, slavery was, in fact, recreated on an extended scale in new geographic zones in response to processes of market integration and industrialization even as it was eclipsed in older zones. (Here we might also think of the expansion of slave cotton and coffee production as part of the emergent nineteenth-century division of labor.) In this sense, the making, unmaking, and remaking of slavery was part and parcel of industrialization and the economic and social restructuring of a capitalist world economy.

In like manner, industrialization itself may be reconceptualized, not as a linear sequence of events, but as a process of structural transformation that only attains expressiveness over periods of longer duration within the world economy as a whole. Thus, rather than an autonomous and direct cause of abolition, emancipation, and free trade, the Industrial Revolution in Britain appears as mediated in complex ways by processes of integration of commodity and financial markets, state and class formation, and global political domination, and only gradually contributes to the structural transformation of the world division of labor. In this view, free trade may be interpreted not as a structural imperative deriving directly from industrialization, but as a conjunctural outcome determined by considerations of monetary, financial, and commercial policy, state restructuring, and political will among elites (Ingham 1984; Cain and Hopkins 1993). Its relation to industrial capital, if significant, is nonetheless indirect and highly conditioned by Britain's position in the world economy and relations among classes domestically.

Conversely, Drescher's analysis is compatible with the temporal and spatial characteristics of the cyclical restructuring of the world sugar industry during the first half of the nineteenth century. However, he does not adequately conceptualize the distinct and autonomous character of this structural transformation in its full spatial and temporal extension. He thereby fails to grasp the nature of the decline of the British West Indies. Indeed, viewed from the perspective of the full cycle, the period of expansion between 1792 and 1820 was integrally part of the crisis of the British West Indian sugar economy. It reinforced the hold of those spatial and social structures in the British West Indies that constrained the development of productive activity during the phase of contraction while it created the conditions for the development of new and more efficient sugar zones. Seen in this light, the decline of the British West Indian slave colonies cannot be measured simply by the movements of the price of sugar and slaves or "profitability" in a narrow accounting sense. A whole way of life and complex transnational economic and political organization does not collapse on the morning's sugar quotations. The expansion of world sugar production was independent of British West Indian abolition and emancipation, and it is unlikely that the British

West Indies could have expanded commensurately even without the abolition of the slave trade or slave emancipation. Thus, while Drescher (1977) effectively criticizes Williams' interpretation of abolition and calls into question the causal structure of his argument, he does not address the larger substantive issues of decline raised by Williams. Instead, he comes to premature conclusions.

Consequently, the political events of abolition and emancipation need to be interrogated in relation to the structural transformation of the world economy as a whole. However, it would be a mistake to reduce abolitionism to a reflex of this transformation just as it would be a mistake to discount the importance of the historical context of abolition. Abolition and emancipation were not inevitable. The reorganization of world sugar production did not require either of them. Britain could have allowed market forces to eliminate uncompetitive properties and colonies and permitted the competitive colonies to carry on. Alternatively, Britain could have subsidized its sugar colonies. (It would not have been the first time that a state subsidized special interests. Although, with time, the West Indian colonies would have fallen behind the new production zones precisely at the moment that Britain was becoming the emporium for the world's tropical produce.)

Abolition and emancipation involved certain choices and entailed certain consequences. If, by themselves, they did not create the crisis of the British West Indian sugar industry, at the very least, they shaped the way in which Britain and its colonies experienced the restructuring of the world economy and conditioned their future possibilities. Abolition destroyed the commercial sector most directly linked to slavery, the trade in slaves, which, as Drescher argues, yielded at least average profits at the moment of its prohibition. It also cut off the supply of labor from Africa to the Caribbean. In this sense, Drescher is right to argue that abolition of the trade made an already rigid system even more rigid. But the abolition of the trade in slaves did not, by itself, economically cripple the colonies or lead to emancipation. Between 1807 and the mid-1820s, the British West Indian colonies increased their sugar production despite abolition of the trade. Nonetheless, the old settled colonies were in a difficult position and would most likely have declined even without abolition and emancipation. In contrast, new frontier areas within the empire could have successfully adapted to the new conditions. However, Guiana had its sugar industry undercut by the abolition of the trade and, above all, by slave emancipation. Similarly, Trinidad could have adapted to the new conditions and substantially altered the structure of world sugar production. But because of its status as a Crown colony, anti-slavery forces in Parliament were able to fight for land and labor policies which restricted its potential development, and it never reached its potential as a sugar producer. (Perhaps the idea of "econocide" resonates even more deeply with the historical experiences of Guiana and Trinidad than it does with the abolition of the slave trade.) Thus, abolition mediated the cyclical restructuring of the world sugar industry in significant ways and created diverse consequences for different regions of the British colonial economy.

Abolition and emancipation are, in Sewell's terms, "eventful history," because of their impact on social-economic structures. But that impact is neither immediate nor transparent. Their consequences are only clear when contextualized in relation to the structural transformations of the world economy. Therefore, it is important to consider that the context of abolitionism is not just a cyclical expansion-contraction of the world economy, but one which coincides with what Arrighi (1996) argues is a new "cycle of accumulation" that established British hegemony over the world economy and reorganized the relations between states and markets on a global scale. This conjuncture shaped the conditions for the emergence of ideologies and practices of free trade and anti-imperialism: it at once created potential allies and an effective field of action for abolitionism and groups that could utilize anti-slavery for their own ends. Thus, even if we accept that the abolitionist movement represented no clearly defined economic or political interest group as Drescher contends, abolitionism nonetheless rapidly became implicated in the politics of empire and free trade. Whatever its origins, abolitionism was mobilized by a combination of landed aristocracy, the City, and mercantile interests in an attack on the "Old Corruption," monopoly, and the old colonial system. This alliance of diverse interests, spearheaded by Tory reformers, sought to reform the state bureaucracy and revenue system, stabilize the monetary system, and expand the opportunities for financial and commercial activity deriving from Britain's position in the world economy. Their efforts culminated in the adoption of free trade and the gold-sterling standard (Ingham 1984, esp. 114–117; Cain and Hopkins 1993). Perhaps even more importantly, abolitionism contributed substantively to the construction of the distinctive British variant of liberalism and anti-imperialism which symbolically ordered relations of the nineteenth century world economy and served as the ideological pivot of British economic and political hegemony. In combination with the ideology of free trade, abolition and emancipation reinforced certain notions of formal freedom and offered a graphic demonstration of the benevolence, disinterest, and moral purpose of British expansion, whether through formal or informal empire.

Neither the Industrial Revolution nor an autonomous abolitionist movement by themselves can account for the decline of the British West Indies, abolition of the slave trade, or slave emancipation. Individual causal sequences of events, taken in isolation, tell us little. However, such sequences develop within specific temporal rhythms and spatial configurations which are themselves products of larger networks of social relations. They have different consequences in different spatial-temporal contexts. Thus, it becomes necessary to ground our analysis of specific causal sequences in fields of social action that are temporally and spatially comprehensive. Such an approach requires us to conceive of social relations as possessing definite spatial extensions and changing geo-political boundaries in combination with distinct and autonomous temporal planes, irreversible sequences, and non-arbitrary periodicities. Through their interrelation and interaction, they form a complex and multilevel social whole that is at once unified and differentiated in time and space—ultimately the world economy. The complex interplay of social action and structural condition create multiple sources and directions of change within a global framework. Consequently, it becomes necessary to combine diverse methodological approaches, to move between narration and description, in order to disclose the relevant causal relations and interpretive fields.

This perspective enables us to incorporate into our conceptual scheme the spatial and temporal frameworks through which agencies and acting units, and hence causal sequences, are formed and reformed. It allows us to think of such event sequences as at once partial outcomes of complex causes and partial causes of complex outcomes (Hopkins 1982b, 146–147). Instead of privileging a single cause—industrialization or abolitionism—that initiates a linear sequence of events across homogenous and empty space, such an approach enables us to trace the interaction of event sequences through temporally and spatially complex fields of relations. Causality may be understood here as cumulative, the result of the interaction of events and structures across plural times and differentiated spaces of the world economy. Social action appears as mediated by structural differences, and its consequences may be uneven across time and space. Event sequences may gain or lose causal significance in accordance with their interaction with other sequences or structural changes in the fields of relations. Such contextualization allows us to better understand the conditions under which particular event sequences may be consequential—to comprehend both their possibilities and their limitations. It thus broadens and makes more adequate our explanatory schemes and enlarges our possibilities for historical understanding.

The analytical approach presented here seeks to incorporate time and space as constitutive dimensions of social relations. It focuses on the transformation of social relations in time and space, hence, on the processes continually producing and reproducing those relations. Thus, emphasizing the plurality of social time calls attention to both the unity of world-scale processes and the differentiation of particular social spaces within the world economy. It thereby permits us to register shifts from one temporal plane to another and to locate individual sequences within specifically constituted spatial-temporal configurations. Rather than attempting to establish uniform and consistent causal chains independent of time and space, this approach aims to reconstruct the complex and uneven conditions through which social relations are historically transformed. This perspective at once calls attention to the historical interrelation of the spaces forming the Caribbean over time and embeds them within the broader spaces and temporalities of the world economy. It focuses not on the repetition of similar patterns, but on the relations among diverse patterns. From this perspective, the history of the Caribbean appears not as the history of particular island societies or individual imperial systems viewed as independent sites of autonomous causal sequences, but as a historical mosaic of interrelated, interdependent, mutually formative loci of relations and processes of commodity production and exchange, political power, and social domination—discontinuous, asymmetrical, nonsynchronous, but unified through the multiple spatial-temporal dimensions of the world economy.

Chapter Six

Small Islands and Huge Comparisons

Caribbean Plantations, Historical Unevenness, and Capitalist Modernity

The appearance of world-systems theory and various globalization approaches has called into question the adequacy of the nation-state as the appropriate unit of analysis for macrosocial research. For many scholars, the nation-state can no longer be sustained as an independent analytical unit. Rather, it is perceived to be either part of or embedded in a larger historical system. For world-systems scholars, attention has shifted away from state-centered comparisons of national societies to an emphasis on what they regard as the singular governing unit, the modern world-system. On the other hand, no less prominent comparativist than Charles Tilly (1995) argues that ontological inadequacy and the disintegration of the state system have resulted in the decline of what he terms "Big Case Comparison."

This chapter reformulates the methodological and theoretical principles of the comparative method by means of a study of the transformation of the sugar industry in Martinique and Cuba during the nineteenth century. It follows a strategy that Philip McMichael (1990) has termed "incorporated comparison." Here the units of comparison (cases) and their properties (variables) are not presumed to be independent of and commensurate with one another. Instead, they are treated as historically singular instances of unified global processes which they themselves constitute and modify (Arrighi 1994, 23). The purpose of comparison is to specify their substantive interrelation within the whole and to disclose the systemic relations that differentiate one instance from another. Thus, this approach seeks to at once comprehend particular local histories as products of world economic processes and contribute to our understanding of the historical complexity of the world economy itself.

The examination of the slave sugar plantation in Martinique and Cuba undertaken here reveals contrasting yet interrelated paths of development that suggest the historically complex and differentiated character of slavery in the modern world economy. In Martinique, the intensive exploitation of prevailing forms of socioeconomic organization resulted in the reproduction of an "old" spatial-temporal pattern of slavery that constrained social and technical innovation. At the same time, the slave economy of Cuba underwent a process of dramatic expansion: the rhythm of development accelerated as the elements of slave production were radically recomposed in new social and spatial configurations consistent with emerging global patterns of industrial production and market integration. These contrasting outcomes are not simply the result of properties internal to Martinique and Cuba. Rather, they derive from the interrelation and reciprocal influence of the two plantation systems within the expansion of the nineteenth-century world economy. Thus, what appear to be two spatially separate sugar islands with common attributes may be more adequately conceived as distinct yet mutually conditioning socioeconomic configurations whose divergent trajectories have decisive implications for the recomposition of land, labor, and technology in each instance.

These distinct yet interrelated paths of development raise questions about comparative methods that are central to the concerns of this chapter. Conventional procedures for comparison abstract from time and space and emphasize formal similarities and dissimilarities between cases by treating cases as independent of one another and by regarding their properties as commensurate across cases. They thereby obscure two essential features of the instances being compared: first, their unavoidable relational character and, second, the role and importance of different temporalities in the formation of each of these socioeconomic configurations. In contrast, the comparative strategy presented here grounds comparison in substantive processes of world economy in order to recover the different constitution and historical trajectory of each slave-based sugar complex. It thereby seeks to comprehend the social-historical construction of relations and spatial-temporal heterogeneity. Comparison thus goes beyond external similarities to reveal both the historical diversity of slave relations and the spatial and temporal unevenness of the world economic processes.

THE PROBLEM OF
HISTORICAL COMPARISON

Before beginning the substantive discussion, I must address in greater detail some problems of method raised by the comparison under consideration. The method of formal comparison treats each unit as independent and equivalent and/or uniform in terms of its set of attributes. Comparison attempts to specify variance (contrasts/particularizations) or invariance (generalizations) by observing relations among (or correlating) the attributes of the units. These relations constitute contrasting or generalizable patterns. In turn, these patterns tell us something specific about the units themselves or something general about the relations among their properties. The condition of comprehension within this logical framework is that both the units of comparison and the attributes of those units are defined as independent of and external to one another and that both are treated in terms of their formal equivalence and identity: comparison is intelligible insofar as phenomena differ through occurring in different surroundings (Sartre 1982, 141).

For example, formal comparison would treat the sugar plantations of Martinique and Cuba as comparable constellations of land, labor, and technology that define Martinique and Cuba as separate, comparable units. Any distinctions or similarities between these cases would derive from the correlations among these attributes and the relative presence or absence of other complicating factors or events within each constellation. This method ultimately focuses on configurative distinctions among abstracted conditions of the units, which are themselves abstracted from time and place. From this point, it is but a short step to conceiving of units as discrete and independent social entities, each endowed with its own economy, polity, and society. By isolating units of comparison and their conditions, such as land, labor, or technology, as independent and equivalent phenomena, formal comparison eliminates from consideration both the historical processes forming these relations and the changing patterns among them.

The substantive comparison I am proposing suggests the limitations of such an approach. The divergent historical trajectories of plantation agriculture in Martinique and Cuba indicate the need to ground comparisons within the historical processes under investigation. In contrast to the assumptions of the formal logic of comparative inquiry, the "cases" here are not independent; neither are their attributes equivalent. Rather, in each instance, slavery, land, and technology are constituted differently within relational complexes possessing distinctive spatiotemporal characteristics. Further, sugar production in Martinique and Cuba coexist and mutually influence one another. Cheap Cuban sugar was a major force in the development of a protected market for sugar in France and the intensive exploitation of Martinique. The enormous amounts of American, and, above all, Cuban sugar entering the European market in the decades following the Napoleonic Wars threatened to destroy the French colonial sugar industry (and with it French maritime commerce) and to compromise the recovery and prosperity of the French

Atlantic port cities. On the other hand, the French system of protection pressured Cuba to increase its productive efficiency and the size of its output while the use of French sugar technology made such a response possible for Cuba. Thus, in a sense, Martinique is Martinique because Cuba is Cuba, and vice versa. Indeed, they may be seen to represent divergent outcomes of the unified processes forming the world economy and, more particularly, the world sugar market, during the nineteenth century: it is their historical interdependence and difference that most urgently require understanding.

It is in response to difficulties of this sort that Tilly advocates the use of historically grounded comparisons. Such an approach seeks to attach statements "to specific eras and parts of the world, specifying causes, involving variation from one instance to another within their time-space limits, remaining consistent with the available evidence from the times and places claimed" (Tilly 1984, 60). In particular, he suggests that "encompassing comparisons" represent a fruitful, if risky, strategy for macrohistorical inquiry. Such comparisons "begin with a large structure or process. They *select locations* within the structure or process and explain similarities or differences among those locations as consequences of their *relationships to the whole*" (Tilly 1984, my emphasis). Consequently, he envisions macrohistorical analysis as "the study of big structures and large processes within particular world systems." Its task "is to fix accounts of specific structures and processes within particular world systems to historically grounded generalizations concerning those world systems" (Tilly 1984, 74).

In Tilly's view, encompassing comparisons are promising, but run the danger of falling into a functionalist explanation in which the whole determines the behavior of the parts. The danger is not simply the possibility of functionalism, however, but the very formulation of the terms of comparison. In Tilly's approach, world economies, macrosociological and microsociological structures and processes not only remain conceptually independent of one another, but are treated as if they refer to discrete empirical entities or levels. Encompassing comparison presumes a governing systemic unit and subordinate case units that are related to one another, not as interrelated and mutually formative if asymmetrical processes, but as externally opposed things. Eric Wolf (1982, 3) warns of the limitations of such a conception: "Only by understanding these names as bundles of relationships, and by placing them back into the field from which they were abstracted, can we hope to avoid misleading inferences and increase our share of understanding." By thus presuming the analytical units, encompassing comparison, as presently formulated by Tilly, removes from theoretical consideration the formation and interrelation of these very units. It thereby limits the scope and possibility of historical explanation and jeopardizes the development of the historically grounded social theory it was intended to promote (McMichael 1990, 388–389).

As Wolf's warning implies, it is insufficient simply to *place* phenomena within empirically given chronological and geographical coordinates. Instead, the social-historical construction of temporal and spatial processes and relations must itself become an object of inquiry. To this end, Philip McMichael proposes the use of "incorporated comparison" as an alternative strategy. Here, comparable social phenomena are viewed not as discrete *cases* but as differentiated *outcomes* or *moments* of an historically integrated process (McMichael 1990, 392). This emphasis on the unity of historical process allows the relational character of units to be formulated. Neither whole nor parts are regarded as independent categories or units of analysis; rather, they are treated as units of observation of systemic processes (McMichael 1990, 391). Instead of external contextualization, incorporated comparison seeks to relate apparently separate moments as interconnected components of a broader, world-historical process or conjuncture. Such interrelated instances are "both integral to, and define, the general historical process" (McMichael 1990, 389).

Such an approach avoids treating the world economy as a completed totality whose parts are related functionally to one another. In this latter conception, exemplified particularly by Wallerstein's earlier formulations of the world-system, the whole is greater than its parts, functional descriptive categories dominate, and the system appears as an ever-present "external cause." We are presented with a historical structure without a history. Neither does the strategy presented here treat the terms of comparison as reified national-level units counterposed to or embedded within an equally discrete world-level unit as suggested by Tilly's approach. Instead, it takes them to represent "bundles of relations" that are treated as provisionally isolated instances of a larger unitary process. They are thus regarded as formative of one another and, in unequal and asymmetrical ways, as formed by, and formative of, a larger whole.

Hence, the comparison of the sugar industry in Martinique and Cuba may be grounded in a specific historical complex of relations and processes—here the capitalist world economy at a specific point of its formation. From such a perspective, land, labor, and technology appear not as autonomous and equivalent "factors" but as historically formed social relations that are constituted differently in each instance within the emerging patterns of production, exchange, and consumption of the larger world economy. Here, comparison, instead of abstracting from time and space, seeks to theoretically specify and reconstruct these relations and processes *within* the historical development of the world economy. It thereby attempts to recover the temporal and spatial

dimensions of these relations and processes as themselves products of historical development. Such comparison yields insight into the diversity and interdependence, and therefore spatial and temporal unevenness, of unified
historical processes. In this way, it gives historical content to theoretical categories while at the same time allowing general concepts to be refined so they
more adequately comprehend particular historical instances. This approach
thus contrasts to modernization theory (e.g., Rostow) which posits historical
development as the repetition of multiple linear times ("take off" from traditional to modern), and world-system theory (e.g., Wallerstein) which appears
to account for these same processes by spatial movement within a single cur-
vilinear time.

THE *USINE CENTRALE*

The discussion of the sugar industry in Martinique and Cuba can begin with
a well-known characteristic of sugar cane: it must be harvested when it is ripe
and converted into sugar as soon as it is harvested. This characteristic of
sugar imparts an industrial character to plantation organization. When the
cane is ripe, cutting, transport, grinding, clarification, evaporation, and crystallization must be integrated within a continuous process in order to obtain
sugar. Speed, continuity, and coordination are of vital importance. Consequently, the agricultural operations required for the cultivation and harvesting
of cane and the industrial operations required for processing it into sugar
must be located in close proximity to one another. Further, the efficient operation of a sugar plantation requires that an equilibrium be maintained between
the amount of land cultivated; the capacity of mill, refinery, and the internal
transport system; and the size of the labor force. Innovations that improve
output in one sector of production must be matched by proportional increases
in the output of the other sectors in order to be effective. An examination of
the technical and social conditions under which these various operations are
combined reveals a great deal about the history of the sugar plantation in the
Americas.

The central refinery revolutionized the production of cane sugar during the
nineteenth century. From a technical point of view, it incorporated modern
industrial technologies, most notably the steam mill, the vacuum pan, the centrifuge, and the railroad. The all-metal steam-powered horizontal grinding
mill made it possible both to process a greater quantity of cane and to extract
a higher proportion of juice from the cane stalks than the earlier animal-,
wind-, or water-powered mills. The vacuum pan and the centrifuge dramatically improved the quantity and quality of sugar that could be obtained from

a given quantity of juice and transformed sugar manufacture from an artisanal process depending upon the particular knowledge and skill of the refiner to a scientific process resting upon standardization, measurement, and systematic application of chemistry and physics. The railroad allowed greater quantities of goods to be moved more rapidly over longer distances. It enabled individual plantations to increase the area under cultivation, provided cheap overland transportation, and permitted the exploitation of new regions. These innovations increased the scale of production and transformed the character of plantation agriculture. The centralization of manufacturing, more extensive cultivation, and higher capital investment entailed in their adoption could have diverse implications for social organization, ranging from larger plantations on the one hand to the development of central factories processing the product of cane farmers within a variety of possible property and class relations on the other. The technical and social characteristics of the sugar central have led many investigators to identify it with modern capitalism and free labor. However, its origins lie within the history of Caribbean slavery. I compare the origins and early development of the central refinery, or *usine centrale,* in Martinique with the development of the plantation system in Cuba and to discuss the implications of these two paths of development for some problems of historical interpretation.

THE TRANSFORMATION OF THE WORLD SUGAR MARKET, 1760–1860

The origins of the transformation of sugar production and the emergence of the sugar central both in Martinique and in Cuba are found in the transformation of the world sugar market between 1760 and 1860. World production and consumption increased steadily beginning in 1760, while the period of wars and revolution between 1789 and 1815 dramatically altered the political organization of markets. The "old colonial system" broke up. Saint Domingue— the world's richest colony and the source of nearly half the world's sugar—was destroyed. Britain emerged as the single dominant economic and political power in the European world economy. Under its hegemony there began a process of integration of the world market and a redefinition of the role and significance of colonialism. The growth of world sugar production and consumption accelerated after 1815. Old producing regions expanded their output and new regions emerged. The relations between producers and consumers no longer coincided with previous colonial boundaries, nor were they defined by political control over the sources of production. Instead, economic control over the flow of goods assumed increasing importance. For some planters, colonialism and economic protectionism provided a means of self-defense in an increasingly integrated and competitive market, while for others they were obstacles to their ability to take advantage of the new conditions. For all, however, the underlying processes of market integration, expansion, and competition put the premium, directly or indirectly, on productive efficiency. Thus, new varieties of cane were developed, the technology of sugar grinding and refining underwent almost constant innovation, and, most importantly, labor was reorganized. In some places slavery was abolished; in others, it was expanded and intensified. Contract laborers from Asia, Africa, and elsewhere were brought to the sugar zones. The development of the sugar plantation in Martinique and Cuba during the first half of the nineteenth century represents two different responses to the processes restructuring the world market.

THE *USINE CENTRALE* IN MARTINIQUE

The expansion of the sugar industry in Martinique after 1815 depended upon the development of a protected market for its product in France. The colony had been devastated by war, revolution, foreign occupation, and limited access to overseas markets between 1789 and 1815, and it was unable to withstand competition from the vast amounts of cheap foreign sugar available after the peace. In addition, following the loss of Saint Domingue and without access to other markets, France had to rely on trade with its remaining colonies, and especially their sugar industries, for the recovery of its Atlantic port cities, its merchant marine, and navy. Thus, a system of protective tariffs that virtually excluded foreign sugar from the metropolitan market was the condition for the recovery of the maritime sector of the French economy and the rapid expansion of the sugar industry and slave labor in Martinique, Guadeloupe, and Bourbon (Réunion). By 1830 these three small islands produced as much sugar as Saint Domingue in its peak year (Tomich 1990, 33–61).

The sugar boom initiated by the protective tariffs resulted in the expansion and consolidation of the existing estate system in Martinique between 1815 and 1830. However, there was little opportunity to restructure production after 1815. Martinique was an old sugar colony. Sugar production began there in the 1640s, and by 1720 virtually all of the principal agricultural lands of the island were occupied. The units of property, the scale of production, and the division of labor on the estate had been formed in accordance with the conditions prevailing in the eighteenth century. Thus, between 1815 and 1848, the great majority of properties were too small to effectively utilize the new milling and refining technologies, while the amount of land available for either the expansion of old estates or the formation of new ones was limited. Sixty large estates producing between 150 and 300 tons of sugar annually dominated the island's economy. The largest of these planted about 128 hectares in sugar and had about 200 to 210 slaves, about half of whom were employed in sugar production. In addition, one hundred plantations produced between 75 and 150 metric tons of sugar, while the remaining sugar estates produced less than 75 tons (Tomich 1990, 150).

Consequently, the growth of sugar production in Martinique was the result of greater exploitation of available resources, especially slave labor, within the historically prevailing framework. Existing estates intensified their production, and new estates—often small and inefficient—formed on marginal lands. Coffee, tobacco, and cotton plantations were cannibalized for land and slaves to sustain the growth of the sugar industry. In 1820, there were 351 sugar plantations, ten of which had steam-driven mills. They employed 31,231 slaves on 16,457 hectares of land and produced 26,529 metric tons of sugar. By 1847, the last year before emancipation, the number of sugar plantations had increased to 498 and the number of steam mills to 33 (the majority of which were underpowered). They employed 40,429 slaves on 19,735 hectares and producing 32,093 metric tons (Tomich 1990, 100–103). Thus, with the expansion of sugar production, the existing social and technical organization of the plantation system in Martinique was reinforced and became more rigid. Despite greater total output, the relative inefficiency of colonial sugar producers increased their reliance on protective tariffs.

Paradoxically, the colonial sugar industry came to require such high tariff barriers in order to maintain its position in the national market that the way was opened for the revitalization of the French beet sugar industry. The colonies were then confronted with a powerful and dynamic competitor in the only market open to them. The reemergence of the beet sugar industry initiated a period of crisis for colonial sugar producers. Between 1830 and 1848 French sugar consumption increased, the price of sugar fell, and the processes of sugar production were radically transformed by the technical advances of the beet sugar industry. Colonial producers were under great pressure to increase the quantity and quality of their product. But the plantation system in the colonies froze the framework for organizing land, labor, and technology and blocked innovation. New techniques were either adapted to the existing division of labor or abandoned. The obstacle to change was not technical transformation in one or another sector of production, but the integration of the division of labor on the sugar estate as a whole (Tomich 1990, 61–75, 139–204).

By the late 1830s, the very impossibility of reforming sugar production led to a radical solution to the problem—the complete separation of the agricultural and industrial aspects of sugar production. The *usine centrale* would centralize milling and refining operations while the plantations would specialize in cane cultivation. This arrangement would alter the division of labor prevailing on the sugar estates of Martinique and allow production to be organized on a scale sufficient to take advantage of the new milling and refining technologies. At the same time, cane farmers would no longer have to bear the expense of processing equipment, and the area under cultivation would not be limited by the capacity of the mill and refinery.

However, despite the promise of the *usine centrale*, old forms of social and technical organization persisted in Martinique. Few planters had the resources necessary to establish a *centrale*, and most feared that once they lost control over processing their own sugar, they would become mere cane farmers subordinated to the giant central factories. Indeed, in the view of traditional planters, the *usine centrale* was unsuitable for local conditions, and its adoption would only deliver them into the hands of metropolitan bankers and speculators. In addition, they regarded it as a threat to the social order: its introduction was accompanied by proposals for free labor that contributed to pressure against the slave regime. Finally, so long as planters processed their own sugar, no matter on how small a scale, they could claim the status of *habitant sucrière*. They feared that if they ceased to do so, they would no longer be regarded as members of the planter elite, and that the distinction between them and free mulatto cane farmers would diminish. Consequently, labor and land remained tied to the existing organization of production in Martinique, and the development of the *usine centrale* was blocked (Tomich 1990, 204–213).

THE CUBAN *INGENIO*

Cuba represents a different path of development of the sugar plantation. Over the long term, Cuba benefited most from the crisis of world sugar production provoked by the Haitian Revolution. Cuban sugar production increased rapidly and continuously in the years after the Napoleonic Wars. By 1820, sugar was established as the dominant sector of the Cuban economy, and by 1830, Cuba emerged as the world's largest sugar producer. World demand continued to grow at an accelerating rate, and Cuban production more than kept pace with it. Cuba accounted for a little more than 19 percent of world sugar production in 1840, nearly 25 percent by 1850, and nearly 30 percent by 1868 (Moreno Fraginals 1978, I, 46–47, 67–71, 95–102, 167–255; II, 93–97, 106–174; III, 35–36; Scott 1985, 10; Knight 1970, 14–18, 40–4).

Unlike Martinique, Cuba did not enjoy a protected market for its sugar.

Spain could not provide adequate markets for Cuban sugar. By 1818, Cuba gained virtual commercial freedom from Spain in order to export its products to the United States, Britain, Germany, France, Russia, and the Low Countries. By 1830, the United States emerged as Cuba's major trading partner. The United States was the second largest consumer of sugar in the world and had the fastest growing population. With the collapse of the "Old Colonial System" and the Haitian Revolution, it was cut off from its former access to both Saint Domingue and the British West Indies. Cuba provided a dynamic alternative both as a source of supply of sugar and its by-products and as a market for North American goods. The close links between the United States and Cuba were a significant exception to Britain's ability to dominate the markets of peripheral countries through its industrial and commercial superiority. The United States was not only the major consumer of Cuban sugar but increasingly a supplier of lumber, foodstuffs and, significantly, industrial goods to Cuba (Knight 1970, 43–45).

Nevertheless, throughout the nineteenth century, world sugar production increased enormously, and the price of sugar fell steadily. Without a preferential market of its own, Cuba was forced to compete against protected sugar in the highly competitive "free" sugar markets of the United States and continental Europe. In order to maintain their position in these markets, Cuban planters were under constant pressure to expand output, increase efficiency, and lower the costs. They were able to respond successfully to these demands precisely because Cuba was still a "sugar frontier" through most of the nineteenth century. Only 515,820 hectares out of a total area of 12,428, 272 hectares were under cultivation in 1827 (Friedlaender 1978, 197). The unprecedented expansion of the Cuban sugar industry was due to the ability of Cuban planters to increase the area under cultivation, establish new plantations, concentrate labor, and incorporate scientific advances into production processes in combinations and on a scale that were not possible in the older Caribbean slave colonies. The availability of fresh land and labor, especially in the context of a rapidly expanding world market, made possible the remarkable technical evolution of the Cuban sugar mill from animal-powered trapiche to mechanized mill. Land and labor could be combined with the mill in new proportions as the capacity of the latter developed. Indeed, it is not an exaggeration to suggest that technical innovation was the condition for the expansion of sugar and slavery in Cuba (Marrero 1983–1986, II, 179–180; Zanetti Lecuona and García Alvarez 1987, 23–24).

The development of the Cuban sugar industry was centered in the western part of the island. Sugar cultivation spread south and west of Havana displacing coffee and tobacco producers and spreading onto new lands. New and ever larger plantations were established at a rapid pace and old ones increased their capacity. The number of *ingenios* increased almost fourfold between 1800 and 1857. During the initial stages of expansion the multiplication of traditional production units accounted for much of the increase in total production, although even here the scale of production was frequently considerably larger than elsewhere in the Caribbean. Steam power made an early appearance, however, and the methods of sugar manufacture in Cuba were transformed by the application of modern industrial techniques. Knight estimates that in 1827, only 2.5 percent of the 1,000 *ingenios* in Cuba were steam powered. But according to Moreno Fraginals, in 1860 there were 359 animal-powered mills with an average production capacity of 113 tons; 889 semi-mechanized mills using steam engines with an average production capacity of 411 tons; and 64 mechanized mills using steam power and more advanced processing technology (including vacuum pans), with an average production capacity of 1,176 tons (about 15 percent of total production in the island). In conjunction with the adoption of steam power, there was a steady process of land concentration. The average size of a sugar estate in western Cuba in 1762 was between 300 and 400 acres. By 1860 it had reached 1,400 acres and dwarfed its counterpart in Martinique (Knight 1970, 38–39; Moreno Fraginals 1978, I, 170–173; Scott 1985, 20–21).

Distance and the lack of internal transport limited the land that could be exploited for cane cultivation and raised the price of sugar. Overland transport was slow, difficult, and costly. Thus, the establishment of new plantations was initially limited to the regions around maritime or river ports, particularly Havana. These difficulties made planters look for novel if not audacious solutions to the transportation problem. In 1837, thirteen years after the first steam-driven railway began to operate in England, the first railroad in Latin America or the Caribbean was completed between Havana and Güines (Guerra y Sánchez 1964 54; Marrero 1983–86, II, 169–170; Zanetti Lecuona and García Alvarez 1987, 61–62).

The railroad and the sugar industry developed in the closest interdependence. The railroads were built to serve the sugar industry, and sugar provided most of their profits. The rail network opened new lands and permitted the profitable exploitation of the rich soils of the interior of the island. Sugar replaced coffee and tobacco. Slavery was extended, expanded, and intensified. Shipping costs were reduced drastically, and land use was maximized. Massive amounts of sugar were moved rapidly to ports for shipment overseas, and heavy supplies, such as machinery for the *ingenios*, could be carried distances inland. New, larger, and technically more advanced sugar mills could be established on virgin lands. Following the railroad, the center of gravity of the Cuban sugar industry moved eastward from Havana toward Matanzas and Santa Clara provinces between 1837 and 1851. In these new territories, still larger plantations were founded, incorporating not only the steam engine but also the latest refining technology available from the European beet sugar industry. By 1860, Matanzas had forty-four of the island's fully mechanized mills, followed by Santa Clara with ten. With the highest number of steam-powered mills and the largest number of mills with vacuum pans, Matanzas had the largest total output and the largest average output on the island. Increasing production and lowering costs, in part due to the railroad, allowed the Cuban planters to prosper in the growing world sugar market, despite falling prices. Conversely, the construction of the railroads was predominantly financed by Cuban planters and merchants from the profits of sugar production and slave labor (Marrero 1983–86, III, 154–159, 191–193, 209, 212–213; Zanetti Lecuona and García Alvarez 1987, 6, 61–62; Guerra y Sánchez 1964, 66; Knight 1970, 32–39; Scott 1985: 21–24).

Cubans enjoyed the technological edge of latecomers. Though they were few in number, the appearance of mechanized sugar mills represented a qualitative transformation in the conditions of sugar production. The Cuban sugar mill developed on a giant scale, and the technology of sugar production there attained the most advanced level known under slavery. Steam-powered mills, the vacuum pan, and the centrifuge increased the capacity of the more advanced plantations and produced more and higher quality sugar. On large estates small rail lines were introduced, often using animal-drawn equipment, to transport canes to the mills from the fields, for transportation within the factories and to the wharves. These developments broke the fixed ratio between land, labor, and mill capacity that had limited the development of the old *ingenio*. It was no longer necessary to limit the acreage under cane. The use of rail transport within estates allowed a greater area to be planted and provided the increased supply of cane required by modern refining techniques. The scale of production increased, and the capital requirements for founding an *ingenio* grew enormously. With the introduction of estate railways, there was bitter competition for land and labor. Small producers were squeezed out, and a monocultural economy emerged that was dominated by large planters who could afford the increased costs of the new mechanized mills. The optimal size of a large sugar estate rose to two or three thousand tons, instead of the previous three or four hundred tons, and the form of plantation organization itself was transformed with the emergence of giant semi-mechanized, and finally fully mechanized, mills (Marrero 1983–86, II, 153–159; Knight 1970, 18–19, 30–40; Guerra y Sánchez 1964, 54, 66; Moreno Fraginals 1978, I, 167–255; II, 106–174; III, 35–36; Scott 1985, 20–21).

CONCLUSION

A comparison of the development of the sugar plantation in Martinique and Cuba reveals firmly linked spatial and temporal differences shaping the nexus of market and productive processes in each situation. Despite apparent formal similarities, land, labor, and technology are in each instance constituted differently within distinct spatiotemporal configurations and result in contrasting historical trajectories.

In Martinique, the evolution of the sugar plantation is constrained and shaped by structures formed in a cycle of slavery and sugar that precedes the integration of world markets and the emergence of industrial capital. The revitalization of the plantation system during the first half of the nineteenth century maintained the old productive and commercial pattern within the new development. However, the tariff barriers which gave new life to the old system led to the emergence of the beet sugar industry in France. The accelerated rhythm of development and greater technical efficiency of beet sugar unified different temporal structures within the French market and pushed the full development of the colonial sector. In Martinique, the process of extensive exploitation requiring new lands found its limit—which appeared to be absolute—in the manner in which it was articulated with technical and social processes. The near impossibility of change created an almost static form of time, virtually imprisoned by the "natural" shortage of land. Persistence and stability, if not a cyclical repetition of the past, characterized temporal experience.

In contrast, the organization of land, labor, and technology in Cuba presupposes integrated world markets and capital circuits increasingly anchored in industrial production. In Cuba, technological development had dynamic consequences. The availability of land—essential to the extensive pattern of exploitation of the Cuban sugar industry—was blocked by difficulties of transport. Nevertheless, this limit—instead of being simply destructive and leading to a regression as in Martinique—resulted in the previous order being surpassed. The introduction of the railroad, integration into the international circulation of capital, and the expansion and intensification of slave labor imposed new social-economic forms and an accelerated rhythm of development. Indeed, one might speak here of a structural change in temporality itself—the "denaturalization of historical time," to borrow Koselleck's phrase—defined by technology, industry, and economy (1985, 96). Movement, increasing speed, and openness to new social-economic arrangements and spatial configurations within and without characterized the temporal dimension of the sugar industry in Cuba.

By conceiving of Martinique and Cuba as parts of a differentiated spatial-temporal whole, a singular historical world economy, the comparative strategy presented here brings the processes of transformation in each plantation system into relation with one another. In contrast to methods of formal comparison, the units of comparison are not treated as discrete, independent, yet comparable "cases" abstracted from their location in time and space. Rather, they are taken to represent "instances" of world processes that are formed and reformed by their relation with one another (Hopkins 1982a, 30). This approach thus recognizes and accounts for the interrelation and mutual conditioning of units within historical processes of world economy.

Within this framework, the purpose of comparison is not to derive general law-like statements from the discovery of "causal regularities" among units treated as comparable replicate "cases" of the processes under investigation (Taylor 1987, 16). Rather, comparison seeks to reconstruct in time and space patterns of relations that shape and reshape the world economy and the connections among them. Time and space are not concepts or variables outside world economy, but are fundamental properties of the system itself. The outcomes of such processes are contingent upon their temporal and spatial relations (Taylor 1987, 16, 34). From this perspective, the question is not simply to locate processes forming the world economy in time and space. Rather, it is to understand the historical production of time and space and the ways in which time and space produce history in the modern world economy. The task of comparison is thus to reconstruct time and space relationally within world economic processes.

Because phenomena are grounded within a theoretically unified historical field, comparison here discloses difference not by establishing the presence or absence of particular universal factors across cases, but by specifying social-historical relations and processes through their relation to the whole (thereby historically specifying the whole itself) (Sartre 1982, 141). (For Sartre, the general concepts of nature and material scarcity provide the totalizing moment that permits comparison of difference. In contrast, the strategy adopted here grounds comparison in the concept of world economy in order to comprehend difference as time and space relations within a specific historical system rather than in human history generally. It thereby attempts to at once disclose the social and historical premises of spatial and temporal relations forming the capitalist world economy and thus the characteristics and conditions of capitalist modernity itself.) This procedure differentiates particular historical sequences and spatial configurations by locating them within the evolving ensemble of relations forming the world economy. It thereby permits the identification of both different temporal orders within individual sequences and the differing role and importance of individual elements within apparently similar sequences. By thus establishing the spatial and temporal relatedness of particular historical developments, I find this approach makes it possible to formulate the changing character of social categories over time and to theoretically reconstruct the complex, interdependent, mutually conditioning processes that shape the trajectory and pace of change. (The potential of theoretically constructed narrative accounts of such sequences for providing both causal explanation and interpretation of meaning in sociological analysis are discussed in articles by Larry J. Griffin, Andrew Abbott, Jill Quadagno and Stan J. Knapp, and Ronald Aminzade in *Sociological Methods and Research* 22, 4 [May 1992].)

This approach calls into question the homogeneity of time and space as processes of world economy. Slavery, land, and technology in Martinique and Cuba derive their role and meaning from their position within specific historically interrelated and changing configurations. Within the expansion of nineteenth century world economy, we have identified the persistence of an "old" spatial temporal pattern of slavery in Martinique that is related to and conditioned by the creation of a new pattern of slavery in Cuba. Comparison thus goes beyond external similarities to reveal the distinctive character of slavery in each instance. Cuba is not simply the repetition of Martinique, but represents the radical reconfiguration of slavery and plantation agriculture within the emergent economic and political conditions of the new world-scale cycle of accumulation.

At the same time, the sugar industries in Martinique and Cuba are not only contemporaneous with one another, but remain interrelated, mutually conditioning parts of a unified whole. Through their development, specific rhythms, sequences, and periods combine within a complex conjuncture of differentiated temporal strata. Such strata can only be understood in relation to one another. Varying in pace and duration, and possessing diverse trajectories, they nonetheless interact in the same historical dimension of modernity. The "old" is created in relation to the "new": "backwardness" appears *not* as the "not yet" but as an integral part of a heterogeneous "now." On a world scale, the processes of capitalist accumulation thus differentiate and stratify "temporal planes" (see Koselleck 1985, esp. 92–104). Not all space is equally susceptible or equally available to rationalization by economy and technology. Here, the more thoroughly and effectively each region exploits the possibilities given within its particular spatial and temporal configuration, the more the gap between the various regions widens. Thus, the historical time of the modern world economy at once unifies temporalities specific to each of its circuits and is differentiated by them. It imposes its conditions on particular temporal strata, shapes the articulation of temporal sequences, trajectories, and rhythms, and hierarchizes the relation between them, thereby producing the temporality of the world economy as a whole which coincides only accidentally with any particular temporal stratum.

Thus, the world economy, understood as a spatial-temporal whole, is neither reducible to the properties of the individual processes comprising it or their sum, nor is it a discrete unit external to its constituent relations and processes. Rather, its character as a world phenomenon derives from the interrelatedness of the processes comprising it. On a world scale, the processes of capitalist development simultaneously unify and differentiate temporal and spatial relations. By establishing spatial and temporal unevenness, the comparative strategy pursued here reconstructs the world economy as a specific historically evolving constellation of processes and relations ("bundle of relations") linked through definite modes of economic and political integration. This approach reveals both the specificity and variety of particular relations and the total structure and dynamic of a larger, unified network of political power, social domination, and economic activity. It thereby suggests the conditions, possibilities, and limits for development imposed by these structures.

Part Three

Work, Time, and Resistance: Shifting the Terms of Confrontation

Chapter Seven

White Days, Black Days

The Working Day and the Crisis of Slavery in the French Caribbean

This chapter draws its title from two expressions, far apart in time and space, and without any apparent connection between them. In the French Antilles, the practice, common throughout the sugar colonies of the Caribbean, of giving slaves a bit of land to grow their own food and a "free day," usually Saturday, to cultivate it was called *samedi nègre*. On the other hand, in Brazil today the phrase *dia de branco* is used to refer to working days and particularly to Mondays. While this expression evokes an image of the slave past, its origins remain unclear. It appears to be unfamiliar to many middle-class Brazilians, and it is described as an expression used by "poor people" (*gente pobre*) or, more provocatively, by "old-timers" (*gente antiga*). There is no evidence that the two terms share a common historical origin, nor is the use of the analogous phrase apparent in either the Caribbean or Brazil. Yet, the juxtaposition of the two expressions remains striking. The first is a term of contempt bestowed by aristocrats of the skin who measured their wealth, power, and prestige in sugar and slaves, while the second registers the resignation and unsubmissiveness of those whose fate it is to have their time and labor appropriated by others. Together, they divide the week into two distinct and contrasting parts distinguished by different types of economic activity that are characterized by antithetical racial identifications and evaluations. The strength of these oppositions suggests both the complexity and the contradictoriness of the social construction, perception, and evaluation of time within the social relations of slavery. They thus provide the occasion for a re-examination of the evolution of the working day and its significance for the historical development of slavery. This task will be undertaken here with reference to the French Caribbean.

The sugar plantation engaged the slaves in a year-round cycle of work that followed the rhythm of the crop. Despite differences of law, religion, and culture, similar yearly and daily routines derived from the material-technical conditions of sugar production evolved in all the slave colonies of the Caribbean, whether French, British, or Spanish. The transformation of sugar from cane to crystals requires a series of agricultural, mechanical, and physical-chemical operations. Each step—planting, cultivating, harvesting, grinding, evaporation, and crystallization—is necessary in the proper sequence, and none can be omitted if a final product is to be obtained. The spatial concentration of these different aspects of sugar production and their integration within a continuous process are required by the physical properties of sugar. The interdependence of these phases is most apparent during the harvest season. While the harvest might last from six months to a year because of the amount of cane planted, each individual stalk had to be converted into sugar within hours after it was cut or the juice would ferment and spoil causing the yield to diminish and the quality of the product to decline. Thus speed, continuity, and coordination were of vital importance throughout the entire manufacturing process (Ortiz 1970, 21–36).

Large-scale commercial production required that the distinct technical operations entailed in sugar manufacture form a complex division of labor. All the sequential phases of the manufacturing process had to be carried out simultaneously, continuously, and as quickly as possible. To achieve this, each of these various constituent tasks was permanently assigned to different groups of workers who specialized in them. This division of labor not only established the qualitative differentiation of tasks but also created a quantitative relation between these different sectors of production. The process of sugar production formed an organic whole whose constituent parts were related to one another in definite proportions. It was of crucial importance to coordinate the various separate yet interdependent operations throughout the crop cycle from planting to harvest. The capacity of the fields, transport system, mill, refinery, and curing house had to be assessed and synchronized with one another (Marx 1976, 461–470; Ortiz 1970, 33, 41).

The integration of the labor process could only be achieved on the assumption that a given amount of product could be obtained during a given period of time. The allocation of labor and resources was thus governed by a fixed mathematical ratio that set the parameters of the duration of labor time and the conditions for the possible transformation of the labor process. Regularity in the performance of each partial task was necessary to maintain the continuity of production. The specialized labor of each group of workers provided the raw material for the next phase of the process. Direct material dependence compelled each worker or group of workers to spend no more time than was necessary on the performance of their particular task. This regulation of the amount of time necessary to perform a particular task was imposed on the workers as a technical condition of the labor process itself and determined the number of workers in each sector and the intensity and duration of their efforts (Marx 1976, 461–470).

The imperatives of the market and the demand for surplus labor were imposed upon these material-technical conditions of sugar production and exerted pressure for the optimal utilization of available labor time. Within the limits established by the technically determined proportional relations between the various sectors, the need to maximize output and "efficiency" integrated the division of labor on each plantation ever more closely and filled in the "empty spaces" in the potentially available labor time. Historically, these conditions of commercial sugar production were developed through African slavery. Slavery provided the means by which the combination of laborers into the collective social force necessary for large-scale production was organized and molded to the technical and economic requirements of the labor process. The superiority of slavery as a form of social labor lies in its capacity to forcibly concentrate large masses of workers and compel their cooperation. It secured a labor force that was abundant, cheap, and subject to strict work discipline and social control. Through coercion the level of slave subsistence was reduced to a minimum while the time spent in commodity production was extended. Their labor was technically and socially disciplined to the requirements of commercial sugar production, and they were compelled to perform repetitive tasks for long hours over the course of the crop cycle for the duration of their working lives. Thus, the relations of slavery organized sugar production as the production of commodities and gave labor time its specific social form.

Planting and harvesting dominated the agricultural year and defined its division. However, the agrarian rhythm formed by their alternation was not simply natural but rather was manipulated to make full use of the productive capacity of the slave gang over the entire course of the planting and harvest seasons. An agricultural routine was adopted that minimized the effects of the natural seasonal break while the crop matured and kept the slaves continuously engaged in sugar production throughout the greater part of the year. The rotation of the fields was carefully planned so that over the fifteen to eighteen month maturation period of the sugar cane, the planting of one crop could be constantly alternated with the harvesting of a previous crop. Planting and harvesting the crop each took place over the course of a period of several months, and one followed upon the other as quickly as possible. In this way, the planter was able to extend his utilization of the productive potential of the slave labor force and to obtain an annual crop while increasing the yield within the natural limits of the planting and harvest seasons (Goveia 1965, 127–129).

The demand for labor was most intensive during the harvest season, but even in the so-called dead season between harvests, the slaves were kept continuously busy with a variety of tasks essential to the operation of the plantation. These included not only planting and caring for the cane but also auxiliary tasks such as clearing new fields; planting provisions; carrying manure to the fields; ditching; building and maintaining roads, buildings, and animal pens; cleaning canals; building and repairing carts; and other types of repairs and maintenance. If these jobs were not enough to keep the slaves occupied, new work was created for them to do. Such a routine encouraged the generalization rather than the specialization of slave labor. Individual slaves were constantly shifted from one task to another and thus acquired a broad range of general skills, but at the same time the development of the division of labor on the plantation and therefore the collective level of skill and the productive capacity of the slave gang as a group was retarded. Furthermore, although the dead season was in principle less demanding than the harvest season, this regime harnessed the slaves to a pattern of year-round drudgery which dulled their incentive and efficiency and exposed them to the burdens of prolonged fatigue and overwork. This situation was aggravated when heavy rains or prolonged drought impeded work during the off-season. There then followed a push to make up for lost time and complete these tasks before the harvest season renewed its claims on the full energy of the labor force.

Superimposed on the agricultural calendar was the religious calendar. The Edict of 1685 (the *Code Noir*) and the Royal Ordinance of 1786 exempted slaves from labor on Sundays and holidays, and, according to all available accounts, these provisions were generally observed. In pre-revolutionary Saint Domingue, Dutrône calculated that 52 Sundays, 16 feast days, and about 17 rainy days left the planter with 280 work days a year. (This compares with Kuczynski's figure of 250 days for *ancien régime* France and 300 days for Protestant Britain.) After the French Revolution divine virtues gave way to secular ones, and the number of religious holidays was reduced to four: Christmas, Ascension Day, Assumption, and All Saint's Day. These provisions were suspended during the harvest season when the demands of production were continuous. The days remaining after the deduction of these exemptions were available for the labor of the estate (France. Ministère de la Marine et des Colonies 1844, 301–302).

The unit of labor time in the Caribbean sugar colonies was the day. This was a variable natural unit of measurement lasting from sunrise to sunset.

Marking the length of the parts of the working day depended upon the judgment of the overseer. Beyond the technical problems of measurement, this could lead to conflict between the overseer who was under pressure to produce as much sugar as possible and the master who, particularly after the abolition of the slave trade, was desirous of protecting the well-being of his slaves. Anon [Collins] (1811, 162–163) in Jamaica admonishes:

> In turning out in the morning, it is usual to prepare your negroes by the plantation bell, which, by the carelessness of the watchman, or by the difficulty of distinguishing between the light of the moon, and the first approach of morning, is rung an hour or two earlier than it ought to be. This you should prevent, by directing it not to be rung until twilight is very well ascertained.

Mechanical timekeeping was conspicuous by its absence, particularly in the French Antilles. Indeed, even bells were scarce there, and the elaborate system utilizing the clerical hours of the church bells to mark the working day described by Moreno Fraginals (1976, 148–149) for Cuba appears to have been unknown in Martinique and Guadeloupe. The divisions in the day there were more commonly signaled by the crack of the overseer's whip or the blowing of a whistle or conch shell (Lavollée 1841, 122–123; Le Goff 1980, 44–99).

In the French colonies, work in the fields before sunrise and after sunset was forbidden by law, and, although it was sometimes attempted during the harvest season, fieldwork done in the dark was both dangerous and difficult to supervise. In order to take maximum advantage of the daylight hours, the slaves were awakened before dawn. After assembly for communal prayers, roll call, and the assignment of the day's tasks, they went off to the fields accompanied by the overseer and the drivers. The slaves' workday began between 5:00 and 6:00 a.m. with the rising of the sun. At eight or nine o'clock, they stopped work for between thirty and forty-five minutes while breakfast was brought to them in the fields. Work in the fields was avoided during the hottest part of the day, and the slaves had the period from noon until two o'clock to themselves in order to eat and rest. Many slaves devoted this time to the cultivation of their private garden plots or provision grounds if these were located near enough to the fields. At two o'clock they were summoned back for the afternoon work session which lasted until five o'clock in the summer and sunset in the winter. At the end of the workday, and sometimes during the midday break as well, each slave was required to pick a bundle of Guinea grass for fodder for the animals and carry it back to the animal pens. There was a final assembly and an evening prayer, though this was not as regular or as rigorous as the morning assembly. The remaining time belonged to the slaves. Each household prepared its own evening meal. The slaves were relatively free, and all that was required was that general order and tranquility be maintained (Lavollée 1841, 122–123; Debien 1974, 147–152).

Thus, the effective working day spent in the fields normally lasted between nine and ten hours depending on the amount of daylight. To this must be added the time spent going to and from the work site and gathering and carrying fodder. (Many planters thought that this latter task merely added to the fatigue of the slaves after a long day's work and ought to be given over to a special gang.) The need for continuity in sugar production established a regularity of activity during this period that was uncommon in preindustrial work rhythms. The division of the cane fields into carefully measured and geometric pieces as well as the organization of collective gang labor and its supervision by drivers and overseers represent attempts to guarantee the regular and constant application of labor throughout the day and to achieve a standardized and calculable daily output which could permit the integration of the production process over the course of the entire crop cycle. Explicit in the organization of the working day was a concern for the maximization of yield, technical efficiency, and quantification and measurement whose outcome is the increasing standardization of process and product (Lavollée 1841, 123–124; Debien 1974, 153–154).

Both pro- and anti-slavery writers agreed that this regime did not make excessive demands on the strength and health of the slaves even in the tropical climate. In the words of French abolitionist Victor Schoelcher, "The slaves do what they must, and today the masters do not demand more of them than they can do." The technical division of labor left gaps in the working day, and Schoelcher reported that there was much more give and take in the time discipline of the sugar plantations in Martinique than in a European factory. Not infrequently he witnessed the afternoon work period begin at 2:15 or 2:20 rather than at 2:00 p.m. Further, many planters, especially after the abolition of the slave trade, were very attentive to rest periods and meals and thought them to be essential for the efficiency and well-being of their *ateliers* (Schoelcher 1976, 22).

The natural agrarian rhythm of the daily plantation routine was interrupted during the harvest season when the industrial character of sugar manufacture emerged and revealed its dominion over the organization of the entire crop cycle. During this period, the legal restrictions on the working day were suspended. Night work, regarded as what is described by Le Goff (1980) as an "urban heresy" in the agrarian societies of late medieval Europe, proliferated in the sugar mills of the colonial countryside, and the slaves were harnessed to the continuous mechanical movement of the mill and the flow of the boiling house where work went on ceaselessly around the clock. In order to maintain this effort, the *atelier* was divided into three groups called *quarts* that were successively rotated from the fields to the mill and refinery where they worked in seven and one-half hour shifts. According to Sainte-Croix (1822), 150 slaves were necessary to organize a complete system of shifts, and planters with fewer slaves had to restrict themselves to manufacturing sugar only during the day. However, other sources suggest that round-the-clock shifts were carried on with smaller complements of slaves, although night work appears to have been exceptional on small and medium plantations. This schedule placed an enormous physical burden on the slaves. After a full day's work in the fields during the most demanding period of the year, they had to do a shift in the mill or refinery at night as well. During the harvest season, eighteen to twenty hours of intensive effort without a break was common. The exhausting *veillées*, as the night shifts were known, led to fatigue and often to horrible accidents, as tired and overworked slaves got a hand or arm caught in the cylinders of the mill or fell into cauldrons of boiling cane juice (Debien 1974, 149–153; Dutrône 1791, 149–153; Lavollée 1841, 73, 122–123; Sainte-Croix 1822, 135).

The slaves' working activity was not confined only to the production of export commodities. A considerable amount of their time was also devoted to producing for their own subsistence. Commonly, slaves were given plots of marginal land and free time in order to produce at least a portion of their own consumption. This practice directly benefited the master. Imported consumption goods were always expensive and their supply was often irregular, while both the land and the time for provision cultivation emerged almost naturally from the conditions of sugar production itself. Allowing the slaves to produce for their own subsistence from resources already at hand instead of purchasing the necessary items on the market represented a saving to the master and reduction of the cash expenses of the estate. This arrangement shifted the burden of the reproduction costs to the slaves themselves and kept them usefully employed even during periods when there was no work to be done on the sugar crop. In addition, many planters hoped that it would give the slaves a stake in the plantation and instill in them regular habits and the virtues of work and property. Thus, slavery, instead of separating the direct producers from the means of subsistence, provided them with the means of producing a livelihood. While the slaves acquired access to the use of property and the possibility of improving the material conditions of life, for them the price of subsistence was work beyond that required for sugar production. With these developments, the time devoted to the slaves' reproduction became separate from commodity production and a de facto division between necessary and surplus labor time was created.

The practice of giving the slaves gardens and a free day per week to grow their own food was brought by Dutch refugees from Pernambuco who introduced the cultivation of sugar cane into the French Antilles during the first half of the seventeenth century. From the beginning of slavery in the French colonies, the slaves were given small gardens to supplement their rations, but with the introduction of sugar, planters tended to neglect subsistence crops for their slaves in favor of planting sugar cane. With the adoption of the "Brazilian custom," masters no longer distributed rations to their slaves. Instead, the latter were expected to provide their own food, shelter, and clothing from the labor of their free day. But this practice had negative consequences. Food production was anarchic, and the slaves were often poorly nourished. Indeed, frequent food shortages prevented the masters from dispensing with the distribution of rations altogether. Provisions for these rations were produced as an estate crop by compulsory gang labor under the supervision of drivers and overseers. Critics of the custom of free Saturdays claimed that it gave the slaves too much freedom and encouraged theft and disorder. Too many slaves neglected their gardens and preferred to hire themselves out rather than grow food during their free time. They squandered their earnings and robbed their masters and neighboring plantations for food (Debien 1974, 176–186).

The colonial authorities were in agreement with the critics and both sought to stop what they perceived to be the excesses resulting from the free Saturday and to ensure adequate treatment for the slave population. The Royal Edict of 1685 (*Code Noir*), the Royal Ordinance of October 15, 1786, and the Colonial Penal Code of 1828, as well as innumerable local ordinances sought to make the master totally responsible for the maintenance of his slaves and to prescribe standards for food, shelter, and clothing to be provided to the slaves. Masters were expressly forbidden to give their slaves the free Saturday in place of the legal ration or to permit them to furnish their own food. However, such regulations were not easy to enforce in a society dominated by slaveholders, and local authorities made little attempt to carry them out (Debien 1974, 178–186, 205–207).

However, despite the shortcomings and abuses of the practice of free Saturdays and slave provision grounds and the repeated attempts to suppress them, the scale of these activities increased steadily, and they became more and more central to the functioning of the colonial economy. By the 1830s, the masters, with few exceptions, encouraged their slaves to grow their own foodstuffs, and the substitution of free Saturdays for rations had become widespread in the colonies. The slaves were given as much land as they could cultivate. They produced and marketed their crops without supervision, and their produce was an integral part of the colonial food supply. Colonial authorities no longer regarded these practices as threats to order, but rather felt that they contributed to social harmony. The reports of local officials particularly stressed the social benefits of independent cultivation by slaves. One of them expressed the opinion that the free Saturday meant nothing less than bringing the slaves up to the standards of the civilized world:

> But the slaves, for whom the custom of free Saturdays is established, prefer it to the ration because they work on their own account and find some profit from that state of affairs. It is clear evidence that man, even though a slave, has an interest in money and likes to enjoy the fruits of his labors while freely disposing of that which belongs to him. The black is forced to enter into types of social transactions that can only serve as a means of civilizing him. (France. Ministère de la Marine et des Colonies 1844, 183–184)

This latter aspect was seen to be especially important because of the imminent prospect of emancipation. The report continued: "In this regard, the custom of the free Saturday must be preferred to the legally sanctioned ration because, beyond everything else, it is a road toward free labor." In 1846, these practices received the sanction of law. The authorities saw in them not the source of disorder, but the means to regulate slavery and provide a transition to free labor (France. Ministère de la Marine et des Colonies 1844, 183–184, 290).

The evolution of the working day in the French Caribbean needs to be understood not simply as the product of the political economy of the slave plantation, but also as a historical process where the cultural definitions of work and its relation to the larger matrix of plantation life were contested. For the African bondsman, slave labor in the New World required a radical restructuring of the work process under brutal conditions. In the Antilles, the goals and organization of work were very different from what they had been in Africa. The purposes and organization of work were no longer defined by mutual obligation, kinship ties, or social duty. Instead, a complex system of political and legal sanctions established the domination of the master over the person of the slave and imposed work upon the slaves as an alien activity. Work was separated from all other human activities and subordinated to the claims of production embodied in the master, while all other aspects of slave life were subordinated to work. Systematic production for the abstract market, not direct or indirect consumption, required that the slaves adapt to new purposes of production, appropriation, and distribution. The slaves were forced to adopt new work habits, adjust to new work discipline, learn new values, and respond to incentives to work. They had to learn to accept the authority of the master and his supervisors, to become proficient at new skills, and to work together in large gangs continuously and regularly at repetitive tasks for a period of fixed duration, day after day. The burden of this transition was heavy on the minds and bodies of the enslaved, and it required a painful cultural adaptation on a vast scale.

This process of "creolization" can be seen in the historical evolution of the practice of the free Saturday. While the free Saturday never ceased to be functional from the point of view of the interests of the master, it formed a nodal point within the social relations of slavery which allowed slave practices, values, and interests to emerge and develop and to assume autonomous forms of organization and expression. As they became socialized into the routine of plantation labor, the slaves were able to lay claim to the free Saturday and use it for their own ends. By the nineteenth century, the slaves by and large preferred to have an extra day to themselves and raise their own provisions rather than receive an allowance of food from the master. As one government official observed: "This practice . . . is completely to the advantage of the slave who wants to work. A day spent by him cultivating his garden, or in some other manner, will bring him more than the value of the nourishment that the law prescribes for him. I will add that there is no *atelier* which does not prefer this arrangement to the execution of the edict [*Code Noir*]. Once it has been set, it would be dangerous for the master to renounce it" (France. Ministère de la Marine et des Colonies 1844, 183, 290).

Labor time became divided, in practice, between time belonging to the master and time belonging to the slaves. For their part, the slaves felt that they had a right to such "free" time and resisted any encroachment upon it. According to one official:

> It would be almost impossible for a planter to take even a little bit of time belonging to his slave, even if the authorities ignored the situation. There is a spirit of resistance among the slaves that prevents anyone from threatening what they consider to be their rights. (1844, 180–188)

Through this process of the appropriation of a portion of the available labor time, the slaves were able to elaborate what Sidney Mintz (1974) has described as a "proto-peasant" style of life. (Mintz uses this term to characterize those activities by people still enslaved that would allow their subsequent adaptation to a peasant way of life. As Mintz emphasizes, the formation of this proto-peasantry is both a mode of response and a mode of resistance on the part of the enslaved to the conditions imposed upon them by the slave plantation system. Thus, a proto-peasantry is not a traditional peasantry attacked from the outside by commodity production, the market economy, and the colonial state. Rather, it is formed from within the processes of historical development of slavery and the plantation system.) They displayed remarkable energy and skill and used the opportunities presented to them to secure at least relative control over their subsistence and a degree of independence from the master. Their initiative led to the development of new economic and social patterns and the mobilization of productive forces that otherwise would have remained dormant. The slaves who wanted to plant gardens were given as much land as they could cultivate. The plots were frequently extensive, and the slaves had complete responsibility for them. Access to this property meant that the slaves' consumption was no longer entirely dependent on the economic condition of the master. Rather, they could use their free time and the produce of their gardens to improve their standard of living. Beyond supplying the personal consumption needs of the slaves, the provision grounds produced a marketable surplus of food. The slaves sold this produce in the towns and cities and developed a network of markets that were an important feature of the economic and social life of the colonies. In this process, the slaves were able to improve and add variety to the material conditions of their lives as well as to acquire skills, knowledge, and social contacts which increased their independence and allowed them to assert their individuality (France. Ministère de la Marine et des Colonies 1844, 303–305).

The consolidation of this position in subsistence production provided a base for the assertion of the slaves' purposes, needs, and cultural forms in other aspects of plantation life including the organization of work and the composition of the working day. Time became a kind of currency, and a complex system of time accounting emerged. If the master found that he needed the slaves at a time when they were exempted from labor, such work was voluntary, and it was rare that the slaves were not compensated for their services. Often, the master indemnified the slaves with an equivalent amount of time rather than money. In Martinique, it was reported that the slaves on one plantation were made to work on Sunday during the harvest but were given the following Monday off. On the infrequent occasions when the master of another plantation needed the labor of his slaves on a free Saturday or a Sunday for some pressing work which could not be postponed, they were given an equivalent amount of time on a weekday. A government official reported that this latter planter kept a precise account of the extra time that the slaves put in and indemnified them scrupulously (France. Ministère de la Marine et des Colonies 1844, 303–305).

Thus, the time belonging to the slaves not only became distinguished from the time belonging to the masters, but opposed to it. At the extreme, the former encroached upon the latter. In the 1840s, for example, there were persistent attempts by the slaves in Martinique and Guadeloupe to refuse to do night work during the harvest season. More dramatically, in August 1791, at the beginning of the Haitian Revolution, the slaves of Saint Domingue demanded the system of *trois jours*, three days for the master and three days for their own gardens. For the slaves, the time separate from work became a sphere of autonomous activity—free time where they could dispose of their energies as they saw fit and within which they created a community organized around their beliefs, values, and collective action. (According to Monk Lewis, a planter in Jamaica, the slaves on his plantation referred to their free Saturday as "play day.") The slaves' use of their free time became subversive of plantation discipline as one observer in Martinique indicates:

> During the week, when work is finished, the slaves leave the plantation and run to those where they have women. . . . The liberty of the night, that is, the right to use their nights as they wish, is a veritable plague. With this type of liberty, the Negroes have every means to indulge in their debauchery, to commit thefts, to smuggle, to repair to their secret meetings, and to prepare and take their revenge. And what good work can be expected during the day from people who stay out and revel the whole night? When the masters are asked why the slaves are allowed such a fatal liberty, they reply that they cannot take it away from them. (De Cassagnac 1842, 168)

For the slaves, their "free" time represented a social space to be protected and, if possible, expanded, while the master had to contain the slaves' demands within the limits of economic efficiency and social order (Debien 1974, 209; Lavollée 1841, 124; Lewis 1929, 81).

The evolution of the practice of the free Saturday thus suggests the historical trajectory and limits of slave production and the master-slave relation. The relation between master and slave was not static but underwent a process of continual evolution. Europeans and Africans encountered one another through the unequal relations of slavery and engaged in a day-to-day struggle, sometimes implicit, sometimes overt, over the organization of work and the norms and values that it entailed. The master sought to discipline the slaves to the technical and social conditions of plantation production and to inculcate in them appropriate skills, attitudes, and values. But if the enslaved successfully adapted to the exigencies of the new labor regime, their behavior and values were not imitative of those of their masters, nor were their motives, meanings, and goals identical with those of the latter. For their part, the slaves, in a complex mixture of accommodation and resistance, struggled both within and against the framework dictated to them and, in the course of their struggle, developed other values, ideas, and cultural forms. These, in turn, enabled them to assert their own purposes, needs, and rhythms in work and social life and to resist the definitions imposed by their masters. Thus, the very ability of the masters to compel the participation of the slaves in the new conditions of life and labor altered the slave relation itself. New forms, meanings, and goals of social action emerged alongside older ones and became the focal points of a new constellation of conditions, needs, and capacities on both sides which moved the struggle between them to a new terrain.

This process of the appropriation of the free Saturday by the slaves had far-reaching consequences for the development of slavery in the French West Indies and was itself an aspect of the crisis of the slave system. It represents not an attempt to reject or escape the system, but an initiative by a population that over the course of its historical experience had learned to adapt to the labor routine, discipline, and organization of time of the slave plantation and confronted slavery within its own relations and processes. The result was to simultaneously strengthen and weaken the slave system. On the one hand, the slaves became more effectively integrated into slavery and responsive to its rewards and punishments. The operating expenses of the plantation were reduced, and a greater surplus was available to the planter. On the other hand, the amount of labor time at the disposition of the planter was congealed, and the slaves acquired a means of resisting the intensification of work at the very moment that the transformation of the world sugar market demanded higher levels of productivity and greater exploitation of labor from French West Indian planters. In this process, the bonds of slavery began to slowly dissolve, and the activities of the slaves gradually transformed the foundations of slave society itself. Custom, consent, and accommodation assumed a greater weight in the conduct of daily life where coercion had prevailed. The acquisition of skills and property and the establishment of economic and social networks enabled slaves to realize important material and psychological gains. The slaves thus began to fashion an alternative way of life that played an important role not only in eroding the slave regime but also in forming a transition to a new society. In it can be seen nuclei of the postemancipation social structure and the means for resisting the new encroachments of plantation agriculture.

Chapter Eight

Une Petite Guinée

Provision Ground and Plantation in Martinique—Integration, Adaptation, and Appropriation

During the nineteenth century, the working activity of slaves in the French West Indian colony of Martinique extended beyond the production of export commodities. The planters of Martinique, under constant pressure to reduce costs, obliged their slaves to produce for their own subsistence in their "free" time, that is, outside of the time devoted to the plantation's commercial crop. Instead of receiving the legally required amounts of food and clothing, slaves were commonly given plots of marginal land and a free day on Saturday so that they could produce at least a portion of their own consumption needs on their own account. (Some planters gave only half a day on Saturday and continued to supply a part of the slaves' rations themselves. In addition, slaves in Martinique commonly had Sundays free.) By encouraging slaves to work for themselves, masters could avoid the effort and expense of the large-scale cultivation of provisions. Instead, they had only to furnish some clothing, a fixed weekly ration of salt meat or fish and perhaps rum, and occasional medical care (Soleau 1835, 9–10; France. Ministère de la Marine 1840–1843, 205).

This arrangement had obvious benefits for the master. The expense of maintaining the slave population placed heavy economic burdens on a planter. Imported goods were always expensive and their supply was often irregular, while the conditions of sugar production in Martinique made available both the land and time for provision-ground cultivation. Planters perceived it as in their interest to spend as little money, time, or energy as

152

possible on slave maintenance—a perception that did not change appreciably at least as long as the slave trade lasted, and for many extended beyond the end of the slave trade and even of slavery itself. Allowing the slaves to produce for their own subsistence from resources already at hand instead of purchasing the necessary items on the market reduced the slaveholder's cash expenses. The burden of reproduction costs was shifted directly to the slaves themselves, and they were kept usefully employed even during periods when there was no work to be done on the sugar crop. Although such practices meant that after long hours of toil in the cane fields, the slaves had to work still more just to secure the basic necessities of life, many planters hoped that it would give the slaves a stake in the plantation and instill in them regular habits and the virtues of work and property (Sainte-Croix 1822, II, 105).

While provision ground cultivation arose from the planter's attempts to reduce costs and create an interest for the slave in the well-being of the estate, it resulted in the formation of a sphere of slave-organized activity that ultimately became necessary for the operation of the plantation system. This sphere of activity was neither simply integrated into the organization of the sugar estate, nor, as some contend, did it form an independent "peasant breach" with a logic of its own (Cardoso 1979; Lepkowski 1968). Instead, provision-ground production and the commercial production of sugar were intimately bound to each other in ways simultaneously dependent and antagonistic. Although slave provision-ground cultivation was spatially and temporally separate from export commodity production, it developed within the constraints of estate agriculture. Not only did final authority over the use of the land and the disposition of labor reside with the master, but the time and space for provision ground cultivation also arose from the rhythm and organization of sugar production.

Nonetheless, such activity offered an opportunity for slave initiative and self-assertion that cannot simply be deduced from its economic form. The slave provision-ground became in the expression of Maléuvrier, the intendant of Saint Domingue, "*une petite Guinée*," where slaves could organize their own activities for their own purposes (Cardoso 1979, 145). These practices both shaped and were shaped by Afro-Caribbean cultural forms, through which the definitions of social reality of slavery and the plantation were at once mediated and contested. Through this activity, slaves themselves created and controlled a secondary economic network which originated within the social and spatial boundaries of the plantation but which allowed for the construction of an alternative way of life that went beyond it (see Mintz 1974; Mintz 1979, 213–242; Mintz 1964, 248–265; Mintz and Hall 1960, 3–26).

Provision-ground production and the activities associated with it developed within and through the antagonistic relation between master and slave.

If for the master the provision ground was the means to guarantee cheap labor, for the slave it was the means to elaborate an autonomous style of life. From these conflicting perspectives evolved a continuing struggle—at times hidden, at times overt—over the division of the available labor time of the estate into export-crop production and provision crop production. At issue was not only the amount and kind of work to be performed but also its social meaning and purpose. In this process, as much cultural as economic in both its causes and consequences, the slaves contested the definition and meaning of time and space, labor and power.

The condition for the autonomous development of provision-ground cultivation and marketing was the slaves' appropriation of a portion of the labor time of the estate and its redefinition around their individual and collective interests, needs, and values within and against the predominant slave relation. The slaves' struggle for "free" time entailed and was conditioned by struggles to appropriate physical space, the right to property, and the disposition of their own activity. In turn, the consolidation of slave autonomy in provision-ground cultivation provided leverage to contest the conditions of staple crop production. These interrelated practices transformed and subverted the organization of labor within slavery even as they reinforced it. In this process, the bonds of dependence of slave upon master began slowly to dissolve, and the slaves' activities gradually transformed the foundation of slave society itself. The changing role and meaning of these independent activities were both the cause of and response to the increased pressure for profitability on the plantation system during the first half of the nineteenth century. While these practices had existed virtually since the beginning of slavery in the colony, they assumed new importance with changing economic and political conditions and the imminent prospect of emancipation (Rodney 1981, 643–666; Mintz 1982, 209–225).

EVOLUTION

Masters had provided slaves with small gardens to supplement their rations since the beginning of slavery in the French colonies, but the practice of giving the slaves provision-grounds and a free day each week to grow their own food dated from the introduction of sugarcane into the French Antilles by Dutch refugees from Pernambuco during the first half of the seventeenth century. The origins of this latter practice can be traced back further still to São Tomé in the sixteenth century (Debien 1974, 178–179; Malowist 1969, 9–30). Thus, the diffusion of sugar cane entailed not merely the movement of a commodity, but the spread of a whole way of life. With the appearance of sugar cultivation in the French Caribbean, subsistence crops for the slaves were neglected in favor of planting cane, and the "Brazilian custom" was rapidly adopted by planters eager to reduce their expenses. Masters no longer distributed rations to their slaves. Instead, the latter were expected to provide their own food, shelter, clothing, and other material needs from the labor of their "free" day.

But this practice failed to ensure a regular and sufficient supply of food. Slaves were often poorly nourished. Indeed, frequent food shortages prevented the masters from dispensing with the distribution of rations altogether. Provisions for these rations were produced as an estate crop by compulsory gang labor under the supervision of drivers and overseers. Further, critics of the custom of free Saturdays claimed that the custom gave the slaves too much freedom and encouraged theft and disorder. Too many slaves neglected their gardens, preferring to hire themselves out rather than grow food during their free time. They were said to squander their earnings and rob their masters and neighboring plantations for food. Nevertheless, despite these problems, the custom continued to spread slowly but steadily throughout the French colonies (Debien 1974, 178–186; Peytraud 1973, 217).

Metropolitan authorities agreed with the critics and sought both to stop what they perceived to be the excesses resulting from the free Saturday and to ensure adequate nourishment for the slave population. The proclamation of the Royal Edict of 1685 or *Code Noir* by the metropolitan government was the first attempt to establish a uniform dietary standard for slaves in all the French colonies and to end to the prevailing disorder. It sought to make masters totally responsible for the maintenance of their slaves and to prescribe standards for the food, shelter, and clothing to be provided to the slaves. Under the regulations the practice of relying on individual slave gardens and free Saturdays in lieu of rations was to be suppressed in favor of regular weekly food allowances of determined composition and quantity (The *Code Noir* legally prescribed the weekly food ration for an adult at 2.5 pots of manioc flour (1 pot = 2.75 livres) or 7.5 livres of cassava and 3 livres of fish or 2 livres of salt beef. This allotment was known as the *ordinaire*. The master was also obligated to provide the slave with two changes of clothes per year, one change to be distributed every six months. The men were to receive a shirt, trousers, and hat, while the women were given a shirt, skirt, scarf, and hat. Children received only a shirt. In addition, each individual was given one cloth jacket each year. (France. Ministère de la Marine 1844, 177, 219–225; Debien 1974, 176–177, 181, 183–185; Gisler 1965, 23–25, 35–38; Peytraud 1973, 216–224).

This edict remained the fundamental legislation governing slavery in the French colonies throughout the *ancien régime*. The distribution of slave

rations seems to have been more widely practiced in Martinique than elsewhere in the French Antilles, and the slaves there had the reputation of being
better fed than elsewhere in the French colonies. Even so, the writings of
administrators in Martinique throughout the course of the eighteenth century
complain continually that the slave owners were concerned only with sugar,
and, if they provided a part of the slaves' nourishment, the slaves were
obliged to secure the rest on their own account. The persistent failure to regulate the slaves' diet and treatment and especially to prohibit the practice of
slave provision grounds is evident from the succession of declarations, edicts,
ordinances, regulations, and decrees, too numerous to recount, promulgated
by both metropolitan and colonial authorities during the seventeenth and
eighteenth centuries. Colonial officials lacked the means to enforce the regulations in a society dominated by slaveholders who jealously guarded their
"property rights," particularly when it cost them time or money. Planters
expressed their preference for slave self-subsistence, and their reluctance to
spend money on slave maintenance, especially food, persisted throughout the
ancien régime and into the nineteenth century. Far from dying out, the practice of free Saturdays and slave provision-grounds expanded and increasingly
became an established part of colonial life during these years (Debien 1974,
176–177, 181, 183–186, 215; Gisler 1965, 23–25, 35–38; Peytraud 1973,
216–224; France. Ministère de la Marine 1840–1843, 205).

The revisions of the *Code Noir* enacted in 1784 and 1786 attempted to
ameliorate the lot of slaves and reconcile the law with the growing importance of provision grounds in the colonies. The free Saturday was still forbidden, but, instead of prohibiting slave provision grounds, the new legislation
recognized their existence and attempted to regulate them. It decreed that
each adult slave was to receive a small plot of land to cultivate on his or her
own account. The law still, however, required the distribution of rations. The
produce of these plots was to supplement the *ordinaire*, not replace it. The
prohibition against the substitution of the free Saturday for the legal ration
was restated by the Royal Ordinance of October 29, 1828, which reformed
the Colonial Penal Code. But custom was stronger than law, and ministerial
instructions advised colonial authorities to tolerate the replacement of the
ration by the free Saturday when it was voluntary on the part of the slave
(Schoelcher 1976, 8–9; France. Ministère de la Marine 1844, 177, 267; May
1975, 119–121).

These modifications of the earlier legislation were a step toward recogniz-
ing the realities of colonial life, but the law still regarded provision-ground
cultivation only as a supplemental activity, and continued to insist on the distribution of *ordinaire* as the primary means of providing for slave maintenance. However, depressed economic conditions after 1815 made complete

dependence on the ration impractical, and scarcities caused planters to increase their reliance on provision-ground cultivation. In 1829 a parliamentary commission reported that before the sugar boom of 1823 most plantations in the French West Indies could only rarely provide their slaves with the *ordinaire*. Planters had to require slaves to provide for their own subsistence and were thus deprived of a portion of their labor. Yet the commission concluded that "almost all the Negroes now received the quantity of codfish and other food prescribed by the regulations, their masters could employ them full-time in the cultivation of sugar cane." In his testimony before the commission, Jabrun stated that slaves in that colony were better fed, better, dressed, and better housed than they had been some years previously. Nevertheless, he also noted that although produce from provision-grounds normally supplemented the ration, poverty, shortage of credit, and the consequent difficulty in obtaining provisions still caused some planters to substitute the free Saturday for the ration. De Lavigne, a planter from Martinique, testified that in general the substitution of the free Saturday had ceased there. While this latter claim was certainly exaggerated, the evidence presented by both Jabrun and De Lavigne suggests a cyclical aspect to provision-ground cultivation. In contrast to periods of low sugar prices when land and labor could be given over to provision grounds, with the high prices of the sugar boom of the 1820s, many planters may have devoted their attention entirely to sugar cultivation and purchased necessary provisions. Undoubtedly a variety of individual strategies were possible, and while continuous cultivation of provision grounds may be demonstrated for the colony as a whole, it may not necessarily be the case for individual estates (France. Ministère du Commerce et des Manufactures 1829, 23, 52, 67, 156, 248).

Despite the shortcomings and abuses of the practice of free Saturdays and slave provision-grounds and the repeated attempts to suppress them, the scale of these activities increased steadily, and by the nineteenth century they had become more and more central to the functioning of the colonial economy. During the 1830s masters, with few exceptions, encouraged their slaves to grow their own foodstuffs, and the substitution of free Saturdays for the legally prescribed rations became widespread. Slaves were given as much land as they could cultivate. They both produced and marketed their crops without supervision and were so successful that the colony became dependent upon their produce for a substantial portion of its food. As one observer stated in the 1840s, "the plantations which produce foodstuffs [*habitations vivrières*] and the slaves who cultivate gardens more than guarantee that the colony is supplied with local produce." Measures prohibiting these activities were disregarded with the common consent of both masters and slaves. Enforcement would not only have inhibited the efforts of slave cultivators but could also have reduced the island's food supply (Sainte-Croix 1822, II, 105; Lavollée 1841, 10; France. Ministère de la Marine 1844, 182–187; France. Ministère de la Marine 1840–1843, 205).

By the 1840s authorities in both France and the colony no longer regarded these practices as threats to order, but rather felt that they contributed to social harmony. The reports of local officials stressed the social benefits of independent cultivation by slaves. One of them expressed the opinion that the free Saturday was an "effective means of giving [the slave] the taste for property and well-being, and consequently, to make them useful craftsmen and agriculturalists desirous of family ties" (Ministère de la Marine 1844, 183–184, 290). The reforms of the July Monarchy were a decisive step in the recognition of existing practices in the colonies and prepared the way for emancipation. The law of July 18 and 19, 1845, known as the Mackau Law, allowed the substitution of provision grounds for the *ordinaire*. While the land itself remained the property of the master, its produce belonged to the slave, and the state recognized the latter's legal personality and right to chattel property. The Mackau confirmed and regularized what was already a customary practice, giving it legal sanction. In the words of its authors, "The law only recognizes a state that has long existed in practice and makes it a right to the great advantage of the black and without detriment to the master." These legally enforceable rights were less precarious and dependent upon the whim of the proprietor than the previous custom. Slaves could now assert their purposes with the support of the colonial state. The authorities saw in these practices not the source of disorder, but the means to regulate slavery and provide a transition to free labor. The Mackau Law sought to ease the transition to freedom by giving slave skills, property, and therefore a stake in society. In the words of one local official, "on the eve of complete emancipation, it is the interest of the masters to see the taste for labor and the spirit of economy develop in the slaves. Now, without property there is no industrious activity. It is only for oneself that one has the heart to work. Without property there is no economy. One does not economize for another" (France. Ministère de la Marine 1844, 177–188, 288–291, 332–333; France. Ministère de la Marine 1840–1843, 205–206, 208–209).

INTEGRATION AND ADAPTATION

According to French abolitionist Victor Schoelcher, the provision-ground was the principal source of well-being for slaves in Martinique under the July Monarchy. Indeed, its importance grew as the crisis of the sugar industry and mounting indebtedness limited the planters' resources. Customarily, slaves who were given half a free day a week were allotted only half a ration, while those who received a full day were to provide food for themselves. In addition, Sundays belonged to the slaves and could also be devoted to subsistence activities. Schoelcher recorded that on a great number of plantations in Martinique such arrangements had become a sort of exchange between the master and his slaves. "This transaction," he writes, "is very favorable for the master who no longer has capital to lay out to ensure the supply of provisions. And it is accepted with good will by the black who in working Saturday and Sunday in his garden derives great benefits" (Schoelcher 1976, 11; Lavollée 1841, 123).

With few exceptions, masters encouraged their slaves to grow their own foodstuffs wherever possible. The practice of giving free Saturdays to the slaves appears to have been far more common than the distribution of the *ordinaire* as the means of providing subsistence. Although some of the most prosperous planters preferred to give rations to their slaves, provision grounds were almost universal and appear to have existed even where the *ordinaire* was distributed. For example, according to one report, in Lamentin, one of the major sugar-growing regions of the colony, free Saturdays were denied on almost all the plantations and slaves received the legal allotments. Nevertheless, the slaves kept gardens and drew considerable revenues from sales to local markets. Not surprisingly, the distribution of clothing allowances was more widely practiced than that of food rations, although the *procureurs* (public prosecutors) reported that many planters expected their slaves to provide their own clothing as well as their food from the income of their gardens. This practice was especially widespread among the less prosperous planters, particularly in the poorer southern *arrondissement* of Fort Royal. Only wealthy planters could consistently afford to clothe their slaves. Others could do so only when the harvest was good, if at all. Several public prosecutors objected to planters making the slaves provide their own clothing and admonished the slaveholders to stop the practice. Thus, while diverse combinations and possibilities of conditions of subsistence existed, provision grounds and free Saturdays had become a common experience for the majority of slaves in Martinique during the nineteenth century. These slaves provided for their own maintenance, in whole or in part, through independent labor beyond their toil in the cane fields (France. Ministère de la Marine 1844, 89–90, 177, 182–185, 219–225, 288–291, 332–333; France. Archives Nationales. Section Outre-Mer. *Généralités*, 9 (99), De Moges, Mémoire).

The successful development of autonomous provision-ground cultivation and marketing in Martinique depended upon the initiative of the enslaved. It was the result of slaves adapting to the New World conditions and acquiring the skills and habits necessary to produce and market these crops. At least one contemporary observer stressed the importance of cultural adaptation by the slaves in developing subsistence agriculture and also suggested that slave provision grounds became more prevalent after the slave trade ended in the 1830s. "Thus, previously, the progress of the population did not take place in accordance with the laws of nature," he noted. "Each year, the irregular introduction of considerable numbers of blacks increased the possibility of a scarce food supply in the country. These new arrivals in the colonies, knowing neither the soil, the climate, nor the special agriculture of the Antilles, could not count on themselves for their support. It was necessary to provide sufficient and regular nourishment for them, but they had no skills to contribute. Thus, the proprietors were quite properly compelled to plant a certain amount of provisions since their slaves did not know how or were unable to plant enough." He continued, "The slaves of today have less need to constant tutelage than previously. They are able to supply themselves without depending upon the generosity of their masters. The latter hardly plant provisions at all any more because the slaves plant well beyond the amount that is necessary for consumption." Indeed, nineteenth-century accounts indicate that the slaves by and large preferred to have an extra day to themselves and raise their own provisions rather than receive an allowance of food from the master. "This practice is completely to the advantage of the slave who wants to work. A day spent by him cultivating his garden, or is some other manner, will bring him more than the value of the nourishment the law prescribes for him. I will add that there is no *atelier* which does not prefer this arrangement to the execution of the edict [*Code Noir*]. Once it has been set, it would be dangerous for the master to renounce it" (France. Ministère de la Marine 1844, 104–105, 180–188, 290; France. ANSOM *Généralités* 144 (1221). Éxécution de l'ordonnance royale II, 40, 51).

The slaves who wanted to plant provisions were given as much land as they could work. The plots were usually located on uncultivated lands on the margins of the estate, often scattered in the hills above the cane fields. However, both De Cassagnac, a local planter, and Schoelcher write that some planters in the 1840s allowed cane land to be used for provisions as a form of crop rotation. When the sugar cane had exhausted the soil in a field, the slaves were permitted to plant provisions there until the land was again fit for cane. The provision grounds were then shifted to other fields. (According to historian Gabriel Debien, larger grounds located away from the slave quarters only appeared after 1770, but these were still intended to supplement the rations provided by the master rather than furnish the main items of slave diet. The staples of the slave diet—manioc, potatoes, and yams—were grown by the master in the fields belonging to the plantation.) The plots allotted to slaves were frequently quite extensive, as much as one or two acres according to

Schoelcher. All available sources agree that the slave provision grounds were well kept. Produce was abundant, and the land was not allowed to stand idle. Manioc, the principal source of nourishment for the slave population was harvested as often as four times a year. Besides manioc, the slaves raised bananas, potatoes, yams, and other vegetables on these plots (Debien 1974, 178–191, 205–207; France. Ministère de la Marine 1844, 182–187, 290; France. Ministère de la Marine 1840–1843, 206; De Cassagnac 1842, 174–175; Schoelcher 1976, 9–12; Lavollée 1841, 10; Sainte-Croix 1822, II, 105).

In addition to the provision grounds, there were also small gardens in the yards surrounding the slave cabins. They were intended to supplement the weekly ration, not replace it, and all the slaves, including those who received the *ordinaire*, had them. In these gardens slaves grew sorrel, squash, cucumbers, from France and Guinea, green peppers, hot peppers, calabash vines, okra, and perhaps some tobacco, They also planted fruit trees and, if the master permitted, kept a few chickens there as well (France. Ministère de la Marine 1844, 180–188, 290; Schoelcher 1976, 9–13; France. ANSOM. Généralités, Carton 144, Dossier 1221, Éxécution de l'ordonnance royale 1841–1843, 2, 40, 51; Debien 1974, 178–191; Mintz 1974, 362).

Of course, not all slaves were willing or able to endure the burden of extra work in the provision grounds. Infants, the aged, the infirm, expectant mothers or those nursing children—all those who could not provide for themselves—received a food allowance from the master, even on the plantations where the slaves grew their own foodstuffs. Also included among the non-participants were those slaves who refused to raise a garden. A public prosecutor in Fort Royal writes: "Only the lazy receive a ration and they are almost ashamed of it." Of these "lazy" slaves, Schoelcher comments: "We do not want to deny, however, that there are many Negroes who show a great indifference to the benefit of free Saturdays. It is necessary to force them to work for themselves on that day. It does not surprise us that beings, saturated with disgust and struck by malediction, are little concerned to improve their lot during the moments of respite that are given to them. Instead, they prefer to surrender to idleness or become intoxicated to the point of delirium from the melancholy agitation of their African dances." The free Saturday, while generally received enthusiastically by the slaves, was thus not universally accepted. For many slaves, it simply meant more work, and they refused. They withdrew their voluntary cooperation, throwing the burden of maintenance back on the master. De Cassagnac expressed surprise that on many plantations if the slaves were given the free Saturday, they would not work. They had, in his view, to be treated like children and be forced to work for themselves. It was necessary to have a driver lead them to the gardens and

watch them as carefully as when they were working for the estate (De Cassagnac 1842, 176; Schoelcher 1842/1976, 12; Anon. [Collins] 1811, 87–94).

But compulsion was not usually necessary, and often individual planters
went to great lengths to support the efforts of their slaves. Sieur Telliam-Mail-
let, who managed the Ceron plantation in Diamant, plowed his slaves' provision-grounds. Even though he supplied the *ordinaire*, M. de Delite-Loture,
who owned nearly three hundred slaves in the *quartier* of Sainte Anne,
bought or rented land in the highlands of Rivière Pilote which he cleared so
his slaves could work it for themselves. Each week he had them taken nearly
two leagues from the plantation to these gardens, and he paid for the transport
of their produce as well. Schoelcher reports that in some *quartiers*, the masters provided the slaves who worked such gardens with tools, carts, mules,
and a *corvée* of workers, and the masters and the slave cultivators divided the
harvest in half. Other masters considered such an arrangement beneath their
dignity and simply abandoned the land to the slaves (De Cassagnac 1842,
174–175; Schoelcher 1976, 12; France. Ministère de la Marine 1844, 182–
185, 288–391, 332–333; France. ANSOM. *Généralités*, Carton 9, Dossier
99, De Moges, *Mémoire.*).

For even the most industrious slave, the paternalism of the planter was ines-
capable. As Schoelcher remarks, "the greater or lesser wealth of the slaves
depends a great deal on the benevolence of the master." Whichever mode
of providing for the slaves was adopted, one inspection report notes, "their
nourishment is assured everywhere, and the master is always ready . . . to
come to the aid of the slave when the latter has need of him." Indeed, seasonal fluctuations could require the master to come to the assistance of his
slaves. "In years of great drought," De Cassagnac writes, "subsistence crops
do not grow. Then planters who previously gave the free Saturday once again
give the *ordinaire*. Those are disastrous years" (France. Ministère de la
Marine 1844, 180–188, 290; Schoelcher 1976, 12–13; De Cassagnac 1842,
174–175; France. ANSOM. *Martinique*, Carton 7, Dossier 83, Dupotêt à
Ministre de la Marine et des Colonies, Fort Royal, 5 avril 1832).

Even at best, the slaves who produced their own provisions were exposed
to risk and uncertainty. They were generally given land of inferior quality
that was incapable of supporting sugar or coffee. At times the planters
deprived them of their free day under various pretexts. If for some reason
they fell ill and could not work, their food supply was jeopardized. Drought
or bad weather might make cultivation impossible. The prospect of theft and
disorder was then increased, and, at the extreme, the physical well-being of
the labor force was threatened (Soleau 1835, 9–10; Lavollée 1841, 123;
Debien 1974, 178–180; Peytraud 1973, 217; Gisler 1965, 48).

Nevertheless, provision-ground cultivation could be advantageous for the slave. Access to this property meant that the slaves' consumption was no longer entirely dependent on the economic condition of the master. Rather, slaves could use their free time and the produce of their gardens to improve their standard of living. Demonstrating exceptional initiative and skill, they used the opportunities presented to them to secure at least relative control over their subsistence and a degree of independence from the master. According to one contemporary estimate, the incentive provided by the gardens doubled slave output. With the free day and the other free time that could be husbanded during rest periods and after tasks were finished, slaves could produce beyond their immediate subsistence needs. The sale of this produce in the towns and cities allowed the slaves to improve both the quantity and quality of goods available to them and satisfy tastes and desires that the master could not supply. Thus, improvement in the slaves' well-being was due to their own effort, not any amelioration of the regime (Mintz 1974; France. Ministère de la Marine 1844, 110, 188, 303–305; Higman 1976, 129; Soleau 1835, 9–10; France. ANSOM. *Martinique*, Carton 7, Dossier 83, Dupotêt à Ministre de la Marine et des Colonies, Fort Royal, 5 avril 1832).

The slaves developed market networks that were an important feature of the economic and social life of Martinique, and the colony came to rely on the produce of the slave gardens for a substantial portion of its food. Sunday was the major market day in the towns; however, smaller markets were held on other days. Important market towns, such as the ones at Lamentin, François, Trinité, and Robert, attracted slaves from all parts of the island, bringing them into contact with the world beyond the plantation. Soleau, a visitor to the island in 1835, describes the Lamentin market: "This town is one of the most frequently visited by the slaves of the colony. It has a fairly large market where they come to sell their produce on Sunday. I have been told that the number of slaves that gather there is often as high as five or six thousand. I passed through there that day while going to the *quartier* of Robert, and encountered many blacks on the road who were going to the town. All were carrying something that they were doubtlessly going to sell—manioc flour, potatoes, yams, poultry, etc." An astonishing variety of goods were exchanged at the town markets. In addition to manioc, fruits, vegetables, yams, fresh or salted fish, animals, and slave handicrafts, these included manufactured goods such as shoes, dry goods, porcelain, crystal, perfume, jewelry, and furniture. Barter undoubtedly played a large part in these exchanges, especially at local markets, but the money economy was significant, and prices were set in major towns for the main articles of trade. The scale of exchange at these town markets was so great that urban merchants began to complain. But their protests had little effect, for, as one planter noted, the town markets were a great resource for the interior of the island

(Soleau, 1835, 59; France. ANSOM. *Généralités*, Carton 144, Dossier 1221, Exécution de l'ordonance royale 1841–1843, 51; France. ANSOM. *Martinique*, Carton 7, Dossier 83, Mathieu à Ministre de la Marine et des Colonies, 10 mars 847, no. 1508; Sainte-Croix 1822, II, 13–15; De la Cornillère 1843, 123–124).

The Sunday market was as much a social event as an occasion for exchanging goods. Slaves went to town to attend mass, meet friends from other parts of the island, drink tafia, smoke, eat roast corn, exchange news and gossip, and perhaps dance, sing, or gamble. It was an opportunity for display, and the slaves wore their best. An observer painted a striking picture of the appearance of the slaves at the Lamentin market: "These slaves are almost always well-dressed and present the exterior signs of material well-being. The men have trousers, shirts, vests, and hats of oilskin or straw. The women have skirts of Indian cotton, white blouses, and scarves, some of which are luxurious, as well as earrings, pins, and even some chains of gold." According to Soleau, the signs of prosperity presented by slaves of Martinique on market day were unusual in the Caribbean and even rural France: "One thing struck me that I have never seen in Cayenne, Surinam, or Demerara. It is the cleanliness and luxury of the clothing of the slaves that I encountered. The lazy, having nothing to sell, remained on the plantations. In France, generally, the peasants, except for their shoes, were not better dressed on Sunday and did not wear such fine material." The colorful and bustling markets punctuated the drudgery and isolation of plantation life. Slaves from town and country, young and old, male and female, along with freedmen, sailors, merchants, planters, and anyone who wanted to buy and sell, mingled in the crowds. These markets offered incentives to slaves enabling to improve the material conditions of life as well as to acquire skills, knowledge, and social contacts that allowed them to increase their independence, assert their individuality, and vary the texture of their lives. Their initiatives developed new economic and social patterns and mobilized productive forces that otherwise would have remained dormant (De la Cornillère 1843, 123–124; Soleau 1835, 59; France. Ministère de la Marine 1844, 102).

APPROPRIATION

While provision-grounds and free Saturdays never ceased to serve the interests of the slave owner, they were not simply a functional adaptation to the requirements of the plantation economy. Rather, they form what Roger Bastide describes as a "niche" within slavery that allowed collective self-expression by the slaves—a niche where Afro-Caribbean culture could develop. The slaves had complete responsibility for the provision grounds and were thus able to organize their own activities there without supervision. The use of these parcels and their product was not simply a narrow economic activity but was integrated into broader cultural patterns. Preparing the soil, planting, cultivating, harvesting, and disposing of the product were organized through ritual, kinship, and mutual obligation. The provision-grounds were important for aspects of slave life as diverse as kinship, cuisine, and healing practices. There kin were buried, and singing, dancing, and storytelling took place. These practices provided an avenue for the slaves to exercise decision making and demonstrate self-worth that would otherwise have been closed off by slavery. But except for Schoelcher's vague comment that the slaves cultivated them "communally," there is little detailed information on how the slaves organized their activities. This lack of documentation is perhaps mute testimony to the genuine autonomy that the slaves enjoyed in the conduct of these activities (Jean Besson [1984a, 1984b, and 1978] has demonstrated the importance of family land for distinctively Afro-Caribbean conceptions of kinship and property in the free villages of postemancipation Jamaica. See also Melville J. Herskovits 1937, 67–68, 76–81; Schoelcher 1976, 9; Lewis 1929, 88; Bastide 1978, 58).

The provision grounds formed a nodal point within the social relations of slavery that allowed slave practices, values, and interests to emerge and develop and to assume autonomous forms of organization and expression. Long before the promulgation of the Mackau Law, slaves established rights and prerogatives with regard to not only the produce of the land but to the provision grounds and gardens themselves. Masters were compelled to recognize these claims. "The masters no longer acknowledge any rights over the gardens of the *atelier*. The slave is the sovereign master over the terrain that is conceded to him," admits the Colonial Council of Martinique. "This practice has become a custom for the slaves who regard it as a right which cannot be taken from them without the possibility of disrupting the discipline and good order of the *ateliers*," reports one official. Slaves regarded the provision grounds as their own. When they died, the garden and its produce were passed on to their relatives. "They pass them on from father to son, from mother to daughter, and, if they do not have any children, they bequeath them to their nearest kin or even their friends," writes Schoelcher. Often if no relatives remained on the estate, kinsmen came from other plantations to receive their inheritance with the consent of the master. Here, as elsewhere, the autonomous kinship organization of the slave community served as a counterpoint to the economic rationality of the plantation, and the master was obliged to respect its claims (Schoelcher 1976, 9–13; France. Ministère de la Marine 1844, 180–188, 290; France. Ministère de la Marine 1840–1843,

208–209; France. ANSOM. *Généralités*, Carton 144, Dossier 1221, Éxécution de l'ordonnance royale II, 40, 51).

Slaves defended their rights even at the master's expense, and there was
often a subtle game of give and take between the two. While traveling through
the *quartier* of Robert, Schoelcher was surprised to find two small patches of
manioc in the midst of a large, well-tended cane field. The proprietor,
explained that the slaves planted the manioc when the field had been temporarily abandoned. When he wanted to cultivate the field, he offered to buy the
crop, but they demanded an exorbitant price. The master then called upon the
other slaves to set what they considered to be a fair price, but this too was
rejected by the slaves who had planted the manioc. "I'll have to wait six or
seven months until that damned manioc is ripe," the proprietor complained.
Another planter, M. Latuillerie of Lamentin, upon returning from a long trip,
found that his slaves had abandoned the plots allotted to them in favor of his
cane fields. He could not simply reclaim his land. Instead, he first had to agree
to give the occupants another field. Schoelcher also observed large mango
trees in the middle of cane fields which stunted the cane plants in their
shadow. The masters would have cut them down, but they remained standing
because they were bequeathed to some yet unborn slave. He notes that "there
are some planters who do not have fruit trees on their plantations because
tradition establishes that such and such a tree belongs to such and such a
Negro, and they [the planters] have little hope of ever enjoying them because
the slave bequeaths his tree just like the rest of his property (France. Ministère de la Marine 1844, 180–188, 290; Schoelcher 1976, 9–13; France.
ANSOM. *Généralités*, Carton 144, Dossier 1221, Éxécution de l'ordonnance
royale 1841–1843, 40, 51).

The elaboration of autonomous provision-ground cultivation remained
intertwined with and dependent upon the larger organization of plantation
labor not only spatially, but temporally. The practice of the free Saturday
transformed the character of the working day in the French Caribbean. An
examination of this custom calls attention to the historical processes through
which the cultural definitions of work and its relation to the larger matrix of
plantation life were contested. As the slaves became socialized into the routine of plantation labor, they were able to lay claim to the free Saturday and
use it for their own ends. They felt that they had a right to such "free" time
and resisted any encroachment upon it. According to the report of one public
prosecutor published in 1844: "It would be almost impossible for a planter
to take even a little bit of time belonging to his slave, even if the authorities
ignored the situation. There is a spirit of resistance among the slaves that
prevents anyone from threatening what they consider to be their rights."
Another official emphasizes: "There would be discontent if the proprietors
took away the free Saturday to give the provisions prescribed by the edict. . . .

The Negroes prefer this method which assures them of an extra day each week. Everywhere that it has not been adopted the blacks desire it and beg for it. To try to abolish it where it was once been established would be to provoke disorder and revolt" (Mintz 1974; France. Ministère de la Marine 1844, 180–188, 290, 303–305).

The slaves effectively appropriated a part of the disposable labor time as their own. In practice, time on the plantation became divided between time belonging to the master and time belonging to the slaves. The time available for export commodity production was restricted, and the master now had to bargain with the slaves. Time became a kind of currency, and a complex system of time accounting emerged. If masters found that they needed slaves on a Saturday or at another time when they were exempted from labor, such work was voluntary, and slaves were generally compensated for their services. Often, masters indemnified the slaves with an equivalent amount of time rather than money. It was reported that the slaves on one plantation were made to work on Sunday during the harvest but were given the following Monday off. (This report added that the planter would be warned that this change was not in accord with religious rites and the regular habits of the slaves.) On the infrequent occasions when the master of another plantation needed the labor of his slaves on a free Saturday or Sunday for some pressing work, they were given an equivalent amount of time on a weekday. A public prosecutor reported that this planter kept a precise account of the extra time that the slaves put in and indemnified them scrupulously (Mintz 1974; France. Ministère de la Marine 1844, 303–305).

Thus, time belonging to the slaves not only became distinguished from that belonging to the masters but opposed to it. At the extreme, the former encroached upon the latter. For the slaves, the time separate from work became a sphere of autonomous activity—"free" time where they could dispose of their energies as they saw fit and within which they created a community organized around their beliefs, values, and collective action. Their use of this free time could become subversive of plantation discipline. (According to Monk Lewis, a planter in Jamaica, the slaves on his plantation referred to their free Saturday as "play day.") This was especially apparent in the case of the slaves' nocturnal activities. Although prohibited by law from leaving the plantation after dark (and in earlier times the *Code Noir* prescribed whipping and branding and for repeated offenses even death), slaves enjoyed considerable freedom of movement at night. When the masters were asked why slaves were allowed such a fatal liberty, they replied that they were unable to take it away from them. "For the blacks," writes De Cassagnac, "the night is a moment of supreme and incomparable sweetness that the whites will never understand." The night provided an opportunity for the exercise of individual freedom and collective self-expression away from the watchful eye of the authorities. It became the occasion for dancing, music, and religious rites—activities that expressed values antithetical to the subordination of life to work and the rejection of the role of sober, industrious, and self-regulated labor desired by the planters. If the slaves had learned to adapt to the exigencies of plantation labor, they nonetheless refused to reduce themselves to mere instruments of production (Debien 1974, 209; Lavollée 1841, 123–124; Lewis 1929, 81; Peytraud 1973, 156; De Cassagnac 1842, 168, 211; cf. Schoelcher 1976, 53n.; Debbasch 1961, 1962, 131–138).

The free Saturday was important as the appropriation of a quantity of time and as the qualitative transformation of the meaning of that time. Through their activity, slaves were able, in some limited way, to define the nature of freedom for themselves. "Free" time became free for the slave and not merely a period when sugar was not being produced. The appropriation of this time provided a base for the assertion of the slaves' purposes, needs, and cultural forms in other aspects of plantation life, including the organization of work and the composition of the working day. Thus, the free Saturday and the appropriation of free time became significant because of the consequences for the material reproduction of the enslaved population and as an arena in which the slaves were able to contest the conditions of domination and exploitation and the conceptions of social life imposed by the plantation regime. While slaves regarded "free" time as a resource to be protected and, if possible expanded, masters had to contain the slaves' demands within the limits of economic efficiency and social order. In the development of this process, the historical trajectory and limits of slave production and the master-slave relation can be traced.

Instead of separating the direct producers from the means of subsistence, slavery provided them with the means of producing a livelihood. While slaves gained access to the use of property and the opportunity to improve the material conditions of life, the price of subsistence was work beyond that required for sugar production. With these developments, the time devoted to the slaves, maintenance became separate from commodity production and a *de facto* distinction between time belonging to the master and time belonging to the slave was created.

The planters responded to the slaves' appropriation of the free Saturday by attempting to transform their initiative into an instrument of labor discipline and social control. During the 1830s planters in Martinique implemented a system of task work to induce slaves to work and guarantee the performance of a given amount of labor during the day. Through experience, planters were able to calculate for each of the different types of work to be done on the plantation how much the average slave could do in a day without being overworked. Every morning each slave in the gang was assessed his or her daily task based upon this customary amount of labor. On the one hand, slaves could do their daily quota of work as they liked and were free to dispose of the time remaining after its completion as they wished. Under the task system slaves might gain several hours each day which could be spent in the cultivation of their own gardens or in some other employment. The slaves thus had the opportunity to improve their condition, while slave owners obtained the required amount of labor. On the other hand, slaves who did not use the time well had to spend the whole day working in the masters' fields in order to complete the required task. The punishment was proportional to the effort, or lack thereof, and if the slaves' failure to meet their assignment was too great, their free day could be jeopardized (Soleau 1835, 8–10).

Task work could only function when the slave population had sufficiently assimilated the routine of plantation labor to respond to its incentives. For self-regulation to replace external domination, slaves had to understand and accept the rhythm of work, organization of time, and system of rewards and punishments that characterized the plantation regime. Only then could the notion of free time appear as a reward to the slave. Only if the slaves formed a concept of their self-interest and appropriated time for themselves within this larger framework could the task system operate and the larger appropriation of the slaves' activity by the master take place. Such slave initiative and planter response contributed to the mutation of the relations of work. Once slaves had a recognized interest, their relation to the master could no longer rest upon absolute domination and authority. Instead, that relation had to admit bargaining and negotiation between interested parties—however unequal and antagonistic their relationship. Thus, implementation of task work marked a further transformation of the master-slave relation; it bears witness to the adaptation of the African slave to the American environment that was both cause and effect of this change (Soleau 1835, 8–9; Brathwaite 1971, 298–299).

Provision-ground cultivation and task work suggest the limits of pure coercion as a means of enforcing labor discipline. Their success was dependent upon the integration of the enslaved population into the productive and social processes of the slave plantation. For these measures to work, both master and slave had to recognize the existence of certain privileges and at least a limited degree of independence for the slave. Paradoxically, however, both master and slave became more closely tied to the maintenance of these privileges. The possible range of action for each was restricted, and the character if not the content of labor relations was altered decisively.

Task work was thus an expression of the social limit of the slave relation. While planters might influence individual behavior and set the parameters for the action of the group through the systematic manipulation of rewards and punishments, such measures merely adapted the slaves to the existing organization of production—with a greater or lesser degree of freedom on the part of the slaves. The task system guaranteed the completion of a minimum amount of work and perhaps reduced the costs of supervision, but it did not alter the composition of the working day or increase surplus production. The self-interest created by this system was not a reward earned through commodity-producing activity, but was formed outside of this work and through a release from it. After slaves completed their predetermined task, they were free to look after their own affairs; literally, they were free to tend their own gardens. Such as system might provide slaves with an incentive to give a bit more of themselves, but it demonstrated the incapacity of slavery to create self-interest in production itself. Rather, individual self-interest and identification with the job and the plantation were created not in commodity production but in social reproduction. The economy of time and labor was dissolved into the maintenance of a given body of laborers on the one hand and the regular performance of a predetermined quantity of labor on the other: It thus resolved itself into a social-political question as the master-slave relation was challenged from within.

The slaves' appropriation of the free Saturday by the slaves and their autonomous elaboration of the activities associated with it had far-reaching consequences for the development of slavery in the French West Indies and helped to shape the historical limits of the slave system in Martinique. It was an initiative by a population that, over the course of its historical experience, had learned to adapt to the labor routine, discipline, and organization of time of the slave plantation and confronted slavery *within* its own relations and processes. The result was to simultaneously strengthen and weaken the slave system. On the one hand, the slaves became more effectively integrated into slavery and responsive to its rewards and punishments. The operating expenses of the plantation were reduced, and a greater surplus was available to the planter. On the other hand, the slaves were able to appropriate aspects of these processes and thereby establish a degree of control over their own subsistence and reproduction. They claimed rights to property and disposition over time and labor that the masters were forced to recognize, and they were able to resist infringements upon those rights. While provision-ground cultivation meant more work for the slaves, they were able to substantially improve their material well-being and increase their independence from the master. They restricted the master's capacity to exploit labor and presented a fixed obstacle to surplus production. The amount of labor time at the disposition of the planter was limited, and the slaves acquired a means of resisting the intensification of work at the very moment that the transformation of the world sugar market demanded higher levels of productivity and greater exploitation of labor from French West Indian plantations.

The very ability of masters to compel the participation of slaves in the new conditions of life and labor and the complexity and originality of the slaves' response altered the character of the master-slave relation. Within the context of continuing domination, exploitation, and material scarcity, new forms, meanings, and goals of social action emerged alongside older ones, becoming the focal points of a new constellation of conditions, needs, and capacities on both sides. The slaves' assertion of rights to provision-grounds and free time and the autonomous use of these resources reduced their dependence on the master and undermined his authority. Custom, consent, and accommodation assumed greater weight in the conduct of daily life, where coercion had prevailed. The acquisition of skills and property and the establishment of economic and social networks enabled the enslaved to realize important material and psychological gains. The slaves thus began to fashion an alternative way of life that played an important role not only in eroding the slave regime but also in creating a transition to a new form of social and economic organization. Slaves' struggles for autonomy and planters' efforts to maintain their domination developed the slave relation to its fullest extent and created within slavery both the embryo of postemancipation class structure and the conditions for the transition to "free labor" (Mintz 1974).

Significantly, the autonomous provision-ground cultivation and marketing elaborated within slavery provided free people with an alternative to plantation labor after emancipation. These activities played an important role in helping the former slaves to resist the new encroachments of plantation agriculture and shape a new relation between labor and capital. The very practices that planters had encouraged during slavery now incurred their wrath. Carlyle scorned Quashee and his pumpkin, but far from representing the "lazy Negro," Carlyle's ridicule was testimony to the capacity of the Afro-Caribbean population to learn, adapt, create, and articulate an alternative conception of their needs, despite the harshness of slavery. Probably few could escape the plantation entirely after emancipation, but provision-ground cultivation and marketing networks enabled for the great majority of the freed slaves to struggle effectively over the conditions of their labor. The skills, resources, and associations formed through these activities during slavery were of decisive importance in enabling the free population to secure control over their own conditions of reproduction and establish an independent bargaining position vis-à-vis the planters after slavery (Hall 1978).

The immediate consequences of emancipation in Martinique, as throughout the French and British Caribbean, were the withdrawal of labor—particularly the labor of women and children—from the plantation sector and from the struggles with the planters over time, wages, and conditions of work, struggles in which the laboring population asserted its independence and initiative. The success of these efforts forced a new relation of production on the plantation system itself as the planters attempted to recapture the labor of the emancipated population or find a substitute for it under conditions that guaranteed profitability. This resulted in the formation of new coercive forms of labor extraction in which the laboring population maintained control over subsistence activities and petty commodity production to one degree or another. Seen from this perspective, the reconstruction of the postemancipation plantation system and the transition from one form of coerced labor to another were not the inevitable results of unfolding capitalist rationality. Rather, both were processes whose outcome was problematic, requiring violence and compulsion on the part of the planters and the colonial state to reassert control over labor in the face of material and social resources acquired by the laboring population while still enslaved. The transition is best understood as the product of the contradictory relation between production and social reproduction within slavery and of the struggle between masters and slaves over alternative purposes, conceptions of needs, and modes of organization of social and material life.

Chapter Nine

Contested Terrains

Houses, Provision Grounds, and the Reconstitution of Labor in Postemancipation Martinique

The history of slave emancipation in the French West Indian colony of Martinique suggests the complexity of social forces and political projects involved
in the abolition of slavery. (Slavery was first abolished in the French colonies
in 1792 by the government of the First Republic only to be restored by Napo-
leon in 1802. In 1830, the government of the July Monarchy committed itself
in principle to slave emancipation but, after eighteen years of debate, was
unable to reach agreement on the proper formula for emancipation. The final
abolition of slavery accompanied the Revolution of 1848 and the establishment of the Second Republic in France.) To speak schematically, a "revolution from above" converged with a "revolution from below." The Revolution
of 1848 brought anti-slavery forces to power in France. Most notably, Victor
Schoelcher, the most vigorous and uncompromising advocate of immediate
emancipation and the symbol of French anti-slavery, became undersecretary
of state for the Colonies and was later elected deputy to the National Assembly for Martinique and Guadeloupe. Under his tutelage, one of the first acts
of the provisional government (March 4, 1848) was to declare its intention to
abolish slavery immediately. A commission was appointed under Schoelcher's direction to organize the transition to freedom; emancipation was
decreed on April 27, 1848. Ironically, the arrival in Martinique of the news
of the fall of the July Monarchy provoked a local slave uprising (May 22–23,
1848) which compelled authorities in the colony to declare slavery abolished
before word of emancipation arrived from France.

The slave uprising appears to have been an episodic flash. Little overt resistance followed upon the May events. Nonetheless, in the aftermath of emancipation, metropolitan authorities, colonial planters and the freed population engaged in a struggle over the political and social organization of labor and property, and, consequently, the nature and content of the new freedom. Central to this confrontation was the disposition of houses, provision grounds, and other resources to which the laboring population had established customary rights while still enslaved. Slaves in nineteenth-century Martinique engaged in extensive provision-ground cultivation, fishing, gathering, and handicraft production both for their own consumption and for sale in local markets. By developing such proto-peasant activities, they not only improved the material quality of their lives but also established customary rights to property and to free time. They thus fashioned a sphere of independent activity, at once within and against the slave relation, that allowed them to assert their own needs, purposes, and cultural forms (see chapter 8). With the end of slavery, the laboring population consolidated and expanded these practices in an effort to redefine the character and purposes of plantation labor and its place in social life.

Sidney Mintz has emphasized the importance of house and yard, provision ground, and internal markets for understanding the subtle yet significant processes of adaptation and resistance through which Afro-Caribbean slaves sought to shape their material and social environment during slavery and after (Mintz 1964, 1979, 1982; Mintz and Hall 1960). His approach suggests the links between slavery and postemancipation developments as well as the originality and the diversity of Caribbean peasantries, and, indeed, of Caribbean history.

This perspective has properly drawn the attention of scholars to the movement of freed populations off the estates; the acquisition of land by squatting, purchase, or rental; and the diverse ways in which subsistence and market production combined with plantation labor in the peasant households. However, the historical experience of emancipation in Martinique calls attention to another dimension of the interrelation of proto-peasant practices and the formation of a plantation labor force. Rather than deserting the plantation, the freed population of Martinique sought to redefine the character of plantation labor while remaining resident on the estate. House and yard, provision ground, and the activities associated with them emerged as strategic terrains of contention in the attempts to fashion the postemancipation labor regime. They provided the former slaves with a means of controlling the conditions of their labor and resisting the reimposition of work routines and labor discipline even as they were being incorporated into the internal organization of the plantation.

This chapter investigates the reconstruction of labor relations in Martinique during the first nine months of the Second Republic. It is particularly concerned with the ways in which housing and provision grounds were implicated in the struggles to reconstitute a labor force and maintain sugar production after emancipation. It draws primarily on the correspondence of François-Auguste Perrinon, commissioner general of the Republic and member of the Schoelcher Commission, between his arrival in Martinique in June 1848 and his departure in October of that same year. Perrinon undertook a series of tours of the rural districts to implement the emancipation decrees and organize labor. His correspondence documents not only the ways in which workers sought to subordinate the rhythm and organization of work to their individual and collective needs in the first moments after emancipation but also the attempts of the Republican regime to regulate labor and property. (The majority of this material is contained in France. Archives Nationales. Section Outre-Mer [hereafter ANSOM]. *Martinique*, Carton 56, Dossier 464. Unless otherwise specified, all further citations of Perrinon's correspondence refer to this source.)

THE AFTERMATH OF EMANCIPATION

Martinique's plantation system was in crisis even before emancipation. Although sugar cane had been cultivated there since the mid-seventeenth century, the island's sugar industry underwent intensive development during the first half of the nineteenth century after the Haitian Revolution deprived France of its wealthiest colony. New plantations were established and old ones increased their output. More land and labor were devoted to sugar at the expense of other crops. By 1847, there were 498 sugar plantations in Martinique. Cane was cultivated on 19,735 hectares and 32,093 metric tons of sugar were produced (France. ANSOM. Martinique, *État des cultures*). The largest and most productive plantations were in the series of fertile valleys running along the northeast coast and on the broad alluvial plain of Lamentin. Plantations in the arid south were smaller and less productive. Despite the rapid growth of sugar monoculture during the first part of the nineteenth century, the end of the slave trade and the reemergence of beet sugar industry in France after 1830 dramatically altered the conditions of production. Unable to renew their labor supply, colonial planters were forced to compete with a dynamic and technically more efficient rival within the French market. As the price of sugar steadily declined, they were unable either to expand onto new land or to modify the social and technical organization of the plantation to reduce costs. Instead, they were compelled to intensify production and increase output within the existing framework. Even as they produced more sugar, they became increasingly impoverished and indebted (Tomich 1990).

With the coming of freedom, some former slaves abandoned life on the plantation and went to settle in the towns. Others occupied land in the mountainous interior of the island or on abandoned estates, by either squatting or purchase; there, they engaged in producing various combinations of subsistence and market crops. If and when members of either group required additional income, they could provide a source of casual labor for the plantations. However, despite the planters' fears that slaves would abandon the plantations after emancipation, the great majority of the rural population remained resident on the estates and engaged in sugar production. Of the 40,429 slaves employed in the production of sugar in 1847, 27,006, or about two-thirds, remained as free workers in 1848 (France. ANSOM. Martinique, *État des cultures*; France. ANSOM, *Martinique*, Carton 11, Dossier 109, Bruat à Ministre de la Marine et des Colonies, Fort-de-France, 9 novembre 1848). Upon his arrival in the colony in June 1848, Perrinon reported that there were few sugar plantations on the island where the present harvest or future harvests were compromised by the inaction of the *nouveaux affranchis* and that in the districts (*quartiers*) of François, Gros-Morne, and Lamentin cultivation had been resumed by the *ateliers* (work gangs) with all the intensity of the past (Perrinon à Ministre de la Marine et des Colonies, St. Pierre, 29 juin 1848). Perrinon was favorably impressed with the capacity of the former slaves to adapt to the rights and duties of freedmen, and was enthusiastic about the possibility of maintaining the continuity of production. He noted the excellent disposition of the great majority of *affranchis* and thought that their remarkable sense of order, dignity, propriety, and hope for the future would have a favorable impact on the island's production (France. ANSOM. *Martinique*, Carton 11, Dossier 108, Perrinon à Ministre de la Marine et des Colonies, Fort-de-France, 8 octobre 1848).

In contrast, the planters were demoralized and had lost political initiative. Deprived of slavery as a source of labor and means of social control, they were faced with unrest and uncertainty at home and their adversaries in power in the metropolis. "The obstacles," Perrinon observes, "do not always emanate from the cultivators, but rather from the proprietors" (Perrinon à Ministre de la Marine et des Colonies, St. Pierre, 29 juin 1848). Some former slaveholders, afraid of a general insurrection, or perhaps of their creditors, abandoned their properties and fled the countryside or even the island, often taking their liquid assets with them. (The Decree of April 27 for the first time permitted sugar plantations to be seized for debt.) Others broke their estates into small plots and rented them to freedmen. Still others sold their property or lost it to their creditors (Renard 1973, 41–42). Although Perrinon encountered some local disorders, he reported that their origins were less in the insubordination of the freed population than in "the impudence of the former masters, some of whom have taken refuge in Saint Pierre leaving their plantations vacant and refusing to send representatives to negotiate with the laborers." He cautioned that the inactivity of these plantations could become a bad example for the colony (Perrinon à Ministre de la Marine et des Colonies, St. Pierre, 29 juin 1848).

However, since emancipation came during the harvest season, there was great pressure to bring in the standing crop and manufacture sugar. Under these conditions, most planters, at times aided by municipal administrations, spontaneously reorganized work and improvised new forms of labor relations in conjunction with the workers. In order to maintain an adequate and regular labor force, planters allowed the former slaves to keep their cabins and provision grounds, and, as during slavery, free Saturdays to grow and market their own crops. Wage labor was uncommon. Except on the larger and more prosperous plantations in the northern part of the island, few planters had sufficient cash with which to pay wages, especially in the absence of an indemnity for their "lost property" (Perrinon à Ministre de la Marine et des Colonies, Macouba, 10 juillet 1848). Even where wages were paid, they could be the simple allocation of money or goods or both in kind that the proprietors and the workers arranged among themselves. More common were various sharecropping arrangements (*contrats d'association*). Workers received a portion of the proceeds from the sugar crop, generally either a half or a third, in return for their services. Depending upon how the crop was divided, the costs of production fell upon the proprietors alone or were shared jointly with the workers (Perrinon à Ministre de la Marine et des Colonies, St. Pierre, 29 juin 1848).

The income from sugar production, whether as wages, shares, or profits, whether in money or kind, may have represented an important economic resource for the laboring population. Indeed, Perrinon reports a number of estates where workers themselves organized cane production under the direction of the former slave drivers after the planter or overseer deserted the property. Beyond purely economic considerations, Perrinon emphasized the attachment of most new citizens to their birthplace: "Leaving the plantation on which they had previously been employed is generally repugnant to them." Because of this sentiment, emigration and changes of occupation were rare. In his view, such a disposition, which he sharply contrasted to the situation following emancipation in the British West Indies, ensured public order, the success of agriculture, and the interests of the proprietors of the soil (Perrinon à Ministre de la Marine et des Colonies, Macouba, 10 juillet 1848; Perrinon à Ministre de la Marine et des Colonies, St. Pierre, 29 juin

1848; Perrinon à Ministre de la Marine et des Colonies, Fort-de-France, 21 octobre 1848).

Yet, despite Perrinon's optimism about the attitude of labor, he encountered a stubborn refusal to submit to conditions that recalled slavery. Thus in Trou-au-Chat, Perrinon reports that

> The attitude is good, but there as almost everywhere else, exactitude of labor is lacking. The associated workers do not completely give the days and hours agreed upon. Subordination to an overseer is repugnant to them as is submitting to roll-call. They see in these formalities reminders of slavery. (Perrinon à Ministre de la Marine et des Colonies, Fort-de-France, 21 octobre 1848)

Similarly, in Vauclin, a prosperous commune during slavery, Perrinon describes the laborers as docile and intelligent. Nonetheless, the commune is distinguished by the difficult and insubordinate attitude of its workers.

> They believe themselves exempt from coming to work at fixed hours or at any time other than at their own convenience, from receiving direction from the proprietor or the overseer, and finally from keeping the commitments that they find too demanding or too analogous to the obligations of slavery. (Perrinon à Ministre de la Marine et des Colonies, Fort-de-France, 21 octobre 1848)

The newly freed workers responded to emancipation not by open resistance, but by a persistent refusal to submit to supervision and regular hours of work. They utilized the threat of unrest, the fear of a labor shortage, and the need to harvest the current sugar crop to assert their control over houses, provision grounds, and petty marketing activities and to thereby contest the conditions of life and labor on the sugar estates.

HOUSE, YARD, PROVISION GROUND, AND THE STRUGGLE OVER LABOR

Attachment to their houses and provision grounds was a fundamental factor in keeping the former slaves resident on the plantations. (All slaves stayed in housing furnished by the master. There were, in general, three types of slave houses in Martinique: those made of stone or masonry with tile roofs; those made of boards with straw roofs; and those made with bamboo laths plastered with mud, also with straw roofs. Some houses, particularly those of stone or masonry, were well built, but much of the housing was poorly built and maintained. The cabin, whichever the type, was generally sixteen to twenty feet long and twelve feet wide. A partition divided it into a kitchen and a sleeping room. There was no chimney and the only light came through the door which was never more than four feet high. The house belonged to the master, and there is little evidence of slaves trying to improve their houses or using their free time to build one. Perrinon found only a single worker who furnished the material for the construction of his house at his own expense during the slave regime. But whatever the condition of the house, it was a private space, a place where slaves could escape the surveillance of the master. They jealously guarded this privacy. Schoelcher writes that the slaves did not like whites to enter their homes, and some masters only showed him the slave quarters with great discretion (France. Ministère de la Marine et des Colonies 1844, 267–281; Schoelcher 1976, 2–4; Perrinon à Ministre de la Marine et des Colonies, Fort-de-France, 21 octobre 1848). During slavery, house, yard, and provision ground were sources of shelter, a more adequate and varied diet, and perhaps marketable produce. They formed "niches" within the slave system that allowed slave families to improve the quantity and quality of goods available to them and permitted individual and collective self-expression. They were thus interwoven in a multiplicity of ways with the formation of proto-peasant activities, slave community, and Afro-Caribbean culture.

With the coming of emancipation, the freed population treated such property as their own. Reasserting customary rights established under slavery, they refused to abandon their houses and provision grounds or to compensate the planters for their use. According to Perrinon: "There generally exists among the workers a very pronounced pretension regarding the possession of houses and gardens. Persuaded of their right to property, they refuse to abandon their customary premises and believe that they should be able to continue to enjoy them without having to make arrangements with the real proprietor" (Perrinon à Ministre de la Marine et des Colonies, Fort-de-France, 19 août 1848; Perrinon à Ministre de la Marine et des Colonies, Fort-de-France, 21 octobre 1848). Not only did the workers' attempt to consolidate their hold on houses and provision grounds engender conflict with planters and the colonial state over property rights but by asserting control over these resources the workers were able to expand individual and collective resistance to the imposition of work routines and labor discipline and even to subordinate the plantation to their domestic economy.

According to Perrinon, wage labor enjoyed great prestige in the eyes of the newly emancipated workers, and they greatly preferred it to *association*. However, while workers asserted their claims to houses and provision grounds, they frequently refused to labor on the estate where they lived. They would either work on another plantation or, if they possessed sufficient resources, live off the income of their garden plot or other subsidiary occupations. In Lamentin, a major sugar district, Perrinon reported a number of plantations where few of the former slaves who remained resident on the property worked there. They preferred instead to hire themselves out elsewhere for a franc a day. Thus, on the Volmenier estate, thirty-five individuals were employed, but only eight were former slaves on the plantation. The workers constantly rejected *association*. Production was instead carried on with the assistance of day laborers from outside the property for a wage of one franc a day (Perrinon à Ministre de la Marine et des Colonies, Fort-de-France, 21 octobre 1848; Perrinon à Ministre de la Marine et des Colonies, Fort-de-France, 19 août 1848). Similarly, the new citizens on the nearby Prix Garnier estate all kept their houses and gardens against the wishes of the proprietor and hired themselves out as day laborers on the neighboring plantations (Perrinon à Ministre de la Marine et des Colonies, Fort-de-France, 19 août 1848).

If pervasive efforts by workers to separate the places of work and residence reduced their dependence on the planter and increased their space for maneuver, from the perspective of the landowner, such initiatives subverted labor discipline and undermined the effectiveness of wage labor (for a comparison with Jamaica, see Hall 1978, 7–23). For many planters, even for those who could afford to pay wages, labor by the day or week was unsuitable. It resulted in an unstable and irregular labor force that was not subject to discipline. In the words of one planter, wage labor demoralized the Negro and maintained "all of his habits of insubordination and capricious idleness." He complained that it was impossible to force the Blacks to perform the amount of work agreed upon for a day or week and that controls could not be established to verify that work was done properly. They arrived late, put down their tools, returned to their homes, or followed any other whim—but the proprietor still had to pay them their wage. Irregular and undependable labor resulted in growing losses. Extensive fields were left uncultivated. Slow and careless manufacture reduced the quantity and quality of the sugar. Production declined to the point of ruining the planter. Recourse to the local magistrates provided no relief. It was so difficult for planters to obtain laborers that they did not dare to take their complaints to the authorities for fear that the workers would abandon the plantation (Charroppin 1848, 9–10).

In the absence of generalized wage labor, the majority of rural laborers worked on the plantations where they resided. However, although *association* gave them a stake in sugar production, the former slaves were not profit maximizers. Instead, they utilized their control over houses and provisions grounds to define their labor around a variety of activities that included not only cane cultivation and manufacture but also the production and marketing of crops from their provision grounds, fishing, pottery making, and charcoal burning. They not only rejected regular hours of work and the supervision of overseers but appropriated the labor time of the estate and sought to subordinate *association* to their own purposes. Thus, for example, in the commune of Saint Anne, Perrinon reports:

> The associated workers whether on half or on third shares, all take Friday to cultivate their gardens, to fish, to make pottery or other objects of personal interest. On the four days that they do work, none of them furnish the hours due to the society. (Perrinon à Ministre de la Marine et des Colonies, Trou-au-Chat, 9 octobre 1848)

Similarly, in St. Luce and Diamant, where *association* by half shares prevailed, almost the entire former population remained in occupation of its houses. Workers combined fishing with agriculture. Perrinon reported that estate labor was weak and irregular. "Work is deserted on Fridays and irregularly done on the other days. Management is not recognized. Property right to houses and gardens are contested" (Perrinon à Ministre de la Marine et des Colonies, Fort-de-France, 21 octobre 1848; Perrinon à Ministre de la Marine et des Colonies, Trou-au-Chat, 9 octobre 1848). There was widespread resistance to his efforts to regularize labor in these districts. Perrinon reported similar appropriations of labor time elsewhere in the south. The population of neighboring Trois-Ilets was described as insubordinate, inexact in the hours of work, and disposed to desert work altogether on Fridays (Perrinon à Ministre de la Marine et des Colonies, Fort-de-France, 21 octobre 1848). Even in Rivière Pilote, where Perrinon recorded that *association* was operating reasonably well, he nonetheless had to demonstrate to the laborers "the necessity and the advantages of exactitude of daily labor and of five days due to the society" (Perrinon à Ministre de la Marine et des Colonies, Trou-au-Chat, 9 octobre 1848).

FREEDOM, PROPERTY, AND ORDER

Although some of the arrangements between planters and workers had been legalized by the competent municipal authorities and had the status of contracts even before Perrinon's arrival, the majority of such agreements, whether for wage labor or *association*, were provisory. In general, the parties waited for the Commissioner General's arrival in order to regularize these relationships by registering them as legally valid contracts (Perrinon à Ministre de la Marine et des Colonies, St. Pierre, 29 juin 1848). Perrinon was faced with the problem of reconciling Republican political principles and the idea of liberty with the necessity of maintaining a viable labor force and social order in the colony (Perrinon à Ministre de la Marine et des Colonies, Fort-de-France, 21 octobre 1848). While an uncompromising enemy of slavery and partisan of immediate and general emancipation, he saw the maintenance of the sugar industry as the only alternative for the colonial economy (see Schoelcher 1847, II, 373–380). He sought to secure labor, but without coercion. In his view, "all compulsion . . . would be incompatible with the principles of liberty. Furthermore, it would be impolitic and would become a source of danger for the colonies because the freed population would only see the continuation of servitude in every attempt of that nature." Instead, he defined the goal of his mission as ensuring equitable arrangements for a prompt return to labor and educating former masters and slaves in their new rights and duties (cited in Renard 1973, 74).

For Perrinon, the problems arising from the arrangements that had been made between planters and workers were minor ones that would be resolved when the new basis of freedom was established. The very existence of these acts, the good faith and ease with which they were made, were, for him, proof that the abolition of slavery was not the abolition of labor. In his view: "The principal difficulty in the present situation resides uniquely in the mode of remuneration applicable to labor. The urgency of this latter problem is generally recognized" (Perrinon à Ministre de la Marine et des Colonies, St. Pierre, 29 juin 1848).

While there were some successful examples of plantations operating with wage labor, Perrinon was persuaded that the extreme poverty of the colony precluded wage labor as a viable option and that *association* was more suited to the conditions prevailing in Martinique (Perrinon à Ministre de la Marine et des Colonies, Fort-de-France, 21 octobre 1848). In his view, the benefits of *association* were social, moral, and economic. It provided the best way to educate the laboring classes, create habits of order, and reestablish mutual trust between proprietors and workers. It would thereby revive and perfect agricultural labor, increase production, and bring the country to its fullest prosperity. Indeed, he was so convinced of the superiority of *association* that he envisioned converting to it even those plantations where wage labor was successful. (Perrinon speculated that wages ought to provide a transition to *association*. "I have the conviction that substantial sums of money circulated in the colony would be an immense benefit for agriculture, by giving the proprietors the means of preparing the workers for association and of leading them there bit by bit provisionally from the wage, the most efficacious means of establishing confidence among the parties." Perrinon à Ministre de la Marine et des Colonies, Fort-de-France, 19 août 1848; Perrinon à Ministre de la Marine et des Colonies, Fort-de-France, 21 octobre 1848; Perrinon à Ministre de la Marine et des Colonies, Macouba, 10 juillet 1848; Renard 1973, 74.)

By modifying the experience of several successful planters, Perrinon formulated a standardized contract of *association* (*contrat d'association*) and propagated it throughout the colony. "This document," he writes, "seems to me to satisfy the needs of the moment and equitably assure the rights of workers and proprietors" (Perrinon à Ministre de la Marine et des Colonies, Macouba, 10 juillet 1848). With it, he sought to create model plantations that would educate former masters and former slaves to the new conditions of production.

The contract formed an annually renewable *association* between the owner and the worker for the exploitation of the estate. The proprietor provided land, animals, machinery, and buildings (except the owners' house). These became the property of the *association*. The associated workers had to provide for their own food, clothing, and care when sick. They had the right to enjoy the use of houses and gardens on the property. Saturdays were set aside for the cultivation of their provision grounds and the sale of its produce. The contract prohibited workers from keeping animals other than pigs and fowl (France. ANSOM. *Martinique*, Carton 56, Dossier 464. *Projet d'Association Formulé sous l'Approbation du Commissaire Général, pour l'Exploitation des Usines à Sucre de la Colonie, soit Tiers Brut, soit à la Moitié Nette*).

The workday was set at nine hours a day. The laborers were to divide themselves into work groups and designate one of their number to act as chief. The latter was to work alongside the others. In exchange for their labor, the workers received a portion of the crop. There were two ways of sharing the product of the *association*. In the first, the product was divided into three equal parts: one for the owner; one for the expenses of the society; and one for the workers. In the second, after having deducted the expenses of the society, the remaining product was divided in halves between owner and workers. Division among the workers was to be made after the manufacture or after sale of the produce. Each associate was to receive a part proportional to the number of working days he or she furnished to the society (France. ANSOM. *Martinique*, Carton 56, Dossier 464. *Projet d'Association . . . pour l'Exploitation des Usines à Sucre de la Colonie*).

Further, the workers elected from among their ranks a council of five members who were to resolve any difficulties that might arise among them. They presided over the division of shares among the workers and served as the intermediary between the workers and the proprietor or the administrator. In addition, the council determined the size and location of provision grounds, assigned responsibility for collective tasks such as watching animals or collecting fodder for them. Finally, the council had the right to exclude workers from the *association* for misconduct or laziness (France. ANSOM. *Martinique*, Carton 56, Dossier 464. *Projet d'Association . . . pour l'Exploitation des Usines à Sucre de la Colonie*).

This contract demonstrates Perrinon's attempt not only to subordinate proto-peasant activities to sugar cultivation but to transform them into mechanisms of labor discipline and social control. On the one hand, the use of housing and provision grounds were made conditional upon labor for the estate. On the other hand, the owners' property rights to land, buildings, and other assets were secured and used to constrain the activities of the laborers. In addition, aspects of worker self-organization were incorporated into the operation of the estate, and the half or third share of the crop due to the associated workers promised greater reward than did the wage. The workers' direct stake in the success of the plantation was to replace the coercion of slavery with self-interest. In this way, Perrinon attempted to reconcile freedom, labor, and property; to balance the interests of planters and workers; and to create a stable and disciplined labor force bound to the estate.

Perrinon initiated a series of tours of the colony's rural districts in order to "organize agricultural labor and, at the same time, enlighten the new citizens about their true interests as well as their duties" (France. ANSOM. *Martinique*, Carton 11, Dossier 108, Perrinon à Ministre de la Marine et des Colonies, Fort-de-France, 8 octobre 1848; Perrinon à Ministre de la Marine et des Colonies, Macouba, 10 juillet 1848). In order to establish his model of *association*, Perrinon urged severe measures in order to chase off those "idlers" who attempted to keep their houses and their gardens without making arrangements with the proprietors. He comments, "Many of them seem to ignore the limits of their rights in this respect and insist in wanting to remain in possession of their houses and gardens without any compensation for the proprietor" (Perrinon à Ministre de la Marine et des Colonies, Fort-de-France, 19 août 1848). Thus, he exhorted the laborers to enter into contracts of *association* with the owners, but used the clause regarding vagrancy in the April 27 emancipation decree to expel from the property any workers who failed to enter into such an agreement. (However, it should also be noted that he often delayed evictions until the crops in the provision grounds were harvested. During the deliberations of the Schoelcher Commission, Citizen Chéry, a member of the delegation of Blacks and mulattos, claimed that since the slave generally built his own cabin, it belonged to him. However, in response to Perrinon's question, he conceded that, although the slaves built the houses, the land belonged to the master and that the latter had the right to compel the *affranchis* to leave. During this exchange, Schoelcher stated that the cabin could not be treated as the slave's property as it was constructed with materials furnished by the master and during work time belonging to him (France. ANSOM. *Généralités*, Carton 43, Dossier 350, Procès-Verbaux des délibérations de la Commission Schoelcher, 45–46. Perrinon à Ministre de la Marine et des Colonies, Fort-de-France, 21 octobre 1848). Perrinon reports from his tour, "I have only found a single worker who has furnished the material for the construction of his house at his own expense during the slave regime. At my suggestion, the proprietor consented to indemnify him although he was not obliged to do so by the law" (Perrinon à Ministre de la Marine et des Colonies, Fort-de-France, 21 octobre 1848; Perrinon à Ministre de la Marine et des Colonies, Fort-de-France, 19 août 1848). Of such expulsions, Perrinon remarks: "But what are these petty inconveniences in the presence of such evident hope that emerges from them for the organization of agricultural labor with free laborers, for the future of the country" (Perrinon à Ministre de la Marine et des Colonies, Fort-de-France, 21 octobre 1848).

For Perrinon, the purpose of such evictions was not simply to expel unsubmissive workers from the plantation and secure order and discipline. They were also intended to provide the new citizens with a moral lesson regarding the nature of the relation of liberty and property in the new order. Thus, on the Trompeuse estate in Lamentin, where a part of the *atelier* worked on shares, but the remainder kept possession of their cabins and gardens while refusing to join the *association*, Perrinon reports:

> I congratulated the associates on their laudable conduct, I caused several admissions in the society, and finally, I made the recalcitrant ones understand that though they are entirely free in the legal limit of their behavior and their will, they cannot restrict the liberty nor violate the property of another by remaining against his wishes in possession of his things. These individuals will leave in a week if they have not enrolled in the society by that time. (Perrinon à Ministre de la Marine et des Colonies, Fort-de-France, 19 août 1848)

For Perrinon, the changes of place, of habits, and of supervision resulting from eviction were among the most important elements in the success of his undertaking. "Such workers, demanding and insubordinate with their former master in the place where they live with the memories and habits of slavery, are the most docile and hard-working when a change of residence makes them understand that it is at the price of their labor that they acquire the enjoyment of house and garden as well as the benefits [*bénéfices*] that provide them with the means of existence" (Perrinon à Ministre de la Marine et des Colonies, Fort-de-France, 21 octobre 1848).

Perrinon also moved vigorously to suppress what he viewed as excessive involvement in secondary activities and to subordinate them to plantation labor and sugar cultivation. He not only sought to delimit the extent of provision grounds, but to restrict other practices such as fishing and charcoal burning (Perrinon à Ministre de la Marine et des Colonies, Trou-au-Chat, 9 octobre 1848). The unrestrained development of these activities infringed upon the property rights of the owner, disrupted discipline, and reduced the labor time available for estate agriculture. Thus, in Vauclin, he prohibited charcoal making and fishing during the hours of work due to the *association*. From Marin, he reports: "My exhortations have attempted to . . . have the cultivators give all the time that they owe to the society and to make them understand that they cannot, without the formal consent of the proprietor dispose of the wood in order to make charcoal for their individual profit" (Perrinon à Ministre de la Marine et des Colonies, Trou-au-Chat, 9 octobre 1848). Similarly, while in Case Pilote, he recommended restrictions on the unauthorized production of charcoal made in the proprietors' forest, arguing that this activity not only violated property rights, but greatly harmed cultivation (Perrinon à Ministre de la Marine et des Colonies, Fort-de-France, 21 octobre 1848).

Beyond asserting property rights, social order, and labor discipline, Perrinon's restrictions were intended to provide workers with a lesson in self-interest and comparative advantage. He urged workers to maximize the return to their labor by devoting their efforts to the more profitable sugar production instead of provision-ground cultivation. (He also made a similar argument about the advantages of *association* over wage labor.) Thus, in Saint Anne, he instructed the workers "about the damage they cause to themselves by deserting the *grande culture* for less profitable work for which unlimited competition depreciates the price" (Perrinon à Ministre de la Marine et des Colonies, Trou-au-Chat, 9 octobre 1848).

Successful implementation of *association* required not only that Perrinon discipline the laborers but that he strengthen the resolve of the proprietors as well. The majority of planters feared that if they tried to impose control over the workers, they would lose their cultivators and not be able to easily recruit others (Perrinon à Ministre de la Marine et des Colonies, Fort-de-France, 21 octobre 1848; Perrinon à Ministre de la Marine et des Colonies, Trou-au-Chat, 9 octobre 1848). Perrinon had to encourage them to adopt a more rigorous attitude toward their workers and show them that the power of the state was behind them. Thus, he reported that in Rivière Pilote, the planters lacked initiative and abandoned themselves entirely to the mercy of their laborers. They did not dare limit the extent of their laborers' gardens, the large number of animals they kept, or punish them for their absence from the agreed upon hours and days of work. This situation was aggravated by the inaction of the mayor. Perrinon encouraged the planters to abandon their fatal inertia, establish the conditions for *association*, and take control there. He left behind the inspector of police who restored labor and discipline after arresting several vagabonds who had been sheltered by the proprietors themselves (France. ANSOM. *Martinique*, Carton 7, Dossier 83, Bruat à Ministre de la Marine et des Colonies, Fort-de-France, 23 Novembre 1850. Such eviction could take place on a substantial scale. Perrinon writes from Diamant: "Citizen Telliam

Maillet the largest proprietor in the commune, has just asked me to expel 50 unsubmissive workers from his property. I complied immediately." Perrinon à Ministre de la Marine et des Colonies, Fort-de-France, 21 octobre 1848). Ironically, the very success of *association* later compelled Perrinon to restrain the excesses of planters. Among some proprietors, the reestablishment of labor resulted in "pretensions that they were far from having a few months ago when the authorities had to intervene to limit their concessions. Seduced by the good appearance of their crops and immoderate in their claims for exorbitant revenues, they want to cancel the contracts of *association* under the strength of which their workers have redoubled their efforts. Six or eight persons have been pointed out to me as having this intention" (Perrinon à Ministre de la Marine et des Colonies, Fort-de-France, 21 octobre 1848).

Perrinon was well received during his tours of the island. He spoke before gatherings of laborers in every rural neighborhood and at each significant plantation in the colony, extolling the nobility of agricultural labor and urging the new citizens to return to work. At each meeting, he spent several hours explaining the new legislation and the advantages of *association* (Perrinon à Ministre de la Marine et des Colonies, Fort-de-France, 9 août 1848). There were a few instances of resistance to *association*. On the Jambette estate in Lamentin, *association* by half shares was agreed upon, but the workers drew back from a contract, which they felt would bind them too tightly. Perrinon persuaded them that the formality of a contract was as much in their interest as in the interest of their proprietor. While waiting to formalize a contract, the workers processed all the cane that was ready to harvest averaging a daily wage of one franc and working with the assistance of laborers from the vicinity (Perrinon à Ministre de la Marine et des Colonies, Fort-de-France, 19 août 1848). In the commune of Robert, Perrinon encountered many gangs composed of *noirs de traite*. He described them as "ignorant and defiant, confounding subordination with slavery, doubting the advantages of *association* which they willingly sacrificed for the simple, positive immediate regularity of a daily salary." Many among them refused *association* in favor of work at a fixed price. They harvested and manufactured sugar for 35 francs per barrel. "I made them understand by comparative calculations that such a mode was disadvantageous for their interests. I had to rudely advise these workers of the privileges and obligations of their new social position," writes Perrinon (Perrinon à Ministre de la Marine et des Colonies, Fort-de-France, 9 août 1848). However, as a rule, Perrinon's encounters with the new citizens generated enthusiasm and goodwill, and in most instances agreements were immediately made on the basis of the model contract of *association* (Perrinon à Ministre de la Marine et des Colonies, Fort-de-France, 9 août 1848).

CONCLUSION

After seeing first-hand conditions in the countryside, Perrinon reappraised the impact of emancipation on Martinique. Even though the freed population did not leave the plantations, two months of labor in the middle of the harvest season, from May to July 1848, had in fact been lost. This interruption caused immense damage to the current harvest and prejudiced future ones (Perrinon à Ministre de la Marine et des Colonies, St. Esprit, 25 septembre 1848). Nonetheless, on the eve of his departure from the colony in October 1848, Perrinon felt that his efforts had been successful. In his final report, he wrote that labor was reorganized throughout the colony. On a few elite plantations the new organization gave results superior to those obtained under slavery. On almost all the others, it promised to maintain the equilibrium even at the price of diminished labor time. Finally, those plantations that did not function at all were the exceptions. On these latter, he asserted, it was only a matter of the proprietors acting within their rights and expelling those associates who refused to completely fulfill their obligations. He adds: "I have not ceased to advise them to act thus in case of prolonged disagreement; I have not failed to inform them that recourse to public force is assured to them for the realization of rigorous measures" (Perrinon à Ministre de la Marine et des Colonies, Fort-de-France, 21 octobre 1848).

Sharecropping contracts achieved some outstanding results, and Perrinon reported some exemplary plantations. The Joyau plantation in Robert was a model of order, cooperation, and prosperity. Regulations were simple and strictly obeyed. Work was performed promptly and regularly under the supervision of an elected council. The associated workers received half shares and enjoyed the added advantage of having the crop processed at the neighboring central refinery, Usine Laguigneraye. Similarly, Perrinon reported that the Berté Saint-Auge plantation in Gros Morne was exceptionally well kept. Its owner directed operations and kept the accounts of the society with equal care. Its thirty-six associated workers produced more than before emancipation. During the harvest, they stayed in the refinery until two each morning on their own initiative and produced up to fifteen hogsheads of sugar a week (Perrinon à Ministre de la Marine et des Colonies, St. Esprit, 25 septembre 1848. Also see Perrinon à Ministre de la Marine et des Colonies, St. Esprit, 25 septembre 1848).

Perrinon observed that the best labor gangs were those that had been well treated by their masters during slavery (Perrinon à Ministre de la Marine et des Colonies, Macouba, 10 juillet 1848). Yet, benevolent, generous, and enlightened administration was not by itself sufficient to secure order and cooperation. Perrinon cited the Ithier estate in suburban Saint-Pierre as a model for the commune. Yet, on the contiguous Morne l'Etoile plantation, belonging to the same owner, not one-tenth of the workers were assiduous in the performance of their work. Perrinon reprimanded them strongly, and recommended that the proprietor indicate the bad subjects so that they could be promptly expelled. However, he noted that Citizen Ithier was too indulgent to impose the necessary severity (Perrinon à Ministre de la Marine et des Colonies, 9 septembre 1848).

However, despite the enthusiasm with which the workers greeted Perrinon and embraced *association* and the numerous examples of successful plantations, irregularity of labor and the persistence of proto-peasant activities remained pervasive problems throughout the colony. Thus, in Lamentin, one of the largest sugar districts, Perrinon found that order had been maintained and production reorganized due in large measure to the vigorous activity of the local administration. Contracts of *association* had been concluded throughout the commune. Nonetheless, they were executed with a certain defiance and indolence against which all efforts had failed (Perrinon à Ministre de la Marine et des Colonies, Fort-de-France, 9 août 1848). After his visit to Diamant, he warned that vigorous action was necessary in order to restore labor: "It is insufficiently supplied despite my efforts. Absence on Friday, inexactitude in hours of work, refusal of supervision, pretension to ownership of cabins are the vices I have fought in Diamant. I have not sufficiently extirpated them" (Perrinon à Ministre de la Marine et des Colonies, Fort-de-France, 21 octobre 1848; Perrinon à Ministre de la Marine et des Colonies, Trou-au-Chat, 9 octobre 1848; Perrinon à Ministre de la Marine et des Colonies, St. Esprit, 25 September 1848). Indeed, in his final report, Perrinon cautioned that the failure of workers to perform punctually and regularly during the agreed upon hours and days was a general vice. With the exception of a few elite *ateliers* who worked longer, the normal amount of labor was not given, but, he reassured his superiors, it was generally recognized that six or six and one-half hours of labor under freedom are more productive than nine hours under slavery (Perrinon à Ministre de la Marine et des Colonies, Trou-au-Chat, 9 octobre 1848).

Perrinon remained optimistic about the results of *association* and declared that free labor gave results superior to those of slavery. Indeed, while the number of workers employed in sugar declined by a third in the first year after emancipation, the amount of sugar produced fell by only a bit more than 20 percent (from 23,668 to 18,736 metric tons) (France. ANSOM. Martinique, *État des cultures*). Nonetheless, the absolute decline in production was sufficient to put hard-pressed planters in jeopardy. Emile Thomas, the organizer of the *ateliers nationaux* in Paris who had been sent to Martinique to report on labor conditions, remarked that the ruin of the planters there was complete (ANSOM. *Martinique*, Carton 11, Dossier 109, Emile Thomas à Ministre de la Marine et des Colonies, Fort-de-France, 9 novembre 1848). One prominent planter complained: "Rural labor has not recovered. The continuity, the regularity which alone produce results do not exist anywhere. The efforts of the Commissioner-General, [those] of the proprietors are to no avail. The present harvest, the next harvest are lost. A plantation that ordinarily produces 15 thousand kilograms of sugar per week, now only makes 500." He urged the government of the colony to form disciplinary labor gangs and severely enforce the laws against vagrancy. Only then could labor be reconstituted on a basis that was adequate for the future (France. ANSOM. *Martinique*, Carton 56, Dossier 464, A. Joyau à Ministre de la Marine et des Colonies, Saint Pierre, 29 août 1848).

After inspection of plantations in a number of districts, Emile Thomas confirmed these judgments in a confidential report to metropolitan authorities. He writes: "Everywhere that association is in existence, work is illusory. Where a regular wage is established, work begins to merit the name." He estimated that in the richest districts of the island more than half the able workers were engaged in regular labor on the plantations, but the average working day was not more than five hours. The coming harvest would be only one-third of the normal one, that of 1849 only one-half, and it was difficult to see where such a decline would lead by 1850. In order to resolve the crisis, he, too, recommended the establishment of disciplinary labor gangs as the only remedy for growing vagrancy and urged planters to return to their properties and resume an active role in their direction (France. ANSOM. *Martinique*, Carton 11, Dossier 109, Emile Thomas à Ministre de la Marine et des Colonies, Fort-de-France, 28 septembre 1848).

The sharecropping contract indicates the complexity of the historical processes forming the labor regime in postemancipation Martinique. It developed as a response to the efforts of the working population to shape the plantation regime according to their needs and perspectives. It played an important role in maintaining the continuity of labor and ensuring the survival of the sugar industry. But, it was an inadequate form of social and economic organization. It did not provide the sugar plantation with labor in sufficient quantity and quality. Instead, house, yard, and provision ground remained important terrains of conflict through which workers sought to assert a peasant economy small-scale production and exchange within the processes of reorganization of the plantation and reconstitution of the labor force. Persistent resistance by the workers would call forth more repressive labor codes under Perrinon's successors, Bruat and, especially, Gueydon. But repression alone was an insufficient response to resistance. In the words of Bruat, labor is "the regenerative element of the colonies, the source of their strength and of their prosperity" (France. ANSOM. *Martinique*, Carton 11, Dossier 109, Extrait des Procès-Verbaux des déliberations de la Session ordinaire du mois de Novembre 1848. Séance de 7. Conseil Privé). For both Bruat and Thomas, wage labor appeared as the only means to contain the initiatives of the working population and secure an adequate and regular supply of labor. Yet, the impoverishment of the planters would present a continuing obstacle to the implementation of such a program. Only through the restructuring of the colonial economy could labor be effectively subordinated and the survival of the sugar industry be guaranteed.

Bibliography

PRIMARY SOURCES

Manuscript Sources

France. Archives Nationales. Section Outre-Mer (hereafter ANSOM).

Fonds Généralités

Généralités, Carton 43, Dossier 350. Procès-Verbaux des déliberations de la Commission Schoelcher.
Généralités, Carton 9, Dossier 99. De Moges, *Mémoire à son successeur (1840)*.
Généralités, Carton 144 Dossier 1221. Condition des esclaves. Publication d'une exposé sommaire de mesures prises dans les differents colonies pour l'éxécution de l'ordonnance royale du 4 janvier 1840. 1841–1843.

Fonds Martinique

Martinique, État des cultures, 1831–1850.
Martinique, Carton 7, Dossier 83. Tournées du gouverneur. 1829–1851, 1870.
Martinique, Carton 11, Dossier 108. Correspondance politique. 1848–1851.
Martinique, Carton 11, Dossier 109. Correspondance générale. C.A. Bruat, Gouverneur. Octobre 1848–juin 1851.
Martinique, Carton 56, Dossier 464. Correspondance générale entre le Ministre de la Marine et le Gouverneur Rostoland. 1848–1849.

Printed Sources

France. Ministère de la Marine et des Colonies. 1840, 1841, 1842, 1843. *Commission instituée par décision royale du 26 mai 1840, pour l'examen des questions relatives à l'esclavage et à la constitution politique des colonies.* 2 vols. Paris: Imprimerie Royale.

————. 1844. Exposé général des résultats du patronage des esclaves dans les colonies françaises. Paris: Imprimerie Royale.

France. Ministère du Commerce et des manufactures. 1829. *Commission formée avec l'aprobation du Roi . . . pour l'examen de certaines questions de législation commerciale: Enquête sur les sucres.* Paris: Imprimerie Royale.

SECONDARY SOURCES

Abbott, A. 1992. "From Causes to Events: Notes on Narrative Positivism." *Sociological Methods and Research* 22: 428–455.

Adamson, Alan. 1972. *Sugar without Slaves: The Political Economy of British Guiana, 1838–1904.* New Haven, Conn.: Yale University Press.

Aimes, Hubert. 1967. *A History of Slavery in Cuba, 1511 to 1868.* New York: Octagon Books.

Aminzade, R. 1992. "Historical Sociology and Time." *Sociological Methods and Research* 22: 456–580.

Anonymous (Dr. Collins). 1811. *Practical Rules for the Management and Medical Treatment of Negro Slaves in the Sugar Colonies by a Professional Planter.* London: Vernor, Hood, and Sharp, Hatchard.

Arrighi, Giovanni. 1994. *The Long Twentieth Century: Money, Power, and the Origin of Our Times.* London: Verso Books.

————. 1998. "Capitalism and the Modern World-System: Rethinking the Non-Debates of the 1970s." *Review* XXI, 1: 113–129.

Aston, T.H., and C.H.E. Philpin, eds. 1985. *The Brenner Debate. Agrarian Class Structure and Economic Development in Pre-industrial Europe.* Cambridge: Cambridge University Press.

Bastide, Roger. 1978. *The African Religions of Brazil: Toward a Sociology of the Interpenetration of Civilizations.* Trans. Helen Seba. Baltimore: Johns Hopkins University Press.

Bauer, John. 1970. "International Repercussions of the Haitian Revolution." *The Americas* XXVI, 4: 394–418.

Beckles, Hilary McD. 1987. "'The Williams Effect': Eric William's *Capitalism and Slavery* and the Growth of West Indian Political Economy." In Barbara Solow and Stanley L. Engerman, eds., *British Capitalism and Caribbean Slavery. The Legacy of Eric Williams.* Cambridge: Cambridge University Press, 303–316.

Beiguelman, Paula. 1973. *Pequenos Estudos de Ciência Política.* São Paulo: Biblioteca de Ciências Sociais.

————. 1978. "The Destruction of Modern Slavery: A Theoretical Issue." *Review* II, 1: 71–80.

Bergad, Laird W. 1989. "The Economic Viability of Sugar Production Based on Slave Labor in Cuba, 1859–1878." *Latin American Research Review* XXIV, 1: 95–113.

Besson, Jean. 1984a. "Family Land and Caribbean Society: Toward an Ethnography of Afro-Caribbean Peasantries." In Elizabeth Thomas-Hope, ed., *Perspectives on Carib-*

bean Regional Identity. University of Liverpool, Center for Latin American Studies, Monograph Series, no. 11. Liverpool: University of Liverpool, 57–83.

————. 1984b. "Land Tenure in the Free Villages of Trelawny, Jamaica: A Case Study in the Caribbean Response to Emancipation." *Slavery and Abolition* 5: 3–23.

Braithwaite, Edward. 1971. *The Development of Creole Society in Jamaica, 1770–1820.* Oxford: Oxford University Press.

Braudel, Fernand. 1972. "History and the Social Sciences." In Peter Burke, ed., *Economy and Society in Early Modern Europe.* New York: Harper Torchbooks, 11–42.

Brenner, Robert. 1977. "The Origins of Capitalist Development: A Critique of Neo-Smithian Marxism." *New Left Review* 104: 25–92.

Cain, P.J., and A.G. Hopkins. 1993. *British Imperialism: Innovation and Expansion, 1688–1914.* London: Longman.

Cardoso, Ciro Flammarion S. 1979. *Agricultura, Escravidão, Capitalismo.* Petropolis: Vozes.

Charroppin, A. 1848. *Du travail libre dans les colonies françaises.* Bordeaux: n.p.

Cohen, G.A. 1978. *Karl Marx's Theory of History: A Defence.* Princeton, N.J.: Princeton University Press.

Cohn, D.L. 1956. *The Life and Times of King Cotton.* New York: Oxford University Press.

Conrad, John H., and John R. Meyer. 1964. *The Economics of Slavery and Other Studies in Economic History.* Chicago: Aldine.

Corrigan, Philip. 1977. "Feudal Relics or Capitalist Monuments? Notes on the Sociology of Unfree Labor." *Sociology* 11, 3: 435–463.

Crawford, M.D.C. 1924. *The Heritage of Cotton. The Fibre of Two Worlds and Many Ages.* New York: Grosset & Dunlap.

Curtin, Philip D. 1969. *The Atlantic Slave Trade: A Census.* Madison: University of Wisconsin Press.

Daubrée, Paul. 1841. *Question coloniale sous le rapport industriel.* Paris: n.p.

David, Paul A., Herbert G. Gutman, Richard Sutch, Peter Temin, and Gavin Wright. 1976. *Reckoning with Slavery.* New York: Oxford University Press.

Davis, David Brion. 1984. *Slavery and Human Progress.* New York: Oxford University Press.

Debbasch, Yvan. 1961, 1962. "Le marronage. Essai sur la désertion de l'esclave antillais." *Année Sociologique*: 1–112; 117–195.

Debien, Gabriel. 1974. *Les esclaves aux Antilles françaises (XVIIᵉ-XVIIIᵉ siècles).* Basse-Terre: Société d'histoire de la Guadeloupe. Fort-de-France: Société d'histoire de la Martinique.

De Cassagnac, Adolphe Granier. 1842. *Voyage aux Antilles.* Paris: n.p.

Deerr, Noel. 1945. *The History of Sugar.* 2 vols. London: Chapman and Hall.

De la Cornillère, M. le Conte E. 1843. *La Martinique en 1842: Intérêts coloniaux, souvenirs du voyage.* Paris: n.p.

Derosne, Charles. 1824. *Mémoire sur la fabrication du sucre dans les colonies par de nouveaux procédés.* Paris: n.p.

————. 1833. *Notice on the New Process for Making Sugar, Lately Introduced in the French and English Colonies.* Paris: n.p.

Derosne, Charles, and Jean François Cail. 1844. *De la elaboración del azúcar en las colonias y de los nuevos aparatos destinados a mejorarla.* Havana: n.p.

Dicken, Peter. 1998. *Global Shift: Transforming the World Economy.* New York: Guilford Press.

Dobb, Maurice. 1947. *Studies in the Development of Capitalism.* New York: International Publishers.

Drescher, Seymour M. 1977. *Econocide: British Slavery in the Era of Abolition.* Pittsburgh: University of Pittsburgh Press.

Dunayevskaya, Raya. 1958. *Marxism and Freedom.* New York: Twayne Publishers.

Dutrône de la Couture, J.F. 1791. *Précis sur la canne et sur les moyens d'en extraire le sel essential, suivi de plusieurs mémoires sur le sucre, sur le vin de canne, sur l'indigo, sur les habitations et sur l'état actuel de Saint-Domingue.* Paris: Debure, De Seine.

Engerman, Stanley. 1973. "Some Considerations Relating to Property Rights in Man." *Journal of Economic History* XXXIII, 1: 43–65.

———. 1976. "Some Economic and Demographic Comparisons of Slavery in the United States and the British West Indies." *The Economic History Review,* second ser. XXIX, 2: 258–275.

Fogel, Robert W. 1989. *Without Consent or Contract.* New York: W.W. Norton & Co.

Fogel, Robert W., and Stanley L. Engerman. 1974. *Time on the Cross. The Economics of American Slavery.* 2 vols. Boston: Little, Brown and Company.

Franco, Maria Sylvia de Carvalho. 1976. *Homens Livres no Ordem Escravocrata.* São Paulo: Editora Atica

Frank, André Gunder. 1967. *Capitalism and Underdevelopment in Latin America.* New York: Monthly Review Press.

Friedlaender, Heinrich. 1978. *Historìa Economica de Cuba.* Havana: Editorial de Ciencias Sociales.

Fukuyama, Francis. 1992. *The End of History and the Last Man.* London: Hamish Hamilton.

Furtado, Celso. 1963. *The Economic Growth of Brazil. A Survey from Colonial to Modern Times.* Berkeley: University of California Press.

Genovese, Eugene D. 1967. *The Political Economy of Slavery.* New York: Random House.

Gilroy, Paul. 1993. *The Black Atlantic: Modernity and Double Consciousness.* London: Verso.

Gisler, Antoine. 1965. *L'esclavage aux Antilles françaises (XVIIe–XIXe siècle): Contribution au problème de l'esclavage.* Fribourg: Editions universitaires Fribourg Suisse.

Goveia, E.V. 1965. *Slave Society in the British Leeward Islands at the End of the Eighteenth Century.* New Haven, Conn.: Yale University Press.

Graham, Richard. 1968. *Britain and the Onset of Modernization in Brazil. 1850–1914.* Cambridge: Cambridge University Press.

Gray, L.C. 1958. *History of Agriculture in the Southern United States.* 2 vols. Gloucester, Mass.: Peter Smith. [Originally Carnegie Institution of Washington, n.d.]

Greenberg, Michael. 1977. "The New Economic History and the Understanding of Slavery: A Methodological Critique." *Dialectical Anthropology* 2: 131–141.

Griffin, L.J. 1992. "Temporality, Events, and Explanation in Historical Sociology. An Introduction," *Sociological Methods and Research* 22: 403–427.

Guerra y Sánchez, Ramiro. 1964. *Sugar and Society in the Caribbean. An Economic History of Cuban Agriculture.* New Haven, Conn.: Yale University Press.

Gutman, Herbert G. 1975. *Slavery and the Numbers Game.* Urbana: University of Illinois Press.

Hall, Douglas. 1961. "Incalculability as a Feature of Sugar Production during the Eighteenth Century." *Social and Economic Studies* 10, 3: 305–318.

———. 1978. "The Flight from the Plantations Reconsidered: The British West Indies, 1838–1842." *The Journal of Caribbean History* 10–11: 7–23.

Herskovits, Melville J. 1937. *Life in a Haitian Valley.* New York: Knopf.

Higman, Barry W. 1976. *Slave Population and Economy in Jamaica, 1801–1834.* Cambridge: Cambridge University Press.

———. 1988. *Jamaica Surveyed.* Kingston: Institute of Jamaica Publications, Ltd.

Hilton, Rodney, ed. 1976. *The Transition from Feudalism to Capitalism.* London: New Left Books.

Hobsbawm, Eric. 1968. *Industry and Empire.* Harmondsworth: Penguin Books.

Hoogvelt, Ankie. 1997. *Globalization and the Postcolonial World: The New Political Economy of Development.* Baltimore: The Johns Hopkins University Press.

Hopkins, Terence K. 1982a. "The Study of the Capitalist World-Economy. Some Introductory Considerations." In Terence K. Hopkins and Immanuel Wallerstein et al., eds., *World-Systems Analysis. Theory and Methodology.* Beverly Hills: Sage, 9–38.

———. 1982b. "World-System Analysis: Methodological Considerations." In Terence K. Hopkins and Immanuel Wallerstein, *World-Systems Analysis. Theory and Methodology.* Beverly Hills: Sage Publications, 145–158.

Ingham, Geoffrey. 1984. *Capitalism Divided? The City and Industry in British Social Development.* New York: Schocken Books.

James, C.L.R. 1963. *The Black Jacobins: Toussaint L'Ouverture and the San Domingo Revolution.* New York: Vintage Books.

Jenks, Leland H. 1973. *The Migration of British Capital to 1875.* New York: Barnes & Noble.

Knight, Franklin W. 1970. *Slave Society in Cuba during the Nineteenth Century.* Madison: University of Wisconsin Press.

Korsch, Karl. 1963. *Karl Marx.* New York: Russell and Russell.

Koselleck, Reinhart. 1985. *Futures Past: On the Semantics of Historical Time.* Cambridge, Mass.: MIT Press.

Kosík, Karel. 1976. *Dialectics of the Concrete. A Study of Problems of Man and World.* Trans. Karel Kovanda with James Schmidt. Boston: D. Reidel.

Kuczynski, J. 1945. *A Short History of Labor Conditions under Industrial Capitalism,* vol. IV. London: F. Muller.

Labrousse, C.E. 1954. *Aspects de l'évolution économique et sociale de la France et du Royaume-Uni de 1815 à 1880.* Paris: Centre de Documentation Universitaire.

Laclau, Ernesto. 1971. "Imperialism in Latin America." *New Left Review* 67 (May–June): 19–38.

Lavollée, P. 1841. *Notes sur les cultures et la production de la Martinique et de la Guadeloupe.* Paris: Imprimerie Royale.

Le Goff, J. 1980. *Time, Work, and Culture in the Middle Ages.* Chicago: University of Chicago Press.

Lepkowski, Tadeusz. 1968. *Haiti.* 2 vols. Havana: Estudios del centro de documentación sobre América Latina Juan F. Noyala, Casa de las Americas.

Lewis, M.G. 1929. *Journal of a West India Proprietor.* Boston: Houghton Mifflin.

Linebaugh, Peter. 1992. *The London Hanged: Crime and Civil Society in the Eighteenth Century.* Cambridge: Cambridge University Press.

Lukàcs, Georg. 1960. *Histoire et conscience de classe.* Paris: Éditions de Minuit.

Malowist, Marian. 1969. "Les débuts du système de plantations dans la période des grandes découvertes." *Africana Bulletin* 10: 9–30.

Marrero, Levi. 1983–1986. *Cuba: Economía y Sociedad. Azucar, Ilustracion y Conciencia 1763–1868.* 10 vols. Madrid: Editorial Playor, S.A.

Marx, Karl. 1973. *Grundrisse.* Harmondsworth: Penguin.

———. 1976. *Capital.* Vol. I. Harmondsworth: Penguin.

McMichael, Philip. 1984. *Settlers and the Agrarian Question: Capitalism in Colonial Australia.* Cambridge: The Cambridge University Press.

———. 1990. "Incorporating Comparison within a World-Historical Perspective: An Alternative Comparative Method." *American Sociological Review* 55: 385–397.

———. 1991. "Slavery in the Regime of Wage Labor: Beyond Paternalism in the U.S. Cotton Culture." *Social Concept* 6, 1 (December): 10–28.

———. 2000. *Development and Social Change: A Global Perspective.* Thousand Oaks, Calif.: Pine Forge Press.

Merrington, John. 1968. "Theory and Practice in Gramsci's Marxism." In Ralph Miliband and John Saville, eds., *The Socialist Register 1968.* London: The Merlin Press, 145–176.

———. 1976. "Town and Country in the Transition to Capitalism." In Rodney Hilton, ed., *The Transition from Feudalism to Capitalism.* London: New Left Books, 170–195.

Mintz, Sidney W. 1964. "Currency Problems in Eighteenth-Century Jamaica and Gresham's Law." In Robert A. Manners, ed., *Process and Pattern in Culture.* Chicago: Aldine, 248–265.

———. 1974. *Caribbean Transformations.* Chicago: Aldine.

———. 1977. "The So-Called World System: Local Initiative and Local Response." *Dialectical Anthropology* 2 : 253–270.

———. 1979. "Slavery and the Rise of Peasantries." *Historical Reflections* VI: 213–242.

———. 1982. "Descrying the Peasantry." *Review* VI, 2: 209–225.

———. 1985. *Sweetness and Power: The Place of Sugar in Modern History.* New York: Viking Penguin.

Mintz, Sidney W., and Douglas Hall. 1960. *The Origins of the Jamaican Internal Marketing System.* Yale University Publications in Anthropology, 57. New Haven, Conn.: Department of Anthropology, Yale University.

Moreno Fraginals, Manuel. 1976. *The Sugarmill: The Socioeconomic Complex of Sugar in Cuba, 1760–1860.* Trans. Cedric Belfrage. New York: Monthly Review.

———. 1978. *El ingenio. Complejo económico social cubano del azúcar.* 3 vols. Havana: Editorial de ciencias sociales.

Ortiz, Fernando. 1970. *Cuban Counterpoint: Tobacco and Sugar.* New York: Vintage Books.

———. 1991. *Contrapunteo Cubano del tabaco y el azúcar*. Havana: Editorial de Ciencias Sociales.

Oxaal, Ivar. 1968. *Black Intellectuals Come to Power*. Boston: Schenkman.

Paquette, Robert L. 1988. *Sugar Is Made with Blood: The Conspiracy of La Escalera and the Conflict between Empires over Slavery in Cuba*. Middleton, Conn.: Wesleyan University Press.

Peytraud, Lucien. 1973. *L'esclavage aux Antilles françaises avant 1789 d'après des documents inédits des Archives Coloniales*. Pointe-à-Pitre, Guadeloupe: Désormaux.

Polanyi, Karl. 1957. *The Great Transformation. The Political and Economic Origins of Our Time*. Boston: Beacon Press.

Prado Jùnior, Caio. 1981. *Historia económica do Brasil*. São Paulo: Brasiliense.

Quadagno, J., and S.J. Knapp. 1992. "Have Historical Sociologists Foresaken Theory? Thoughts on the History/Theory Relationship." *Sociological Methods and Research* 22: 481–507.

Quijano, Aníbal. 2000. "Coloniality of Power, Eurocentrism, and Latin America." *Nepantla* I, 3: 533–580.

Ragatz, Lowell. 1971. *The Fall of the Planter Class in the British West Indies, 1763–1833*. New York: Octagon Books.

Renard, Raymond. 1973. *La Martinique de 1848 à 1870*. Pointe-à-Pitre, Guadeloupe, Groupe Universitaire de Recheches Inter-Caraïbes.

Rodney, Walter. 1981. *History of the Guyanese Working People, 1881–1905*. Baltimore: The Johns Hopkins University Press.

Rosdolsky, Roman. 1974. "Comments on the Method of Marx's *Capital*." *New German Critique* 3: 62–72.

———. 1977. *The Making of Marx's "Capital."* London: Pluto Press.

Sainte-Croix, F. Renouard, Marquis de. 1822. *Statistique de la Martinique*. 2 vols. Paris: Chaumerot, Librairie Palais Royale.

Samuel, Raphael. 1977. "The Workshop of the World: Steam Power and Hand Technology in Mid-Victorian Britain." *History Workshop* 3: 6–72.

Sartre, J.-P. 1982. *Critique of Dialectical Reason*. London: Verso.

Sayer, Derek. 1987. *The Violence of Abstraction. The Analytical Foundations of Historical Materialism*. Oxford: Basil Blackwell.

Scherer, J.A.B. 1969. *Cotton as a World Power. A Study in the Economic Interpretation of History*. New York: Greenwood Publishing Corp.

Schmidt, Alfred. 1983. *History and Structure: An Essay on Hegelian-Marxist and Structuralist Theories of History*. Cambridge, Mass.: MIT Press.

Schoelcher, Victor. 1976. *Des Colonies françaises. Abolition immédiate de l'esclavage*. Basse-Terre: Société d'histoire de la Guadeloupe. Fort-de-France: Société d'histoire de la Martinique.

———. 1847. *Histoire de l'esclavage pendant les deux dernières années*. 2 vols. Paris: n.p.

Schumpeter, Joseph A. 1934. *The Theory of Economic Development: An Inquiry into Profits, Capital, Credit, Interest, and the Business Cycle*. Cambridge, Mass.: Harvard University Press.

Scott, Rebecca J. 1985. *Slave Emancipation in Cuba. The Transition to Free Labor, 1860–1899*. Princeton, N.J.: Princeton University Press.

Sewell, William H., Jr. 1997. "Three Temporalities: Toward an Eventful Sociology." In Terrence J. McDonald, ed., *The Historical Turn in the Social Sciences.* Ann Arbor: University of Michigan Press, 245–280.

Soleau, A. 1835. Notes sur les Guyanes française, hollandaise, anglaise, et sur les Antilles françaises (Cayenne, Surinam, Demerary, la Martinique, la Guadeloupe). Paris: n.p.

Smith, Adam. 1976. *An Inquiry into the Nature and Causes of the Wealth of Nation.* Chicago: The University of Chicago Press.

Stiglitz, Joseph E. 2002. *Globalization and Its Discontents.* New York: W.W. Norton & Co.

Taylor, P.J. 1987. "The Poverty of International Comparisons: Some Methodological Lessons from World-Systems Analysis." *Studies in Comparative International Development* (Spring): 12–39.

Tilly, Charles. 1984. *Big Structures, Large Processes, Huge Comparisons.* New York: Russell Sage Foundation.

———. 1995. "Macrosociology, Past and Future." *Newsletter of the Comparative and Historical Sociology Section of the American Sociological Association* 8, 1 and 2: 1, 3–4.

Tomich, Dale W. 1980. "Rapporti Sociali di Produzione e Mercato Mondiale nel Dibattito Recente sulla Transizione dal Feudalismo al Capitalismo." *Studi Storici* 21, 3: 539–564.

———. 1988. "The 'Second Slavery': Bonded Labor and the Transformation of the Nineteenth Century World Economy." In Francisco O. Ramirez, ed., *Rethinking the Nineteenth Century.* Westport, Conn.: Greenwood Press, 103–117.

———. 1990. *Slavery in the Circuit of Sugar: Martinique in the World Economy, 1830–1848.* Baltimore: The Johns Hopkins University Press.

———. 1991. "World Slavery and Caribbean Capitalism: The Cuban Sugar Industry, 1760–1868." *Theory and Society* 20, 3: 297–320.

———. 1994. "Small Islands and Huge Comparisons: Caribbean Plantations, Historical Unevenness, and Capitalist Modernity." *Social Science History* 18, 3: 340–358.

Torras, Jaume. 1993. "The Building of a Market." *Els Espais del Mercat. 2on Coloqui Internacional d'Història Local.* València, Spain: Diputació de València.

Trouillot, Rolph. 1988. *Peasants and Capital: Dominica in the World Economy.* Baltimore: The Johns Hopkins University Press.

———. 1995. *Silencing the Past: Power and the Production of History.* Boston: Beacon Pressn

Wallerstein, Immanuel. 1974. *The Modern World System: Capitalist Agriculture and the Origins of the European World-Economy in the Sixteenth Century.* Vol. 1. New York: Academic Press.

———. 1979. *The Capitalist World-Economy.* New York: Cambridge University Press.

———. 1980. *The Modern World-System Mercantilism and the Consolidation of the European World-Economy, 1600–1750.* Vol. 2. New York: Academic Press.

Weber, Max. 1978. *Economy and Society.* Berkeley: University of California Press.

Williams, Eric. 1966. *Capitalism and Slavery.* New York: Capricorn Books.

———. 1971. *Inward Hunger: The Education of a Prime Minister.* Chicago: University of Chicago Press.

Wolf, Eric R. 1982. *Europe and the People without History.* Berkeley: University of California Press.

Woodman, H.D. 1968. *King Cotton and His Retainers: Financing and Marketing the Cotton Crop of the South*. Lexington: University of Kentucky Press.

Woodruff, William. 1971. "The Emergence of an International Economy, 1700–1914." In Carlo M. Cipolla, ed., *The Fontana Economic History of Europe*. Vol. 4, part 2, *The Emergence of Industrial Societies*. London: Fontana Books, 656–716.

Wright, Gavin. 1978. *The Political Economy of the Cotton South*. New York: W.W. Norton & Company.

Zanetti Lecuona, Oscar, and Alejandro García Alvarez. 1987. *Caminos Para el Azúcar*. Havana: Editorial de Ciencias Sociales.

Index

Arrighi, Giovanni, 33, 117

Bastide, Roger, 164
Braudel, Fernand, 104
Brazil: coffee and slave labor, 67–68; coffee production, 67; geography of coffee production, 68–69
Brenner, Robert, 32, 36, 39–42, 44–46; capital and wage labor, 40–41; conception of world economy, 45–46; critique of "neo-Smithians," 39–40; market and unequal exchange, 41; method of abstraction, 44–46; mode of production, 40; social classes, 44–45; transition to capitalism, 41–42
Britain, hegemony over world economy, 58–61, 63, 70–71, 78

causality, 98–99, 100–101, 117–19
Code Noir (Royal Edict of 1685), 142, 146, 148, 155, 156
comparison: encompassing, 123–24; formal, 121–22; incorporated, 120–21, 122–23, 124, 132–36
Conrad, John H., 4, 5
Cuba: export markets, 82–83, 129–30; geography of sugar production, 64–65, 83–84, 86, 113, 130–31; railroad, 85–86, 131–32; sugar and slave labor, 64, 81, 82, 87, 88–92; sugar and technology, 65, 84–85, 90–92, 130–31, 132; sugar production, 64, 75, 81–82

Debien, Gabriel, 160
Derosne, Charles, 91, 92
Dobb, Maurice, 32, 34–35, 39, 42; crisis of feudalism, 34; mode of production, 34; petty mode of production, 34–35; wage labor and capital, 34–35
Drescher, Seymour, 96, 98, 115–16; critique of Eric Williams, 102–4, 106

economic cycles, 75–76, 106–8
Engerman, Stanley L., 4, 13, 14

Fogel, Robert W., 4, 14
Frank, André Gunder, 32, 35–36, 39, 42

Genovese, Eugene D., 9–13, 14; capitalism and slavery, 10–11, 12–13; irrationality of slavery, 9–10, 11; production and exchange, 10; slavery as social relation, 10; Southern backwardness, 11–12; theoretical dualism, 10–13
Gramsci, Antonio, 27

historical theory, 18, 19–27

internal marketing, 163–64

Jamaica: geography of sugar production, 111–12; slave labor and sugar, 112
James, C.L.R., 97

About the Author

Dale W. Tomich is professor of sociology and history at Binghamton University. He is author of *Slavery in the Circuit of Sugar: Martinique and the World Economy, 1830–1848* (1990) and is currently engaged in a study of slavery in Brazil, Cuba, and the United States and the remaking of the nineteenth-century world economy.

LaVergne, TN USA
07 October 2010
199988LV00004B/153/P